CONTENTS

INTRODUCTION

Please look back through the reviews of Professor Xenia Gąsiorowska's books and you will find that the words often used to characterize her style are "gracious" and "elegant." We hope there is a certain gracious elegance in this collection of studies in Xenia Gąsiorowska's honor, and by this we mean a shared and learned assumption that literature has its own values, that the study of literature — scholarship — is an appreciation of values, that literature is not separable from all of culture, and that to be a cultured person is, by her example, to try to understand the distinctive Slavic, specifically Polish and Russian culture, she brought to us through the grace and elegance of her cultural Diaspora. Almost all the authors of these studies, Xenia Gąsiorowska's students, are native midwesterners, and even those whose names are Slavic discovered Slavic culture in significant part through her, far from its actual milieux. We are Americans, and our perceptions of Polish and Russian literature are American. But to the degree we have tried to appreciate this literature, we understand it was brought to us first, in significant part and with a fascinating European sophistication, by her. There is no "Gąsiorowska method." There is, rather, a Gąsiorowska style, manner, quality. And we like to think these studies have been informed by this example.

The studies offered here are based on papers originally read at a *Symposium on 19th and 20th Century Polish and Russian Literature in Honor of Professor Xenia Gąsiorowska* on 24-25 April 1981 at the University of Wisconsin at Madison. The papers were read and criticized before the Symposium by Professor J. Thomas Shaw, and during the Symposium among ourselves and the present faculty of the Department of Slavic Languages. Subsequently we passed our work around by mail for further criticism, using a basic evaluation compiled from all criticisms, with a view to achieving the best possible scholarly standards. And yes, Mrs. G. offered her criticisms too, on the second day, and she began her remarks, as she always began her criticisms of our work in class and seminar, "Now, my dears ...."

We have not tried to achieve a comprehensive, "representative" view of 19th and 20th century Polish and Russian literature in this collection. Only one study is on a Polish subject alone, and only one other on a comparative Russian-Polish subject. Our studies represent our current interests, after we have moved on to different places and older lives. But we have ranged through the two centuries of the Symposium, and our contributions fall into identifiable categories corresponding to Professor Gąsiorowska's cultural breadth. The collection begins with five studies of THE NINETEENTH CENTURY , from

Denis Davydov to Tolstoj, Dostoevskij, Nekrasov, and Čexov. The studies of MODERNISM include two examinations of the fairy tale in Sologub's prose and a review of the religious component of Russian Symbolism. In the section on ART, POETICS, DRAMA are an explication of a poem by Majakovskij in relation to a painting by Malevič, an analysis of the metrical typology of Anna Axmatova, an examination of Russian silent film, and a comparison of Witkiewicz and Szajna in the Polish theater. THE SOVIET PERIOD contains a new interpretation of Gor'kij's tale "Twenty-Six and One," a study of the transition from Socialist Realism to Solženicynism, and an analysis of the religious symbolism in Rasputin's *Live and Remember*. This diversity is informed by a discernible unity of scholarly manner, if not of subject: the authors' common assumption that study of an individual work or a general literary question ought to rest on careful readings of text, with appropriate reliance on extrinsic evidence, respect for existing scholarship, and appreciation that no literary subject should be defined in a cultural vacuum.

In his study of "Artistic Consistency in *Notes from the Underground* — Part One," Gary Rosenshield demonstrates that the abrupt shift from the deterministic analysis of human actions in the first part of the work to the analysis in the second part based on its antithesis, free will, is negotiated by the artistic logic of the work itself. The diametrically opposed philosophical arguments are not contradictory, but a reflection of Dostoevskij's belief that man can be rational and irrational at once. The work is not marred by contradiction, but unified by a content formed into an artistic whole. Lauren Leighton, in "Denis Davydov and *War and Peace*," shows that the hussar poet served not only as a prototype for the character of Vas'ka Denisov in Tolstoj's novel, but also provided Tolstoj with credible accounts of war, history, and historical figures. Tolstoj, who respected few opinions other than his own, believed that Davydov first provided the tone of historical authenticity he considered so important to *War and Peace*, and he adapted the poet hussar's views almost without change. In a structural analysis of "*The Death of Ivan Il'ič* — Chapter One," Gary Jahn argues that the narrative displacement of the account in chapter one of the announcement of Ivan Il'ič's death to the start rather than the end of this otherwise perfectly chronological story is not, as has been believed, a narrative flaw. Rather, the displacement is intentional, structurally necessary, and in fact the basic key to Tolstoj's development of the theme of death. Sigmund Birkenmayer, in his study of "Polish Themes in the Poetry of Nekrasov," reviews his own and other scholars' treatments of the poet's attitude toward Poland and his own Polish origins. He demonstrates through selections of Nekrasov's poetry that the poet's attitudes were affected by his emotional and psychological attitudes toward his Polish mother. The section on THE NINETEENTH CENTURY concludes with Leonard Polakiewicz's study of Čexov's views of penology, or "Crime and Punishment in Čexov," and the reflection of those views in two works, "The Bet" and "The Head Gardener's Story." Čexov's ideas about crime and punishment were carried over into his art with humane concern: if it is immoral to set a murderer free, it is equally immoral to put him to death.

The section on MODERNISM begins with two studies of fairy tale patterns, motifs, structural and stylistic features in stories by Fedor Sologub: Pierre Hart's "Functions of the Fairy Tale in Sologub's Prose" and Linda Ivanits's "Fairy Tale Motifs in Sologub's 'Dream on the Rocks.'" Both authors add to the growing but still not fully developed scholarship on the relationships between oral genres and fictional works. And both lead us more deeply into the labyrinths of Symbolist erotic fantasy and the perceptions of children. The studies are grounded in theory of myth, folk traditions, the fairy tale as a source of fantasy. In "The Religious Component of Russian Symbolism," David Schaffer argues that religion is the *sine qua non* that separates Symbolism from Decadentism. Schaffer systematically reviews the religious elements in the poetry of the Modernists — Blok, Belyj, Brjusov, Sologub, Gippius — and suggests that these elements are the only credible criterion for defining Russian Symbolism exclusively from Decadentism.

Juliette Stapanian's study of "Majakovskij's 'Street-' and an 'Alogical' Cubo-Futurist Painting by Malevič" is an ambitious venture into a pioneering area of investigation, the intimate connections between poetry and art. Using a reproduction of a painting by Malevič, she shows that Majakovskij's poem *is* a Cubo-Futurist painting, and she offers an intricate explication of the poem in terms of visual devices, spatial position, interrelationship of form, semantic and morphological-etymological phenomena. Equally ambitious is Anthony Hartman's study of "The Metrical Typology of Anna Axmatova," a new contribution to Taranovsky's and Gasparov's pioneer studies of Russian poetics. Metrical typologies of the poetry of Puškin, Blok, Brjusov, and others have appeared, but until now studies of Axmatova' poetry have been concerned more generally with her versification. The complex and exhaustive data of Hartman's study are an attempt to help extend existing metrical typologies into the poetry of major individual poets. Hari Rorlich shows in his study "In Search of Continuity: Russian and Soviet Silent Films," that the great pioneer Soviet film-makers did not create their art from scratch. Rather, they learned from and were indebted to a tradition established well before the revolution. In "Witkacy and Szajna: Prelude to and Requiem for the Holocaust," Edward Czerwinski suggests some of the similarities between Witkiewicz's theory of "Pure Form" and Szajna's "Open Theater." The Polish dramatist of the Absurd who designed and directed some of his stage productions has more than passing similarities with the designer and director who has written some of his own productions. Both are alogical and visual experimenters. Above all, as Witkiewicz could not bear the coming Holocaust, Szajna is obsessed with its reality and its aftermath.

In the section on THE SOVIET PERIOD George Gutsche re-examines "The Role of the 'One' in Gor'kij's 'Twenty-Six and One'" by shifting the emphasis of interpretation from the martyrdom of the twenty-six exploited bakers to the young girl who disappoints their dreams by allowing herself to be seduced. It is the girl Tanja who best expresses Gor'kij's Nietzschean concern with people of will who defy social standards. It is Tanja, previously understood as unworthy of the bakers, and even as immoral, who exemplifies Gor'kij's understanding of human psychology and the values of remaining open to new experience. In "From Socialist Realism to Solženicynism," John Schillinger argues, with close attention to texts, that although Solženicyn defies the demands of official Socialist Realism, he also retains part of its tradition. Solženicyn departs from the Party policy and the stifling conformity of depictions of reality in its revolutionary development of Socialist Realism, and he refuses to mask reality. But in his parodies of Socialist Realism he calls for a confrontation with the real truth, with the true social reality, so that Russia might move toward its Purpose without deceit. In the last contribution to this collection Gerald Mikkelson analyzes "Religious Symbolism in Valentin Rasputin's Tale *Live and Remember*." He shows that this story of a deserter in 1945 who returns to his village and wife in Siberia and hides with her help in the woods is replete with deeply Russian Orthodox symbolism. In the words and attitudes of the Siberian villagers may be found a deeply native adherence to Christian traditions of judgment, repentance, and mercy.

Lauren G. Leighton
University of Illinois at Chicago

PART I

THE NINETEENTH CENTURY

ARTISTIC CONSISTENCY IN
NOTES FROM THE UNDERGROUND — PART ONE

Gary Rosenshield

Perhaps more than any of Dostoevskij's major novels, *Notes from the Underground* is beset with basic problems of interpretation that have still not been satisfactorily resolved. One of the most serious of these concerns is the contradictory philosophical positions on free will and determinism argued by the Underground Man in Part One. For example, in Chapters One through Six of Part One (which I shall for convenience' sake call Section One), the Underground Man maintains that his life has been largely determined by the laws of nature, laws which he dislikes, but the validity of which he accepts intellectually. "You know the direct, lawful, immediate fruit of consciousness is inertia (*inercija*), that is, conscious sitting-with-the-hands-folded …. That is just the essence of every sort of consciousness and reflection. It must be a case of the laws of nature again …. In consequence of those accursed laws of consciousness, anger in me is subject to chemical disintegration. You look into it, the object flies off into air, your reasons evaporate, the guilty one is not to be found, the insult becomes not an insult but fate, something like the toothache, *for which no one is to blame*, and consequently there is only the same outlet left again — that is, to beat the wall as hard as you can."[1] (Emphasis added, G. R.) Here the Underground Man seems to have accepted the iron logic of determinism with respect to human action. If human actions are strictly determined, man cannot be held morally responsible for what he does. Given such a view, there can be no justification for action, or in the Underground Man's particular case, for reaction. If you have been humiliated, he argues, you may desire revenge, but from a rational point of view it is absurd to seek it because your humiliation has invariably been brought about by someone who acted of necessity, that is, who could not have acted other than he did.

However, in Chapters Seven through Eleven of Part One (Section Two), the Underground Man launches into a blistering attack against determinism, arguing that life itself conclusively shows that man's actions are not determined, that man, on the contrary, is first and foremost a free being. Determinism, he holds, is an abstract rational theory that has nothing to do with "the real living man"; it belongs to "the law of logic, but not the law of man" (150).

The problem is apparent. First, how could the Underground Man hold two diametrically opposite views of human action at one and the same time? And second, even more important, how could he shift so abruptly in the course of a sophisticated treatise from a long deterministic analysis of human action in Section One to an analysis based on its antithesis, free will, in Section Two? An attempt can be made to provide an answer to these questions, especially the second, by examining in detail the nature of the transition between the two sections of Part One and by showing there the significant similarities in the Underground Man's seemingly diametrically opposed philosophical arguments.

Since most critics have paid scant attention to the Underground Man's deterministic arguments at the beginning of Part One of the novel, concentrating instead on the hero's passionate defense of free will against determinism, it is not surprising that the problem of the inconsistency of the Underground Man's arguments has not been adequately addressed. When the Underground Man's deterministic explanations of his behavior have been treated at all they have been seen as rationalizations of his inertia.[2] But if such explanations are really rationalizations of inertia, then it would appear that the Underground Man is attempting to eat his cake and have it, too, glorifying free will in Section Two as the highest manifestation of the human personality, while refusing in Section One to take moral responsibility for the destruction it wreaks. However, even Lermontov's Pečorin, who acts as though he can have it both ways — believing in predestination while performing experiments in free will — inwardly knows (as "The Fatalist" demonstrates) that he is engaging in an exercise in self-deception. It would seem that the Underground Man, who is at least Pečorin's intellectual equal, and who shows some knowledge of Lermontov's works, could hardly permit himself to indulge in such an obviously self-serving line of reasoning. This is the type of self-deception that the Underground Man himself says he cannot keep up for more than a day or so.

The most interesting attempt to confront the problem of the Underground Man's contradictory ideological positions, at least in Section One of Part One, is Joseph Frank's "Nihilism and *Notes from Underground*," a seminal study, which will be used here as a basis of comparison.[3] Although Frank also sees Section One as the Underground Man's rationalization of his moral inertia, he argues that it is primarily concerned with presenting the struggle between the hero's intellectual and "moral-emotive" selves. To Frank, the Underground Man is in large part a rationalist who has accepted all the implications of Černyševskij's determinism, as presented in *What Is to Be Done?*, a determinism that precludes the possibility of morally meaningful actions; but morally and emotionally he is an irrationalist who fights an underground war — through masochism, degradation, and debauchery — against the conclusions of his rational intellect.[4] Frank's interpretation of this first section of the novel is an ingenious one and constitutes the main contribution of his study; however, he is much less successful in reconciling the Underground Man's rationalism in Section One with his attack against rationalism and determinism in Section Two.[5] Whereas he discusses Section One in terms of the Underground Man's psychology, in Section Two he leaves the Underground Man as a psychological character and treats him mainly as a spokesman for the author, thus dispensing with the need to reconcile philosophically or psychologically the Underground Man's diametrically opposite positions in Part One. More and more it is not the Underground Man who points out or argues, but Dostoevskij; and for the most part, not even Dostoevskij as implied author, but Dostoevskij the historical figure. Frank evidently does not find it strange that the Underground Man, who at the end of Chapter Six was still a prisoner of determinist thinking, seems, at the beginning of Chapter Seven, just one paragraph later, to have turned into an impassioned intellectual opponent of this very determinism. He does not attempt to explain how the Underground Man could, without even calling attention to it, pass from one philosophical position to its antithesis in the course of a few sentences. What matters to Frank is that Dostoevskij be consistent; however, the Underground Man, who becomes a device of the author in this interpretation, need not be.

One way of lending greater coherence to the Underground Man's transition in Section One from determinism to his advocacy of free will in Section Two would be to look upon Part One not as a depiction of the psychological state of the Underground Man at a particular moment, but as a presentation of the logical progression of consciousness from determinism to freedom, a process that takes place over a long period of time. Although Part One is presented as being written all at one time, one might argue that it is essentially a condensation of a dialectic of consciousness; that the Underground Man's revolt against determinism starts as a moral and emotional struggle, but becomes, ultimately, an intellectual one as well; and that in the two main sections of Part One we see not the psychological transition from one stage of consciousness to another (presumably a higher one), but only a detailed presentation of the stages themselves.[6]

But this interpretation, too, forsakes the psychological Underground Man for the Underground Man as ideologue. In fact, it turns the novel into a "philosophical tale" in which the hero is throughout essentially a mouthpiece for the author — a more ideologically consistent mouthpiece, but a mouthpiece nevertheless.[7] Furthermore, since this interpretation does not approach Part One psychologically, it runs into serious problems when Part One is considered in the context of Part Two; when one, for instance, attempts to interpret Part One as an explanation of the Underground Man's behavior in Part Two, sixteen years earlier.

If we are to retain the Underground Man as a psychological entity and still resolve the problem of the seeming inconsistency in his philosophical positions (as well as the problem of the abrupt transition between them), we must, it seems to me, demonstrate the presence in Section One of the intellectual defender of free will along with the emotional defender of free will; and in Section Two the presence of the rationalist who believes in all the implications of determinism along with the irrationalist who defends the existence of free will; in other words, to show that all aspects of the Underground Man's psychology and philosophy are represented in each of the two main sections of Part One; that there exists no strict separation of the rational and irrational on one hand or the intellectual and emotional on the other.[8]

It may be helpful here, before proceeding to a demonstration in Section Two of the Underground Man's rationalism, to represent diagrammatically the basic aspects of the Underground Man's personality with which we shall be dealing in Part One. The aspects in parentheses are those sides of the Underground Man's personality which Frank speaks very little of or does not mention at all, but which need to be established as existing and significant in order to show the consistency of the Underground Man's personality and philosophical positions throughout both sections of Part One.

Section One (Chapters 1-6)   Section Two (Chapters 7-11)

A. irrationalist   C. irrationalist
    1. moral-emotive   1. (moral-emotive)
    2. (intellectual)   2. intellectual
B. rationalist   D. (rationalist)

The aspect of the Underground Man that has perhaps been least noted and therefore needs to be established first is his rationalism in Section Two of Part One (D on the above chart). In Section One, as Frank has shown, the Underground Man's intellect, which tends to see human action as totally determined by the laws of nature, is pitted against the Underground Man's moral and emotional side. But it is equally true that we see this very same rationalist in Section Two; this time, however, pitted against an irrationalist who argues against determinsim in an intellectually convincing manner. In the second section the Underground Man engages in a heated polemic with the deterministic philosophy of Černyševskij, but the debate is also an internal one, even primarily an internal one: the Underground Man is debating the rationalist in himself, the rationalist as revealed in Section One. In order to see the rationalist in Section Two it is necessary first to go over briefly the structure and substance of the argument we find there.

Section Two of Part One is presented essentially as a debate. First the Underground Man puts forward a number of arguments demonstrating that man is not primarily a rational being and that he has free will, then he cites a short rationalist rebuttal. The irrationalist attempts first to refute the rebuttal and then marshal more arguments in support of his position. There follows the rationalist's rebuttal of the irrationalist's new arguments, and so on for about fifteen pages. For example, the irrationalist argues that throughout history man has acted against his own interest, logically conceived. The rationalist responds with a creditable answer, that men have acted against their own interest only out of ignorance. The irrationalist argues from history and experience that man's greatest interest irrationally conceived, that is, free will, is sometimes against his greatest interest, rationally conceived. The rationalist responds that free will does not exist and that what man calls free will is merely a name he gives to actions which are taken out of self-interest; free will is a mystical category, not a rational one. The irrationalist says that man will go mad on purpose just to be free of reason and the laws of nature. The rationalist responds that even that can be predicted and thus forestalled.

What is at issue here is not the substance of the argument, but the Underground Man's emotional attitude toward the argument.[9] The Underground Man seems to be foaming at the mouth throughout the debate — and it is understandable because his main opponent here is himself:[10] his irrational intellect attempts to refute the deterministic arguments that he himself put forward in Section One. But the irrational self can never convince the rational self with arguments based on evidence from history or the intuitive knowledge of existence. The rational self needs logical proof, it will not be satisfied with an answer that is contrary to reason: that is, the logic of Euclidean geometry and ninety-century natural science, as understood by Černyševskij and his followers. The very intensity of the irrationalist's anger and frustration give testimony to the presence in Section Two of the rational side of his personality that he himself cannot overcome. Thus, far from abruptly shifting from a rationalist to an irrationalist point of view, we see in Section Two the rationalist and irrationalist at nearly equal strength. Just as with Raskol'nikov before the epilogue in *Crime and Punishment*, the irrational forces in the Underground Man have by no means gained complete dominance over the rational ones at the end of Part One.

Although Frank talks about the intellectual irrationalist in Section Two (whom, for the most part, he calls Dostoevskij), he says little in Section Two of the moral-emotive irrationalist (C1 on the chart), an aspect of the Underground Man that he discussed in detail in Section One. Yet there is no one who has read the novel who is not well acquainted with the moral-emotive aspect of the Underground Man's protest against determinism in Section Two. We have already spoken of the Underground Man's passion in arguing his position, his despair at not being able conclusively to disprove the conclusions of determinism, and we shall soon see his spiteful refusal to contribute a brick to the building of the Crystal Palace. In other words, the same moral-emotive revolt against determinism that Frank described in Section One is as present in Section Two as it is in Section One. Again, the closer we look, the more continuity we see between sections.

Now that we have examined the presence in Section Two of both the rationalist and irrationalist sides of the Underground Man (and as far as the irrational side is concerned, specifically its moral-emotive component), the picture may be completed by focusing on the intellectual component of the Underground Man's irrationalism in Section One (A2 on the chart), an aspect of the Underground Man that Frank does not discuss, perhaps because he interprets the opening chapters of the novel as being essentially a revolt against rationalism of only the moral-emotive side of the Underground Man's personality. In fact, this intellectual irrationalism can be found in precisely those passages in which Frank sees only the Underground Man's rationalism. Frank has argued that the Underground Man is unable to act because he has taken the determinist position to its logical conclusion, which makes action meaningless because it denies the existence of free will. But when we turn to Section Two we see that, paradoxically, the irrationalist's argument against determinism and for free will also leads to inertia. It seems, then, that for the Underground Man inertia is the "logical" conclusion not only of rationalism but of irrationalism as well. If the Underground Man, as an intelligent man, can act only in his own self-interest — that is, contribute to the building of the Crystal Palace (a "rational" premise) — then he would rather, even must, do nothing at all, just out of protest (an "irrational" conclusion). "The long and short of it is, gentlemen, that it is better to do nothing! Better conscious inertia! And so long live the underground!" (153.) The Underground Man preserves and asserts his freedom by staying underground, by doing nothing. But does not the Underground Man in Section One come to this very same intellectual, irrational conclusion, asserting his will — that is, consciously doing nothing — *in spite of* the laws of nature, even when he says he is unable to assert his will *because of* the laws of nature? In Section One, for example, the Underground Man argues that he was incapable of becoming anything. He never directly explains why. One explanation, which is never explicitly stated, but nevertheless is strongly implied throughout, lies not in the Underground Man's inability to become something, but in his not wanting to become anything, because to become something is to become something definable, something that ultimately will be entered like any rational number in those logarithmic tables of the future in which all human actions will be registered. The Underground Man craves to be something — every self craves identity — but he mistakes identity for definition (rational definability) and therefore fears it as much as he desires it. Again the Underground Man starts out from a rational premise and ends with an irrational conclusion. To paraphrase the Underground Man himself, he has reached the most revolting conclusions by way of the most inevitable logical combinations.

In Section One, then, the Underground Man takes up the same intellectual position in defense of freedom that he took up at the end of Section Two. At the end of Section Two he refused to act because to act meant to contribute to the building of the Crystal Palace, to his dehumanization, to his reduction to a number. In Section One, the Underground Man refuses to become something because he thinks it would define him and by so doing deprive him of his freedom. The Underground Man's revolt in Section One is not a purely moral-emotive one as Frank makes it out to be; it is just as much an *intellectual* defense of free will as the more obvious defense of free will in Section Two. The emotional revolt reveals itself in masochism and degradation, the intellectual revolt reveals itself in a refusal to act. Furthermore the moral should not be entirely dissociated from the intellectual: because a moral response may not be strictly rational does not mean it cannot be a "reasoned" one. The Underground Man's moral revolt against rationality in Section One is as intellectual as it is emotional.

The break that occurs between Sections One and Two in Part One is then only on the surface a dramatic shift in point of view; it is rather a change of emphasis. Both the personality and philosophy of the Underground Man in Section Two are the same as in Section One. If they were not, the Underground Man would not have arrived at the end of Part One virtually at the same point from which he started: inertia.

This is not to say, however, that the change in emphasis is arbitrary. On the contrary, it is well grounded in the Underground Man's personality. The Underground Man, a volatile mixture of opposite extremes, rapidly and frequently oscillates from one pole of his personality to the other, sometimes within the bounds of a single sentence.[11] (Such a type, of course, is not uncommon in Dostoevskij. In *Crime and Punishment*, a novel written soon after *Notes from the Underground*, the hero, Raskol'nikov, is subject to the same instability: at one moment he may be moved by compassion and give away money that he is in dire need of himself; the next moment he is justifying the murder of thousands for the sake of ambition and an abstract idea.) That the Underground Man should suddenly change gears in the middle of the first

part is perfectly consistent with his personality, as he himself presents it
to us in Section One. That he could adhere to two diametrically opposite
views of human action is characteristic not only of the Underground
Man, but of several of Dostoevskij's other heroes as well. It is not
consistent ideologically, but it is psychologically; and in Dostoevskij it is
what creates artistic consistency. Furthermore, if not just Section Two
but all of Part One is a debate, both in substance and structure, then it is
to be expected that when the other side gets the floor we shall hear the
diametrically opposite point of view. The Underground Man is permit-
ting his rationalist side to have its say first, even if it may only be a means
of quashing its arguments in the rejoinder — though, as we have seen,
the rationalist in him cannot so easily be silenced.

Moreover, the sharp change of emphasis fits in well with the statement
the Underground Man is making about his dilemma. He shows how
diametrically opposite approaches to his problem lead to the same negative
result: inertia. He begins Part One with rational inertia and ends with its
irrationally derived counterpart. It seems as though there can be no solution
to his problem, for he has tried everything.[12] The Underground Man himself
continually emphasizes the extremes and contradictions in his character; and
he underscores the contradictions in his philosophical positions by setting
them in immediate and salient juxtaposition to each other in Part One,
developing first one and then the other.

The Underground Man does not specifically present himself as consciously aware of the contradictions in the philosophical positions that
he espouses, but it is difficult to believe that a man as perceptive as the
hero of *Notes from the Underground* could really be unaware of them
especially when he presents himself as being aware of other contradictions in his views on matters closely related to free will and determinism.
The Underground Man's view of consciousness is a good example. As
the Underground Man emphasizes, consciousness, particularly heightened consciousness, plays an important role in bringing about inertia,
for it is only the man of heightened consciousness that falls prey to
rationalistic notions regarding human actions. In the first chapter of
Section One, the Underground Man presents heightened consciousness
as a disease, perhaps the most debilitating and dangerous disease, leading to
not only inertia but all those other concomitant diseases (boredom, masochism, guilt, frustration, despair, alienation, and resentment) that plague
modern man:

> I would like now to tell you, gentlemen, whether you care to hear it or not, why
> I could not become even an insect. I tell you solemnly, that I have many times

wanted to become an insect. But I was not equal even to that. I swear to you, gentlemen, that to be too conscious is a disease, a real, thorough-going disease. For man's everyday needs, it would have been quite enough to have the ordinary human consciousness, that is, half or a quarter of the amount which falls to the lot of a cultivated man of our unhappy nineteenth century, especially one who has the particular misfortune of inhabiting Petersburg, the most abstract and intentional town on the whole terrestrial globe. (131-32.)

At the end of Chapter Nine, however, the Underground Man, while insisting on the importance of suffering in human life, concludes with a view of consciousness entirely different from the one that he started out with; and here the Underground Man himself calls attention to the contradiction:

And yet I am convinced that man will never renounce real suffering, that is, destruction and chaos. Why suffering is the sole origin of consciousness. *Though I did lay it down at the beginning that consciousness is the greatest misfortune for man,* yet I know man loves it and would not exchange it for any satisfaction. Consciousness, for instance, is infinitely superior to twice two makes four. Once you have mathematical certainty there will be nothing left not only to do but also to understand. All that you could do, then, would be to bottle up your five senses and plunge into contemplation. Whereas with consciousness, even though the same result is attained — that is, there also won't be anything to do — you can at least flog yourself at times, and that will, at any rate, liven you up. Though it may be reactionary, all the same, it is better than nothing." (152; emphasis added, G. R.)

Just as the rational approach at the beginning and the irrational approach at the end lead to the same result, inertia, so do the varying forms of heightened consciousness. In Section One it is responsible for the acceptance of the conclusions of determinism with regard to action, which results in inertia; in Section Two, it is presented as infinitely superior to twice two makes four, but, as the Underground Man states, it also leads to inertia, a higher form of inertia, but inertia just the same. As with determinism and free will, the Underground Man starts off with one proposition in Section One and concludes with its exact opposite in Section Two. The Underground Man is inconsistent, but as he implies here, man's inconsistency and irrationality are part of his nature and there is no good reason why man cannot hold, or even fervently believe in, contradictory positions simultaneously.[13] Man can be rational and irrational at the same moment or he can vacillate between the extremes of rationality and irrationality. We see both these forms in the novel, but the latter, the rapid vacillation between opposite extremes, is evident throughout, perhaps no more strikingly than in the transition from the deterministic arguments of Section One to the advocacy of free will in Section Two. The form reflects the content because it is a manifestation of it. It should be remembered, however, that although the shift of emphasis in Part One has a very important function in the novel, it is a shift of emphasis and not a change in point of view. As has been shown, the Underground Man, despite appearances, is the same entity, both with regard to personality and philosophic position, throughout the entire first part of the novel.

University of Wisconsin at Madison

NOTES

1. *The Short Novels of Dostoevsky*, tr. Constance Garnett (New York: Dial Press, 1945), 139–40. All translations have been checked with the original in F. M. Dostoevskij, *Polnoe sobranie sočinenij*, ed. V. G. Bazanov et al. (30 vols.; Leningrad: Nauka, 1972-), V, 99-179, and revised when necessary.

2. Bernard I. Paris, "'Notes from Underground': A Horneyan Analysis," *PMLA* (1973), 511-22, who bases his psychological study of *Notes from the Underground* on Karen Horney's theory of neurotic defense strategies, argues that the Underground Man's deterministic explanations are rationalizations of the deepest desires of his neurotic self (but not his real self), which is attempting to avoid all emotional involvement with others. See also Joseph Frank, "Nihilism and *Notes from Underground*," *Sewanee Review*, 69 (1961), 8.

3. For a less successful but nevertheless ingenious attempt to resolve the Underground Man's ideological contradictions (by reducing them to the neurotic defense mechanisms of Horney), see Paris, 511-22.

4. Since the terms rationalism and irrationalism have often been imprecisely used by critics of *Notes from the Underground*, I should like to define here how these terms will be used in this article. The term rationalism will designate not Cartesian philosophy, but the view which presupposes that man can be completely understood by means of theorems deducible from axioms and by hypotheses induced from experimental evidence — or to employ the terminology of the Underground Man, by mathematical logic and the natural sciences. The irrationalist is a skeptic of rational philosophy. He believes that the basic truth about man is not rational — is, indeed, irrational — and thus cannot be discovered by rational methods. In *Notes from the Underground* itself, Dostoevskij does not use the word rationalism (*racionalizm*) — though there is one instance of the adjective *neracional'nyj* — but *razum* and *rassudok* instead. For a detailed discussion of the word rationalism in philosophy, see James Ward Smith, *Theme for Reason* (Princeton: Princeton Univ. Press, 1957).

5. The Underground Man's deep-seated rationalism is still ignored in most of the literature on the novel. Only Frank discusses it in detail. For much briefer treatments, see Robert Louis Jackson, *Dostoevsky's Underground Man in Russian Literature* (The Hague: Mouton, 1957), 35-36, 40, 44, 50, and Edward F. Abood, "Fedor Dostoevsky: 'Notes from Underground,'" in his *Underground Man* (San Francisco: Chandler and Sharp, 1973), 27, 29.

6. For several different views of the development of consciousness in the novel, see the interpretations based on Hegel offered by Edward Engelberg, "The Underground Man and Hegel's 'Unhappy Consciousness' and 'The Beautiful Soul,'" *The Unknown Distance: From Consciousness to Conscience, Goethe to Camus* (Cambridge, Mass.: Harvard Univ. Press, 1972), 89-110; Martin Rice, "Dostoevsky's *Notes from Underground* and Hegel's 'Master and Slave,'" *Canadian–American Slavic Studies*, 8 (1974), 359-69. Rice discusses only the master-slave

relationship in Part Two. In a footnote on page 368, however, he suggests that there may also exist a development of consciousness from the master-slave relationship in Part Two to the "unhappy consciousness" (as described in Engelberg) in Part One. The ideological development of the Underground Man from the Romanticism of the forties (Part Two) to the Nihilism of the sixties (Part One) has been discussed in detail in Frank, 1-33. See also Rudolph Neuhäuser, "Romanticism in the Post-Romantic Age: A Typological Study of Antecedents of Dostoevskii's Man from Underground," *Canadian-American Slavic Studies*, 8 (1974), 333-58. Frank and Neuhäuser, however, are concerned only with the more obvious (though very important) ideological relationships between Parts One and Two; they do not treat these relationships within Part One itself.

7.   For the relation between author and narrator in the "philosophical tale," see Northrop Frye's discussion of "analysis" in *Anatomy of Criticism* (New York: Atheneum, 1967), 308-12.

8.   My method will obviously radically differ from several recent Structural and Deconstructionist studies, which look upon *Notes from the Underground* either as anti-fiction, metafiction, or an autonomous system of signs. See, for example, James M. Holquist, "Plot and Counter-Plot in *Notes from Underground*," *Canadian-American Slavic Studies*, 6 (1972), 225-38; Thomas M. Kavanagh, "Dostoevsky's *Notes from Underground*: The Form of the Fiction," *Texas Studies in Language and Literature*, 14 (1972), 491-507; Wolfgang W. Holdheim, "Die Struktur von Dostoevskij's 'Aufzeichnungen aus Kellerloch,'" *Deutsche Vierteljahrsschrift für Literaturwissenschaft und Geistesgeschichte*, 47 (1973), 310-23; Scott Consigny, "The Paradox of Textuality: Writing as Entrapment and Deliverance in *Notes from the Underground*," *Canadian-American Slavic Studies*, 12 (1978), 341-52.

9.   For a strictly philosophical analysis of the Underground Man's arguments, see Joseph Beatty, "From Rebellion and Alienation to Salutary Freedom: A Study on *Notes from Underground*," *Soundings*, 61 (1978), 181-205.

10.   For a psychological interpretation of the Underground Man's dialogue with himself, see James Lethcoe, "Self-Deception in Dostoevskij's *Notes from the Underground*," *Slavic and East European Journal*, 10 (1966), 10-11. For Paris, 511-22, the Underground Man's dialogue with himself is explained by his moving from one neurotic self to the other.

11.   For the best psychological analysis of the extreme and rapid changes of the Underground Man's personality, see Paris, 511-12.

12.   This essentially is the view presented by M. M. Baxtin, *Problemy tvorčestva Dostoevskogo* (Leningrad: Priboj, 1929), 173-88, who argues that the Underground Man is aware of everything that the author is. See also Abood, 13-29. But, as is well known, Dostoevskij originally intended to present faith in Christ as the antithesis to both the rational and irrational approaches of the Underground Man — that is, to present Christ as the only real solution to the Underground Man's seemingly irresolvable dilemma. See F. M. Dostoevskij, *Pis'ma*, ed. A. S. Dolinin (4 vols.; Moscow-Leningrad: GIXL, 1928-59), I, 353. Supporting Dostoevskij in this regard is Reed Merrill, "The Mistaken Endeavor: Dostoevsky's *Notes from Underground*," *Modern Fiction Studies*, 18 (1973), 509, who argues that the Underground Man's situation is a means of showing that "without faith ethical man must struggle from paradox to paradox, through self-examination after self-examination, in a fruitless, often self-destructive attempt to find ontological fixity and that his efforts are doomed to failure without transcendent faith."

13.   Lethcoe, 1-11, citing the Underground Man's numerous contradictions, maintains that the Underground Man's frequent lying shows that he is in a state of self-deception throughout the novel. Yet the Underground Man's contradictory statements can be seen as lies only if we conceive of him as one self. Once we postulate a divided self, almost all of his statements can be taken to be sincere, from the point of view of one of these selves. Thus, at all times, one self will disbelieve what the other self fervently believes; and the stronger one self believes, the stronger the other self disbelieves. It is also difficult to see the Underground Man as self-deceived when he continually exposes all his "lies."

DENIS DAVYDOV AND *WAR AND PEACE*

Lauren G. Leighton

It is generally known that the poet-hussar Denis Davydov (1781-1839) served as the prototype for the character of the hussar and partisan leader Vas'ka Denisov in Tolstoj's *War and Peace*, but it is less well known that Davydov was a serious historian whose military accounts, memoirs, and theories of warfare were used quite extensively in the writing of the novel. Tolstoj found in Davydov's historical writings a wealth of accurate details and personal knowledge of events, and he used them with unusual effect, acknowledging that it was Davydov who "first provided the tone of truth" for his novel about the Napoleonic campaigns.[1] Credit for the "tone of truth" is extremely high praise from Tolstoj, whose own love of truth is one of his rare consistencies, and there is no doubt that he admired Davydov more unreservedly than is usual for him. He once remarked that "the glory belongs to Denis Davydov, who desires so fervently in his works to show himself familiar with all the European codes of war" (*PSS*, XV, 101). He used the glory of Davydov's life and works to substantiate his own emphatic opinions about war and history, and he adapted anecdotes, facts, and whole descriptions to add depth and reality to *War and Peace*.

According to materials in Tolstoj's *Complete Collected Works*, the author used two of Davydov's published works in the writing of *War and Peace*: the fourth edition of his *Works in Three Volumes* published in 1860, and *An Analysis of Three Articles Contained in Napoleon's Memoirs* published in 1825.[2] The latter work, a refutation of certain claims made by Napoleon regarding partisan warfare and the Russian frost in the Moscow Campaign, is available in *Works* and was not used extensively. The former contains many of Davydov's poems and prose works, but is not a complete collection of his writings.[3] Tolstoj's favorite work and source of greatest use was Davydov's famed "Diary of my Partisan Operations in 1812," briefly titled "Partisan's Diary," and he also showed an interest in "A Meeting with Kamenskij" and "Tilsit in 1807."[4] Tolstoj must also have used Davydov's proscribed *Memoirs*, published abroad in 1863 during the writing of *War and Peace*, for he was more than slightly familiar with "Various Anecdotes, Predominantly about Aleksej Petrovič Ermolov," available only in this text.[5] Tolstoj found Davydov valuable first of all as the prototype of the character of Vas'ka Denisov, and then for his accounts of battles, particularly his reports of partisan raids, characterizations of historical figures, anecdotes with the authentic flavor of history, credible attitudes towards war, and descriptions of places and events. Davydov was an excellent writer whose works are written in an adventurous, unabashedly boastful style and filled with exciting events and original impressions. Davydov was also a perfect representation of Tolstoj's strong ideas about history as a force of the people, and the author appreciated him as a man of natural Russian instinct who understood perfectly that the Moscow Campaign was a people's war.

Existing studies of Davydov's influence on *War and Peace* are brief and to two points: they compare the character of Denisov to his real-life prototype and they compare texts to demonstrate how Tolstoj adapted Davydov's writings to his own needs. These studies are concerned with the way Russia's great Realist used factual materials to create Realist fiction.[6] Not yet noted is that there is a curious duality to Tolstoj's use of Davydov and his works. Tolstoj did indeed create a Denisov who is very much like Davydov, and he did accept Davydov's testimonies with unusual lack of reserve. But although Denisov looks like Davydov, and has Davydov's mannerisms, and speaks Davydov's words, he is ultimately unlike Davydov. At issue here is not the question of the difference between prototypes and fictional characters but Tolstoj's ability to copy an actual personality with marked thoroughness and yet create a completely different character. This duality is equally true of Tolstoj's use of Davydov's writings. Tolstoj agreed with Davydov's views to an extent not at all in keeping with his notorious arbitrariness, and yet he managed to be as opinionated here as elsewhere. His use of Davydov's works is thus as important for what he ignores and changes, as for what he accepts without challenge. For this reason, any consideration of Davydov's influence on Tolstoj has to show that the character of Denisov manages to be both a copy of Davydov and yet a completely different personality, and that Tolstoj managed to be both unusually receptive to Davydov's ideas, and typically arbitrary.

Tolstoj's descriptions of Vasilij Fedorovič Denisov, hussar officer, partisan leader, friend and commander of Nikolaj Rostov, and the lonely soldier who honored Nataša Rostova with her first proposal, match perfectly the portraits of Denis Vasil'evič Davydov:

> Denisov was a little man with a red face, sparkling black eyes, tousled black hair and whiskers. He was wearing an unbuttoned tunic, wide breeches that fell in folds, and on the back of his head a crushed hussar's cap.

> ...puckering up his face as if he were smiling, and showing his short, strong teeth, Denisov began with his short-fingered hands ruffling his thick, black hair that was tangled like a forest.[7]

Davydov was indeed a little man with a red face, black eyes, and tousled black hair. He was acutely conscious of his tiny stature — a good case could be made for his heroism as a compensation for his size — and he was every bit as dark as his Tatar ancestors. We do not have a portrait of Davydov in battle, but surely he must have looked like Denisov at the crossing of the River Enns in Austria in 1805:

> The snub-nosed, black hairy face of Vas'ka Denisov, and his little, battered figure, and the sinewy, short-fingered hand in which he held the hilt of his naked sword — his whole figure was just as it always was, especially in the evening after he had drunk a couple of bottles. He was only rather more red in the face than usual, and tossing back his shaggy head, as birds do when they drink, his little legs mercilessly driving the spurs into his good horse Bedouin, he galloped to the other flank of the squadron, looking as though he were falling backwards in the saddle. (One, two, VIII.)

Davydov lived according to the code of Hussarism (*gusarščina*), which required a hussar to be as refined in society as he was crude in battle, and Tolstoj understood this perfectly when he wrote that "to Rostov's surprise Denisov ... was quite as dashing a figure in a drawing-room as on the field of battle, and was polite to the ladies and gentlemen as Rostov had never expected to see him" (One, four, I). So also did Tolstoj appreciate Davydov's sensitivity about his size: "... it was only on horseback and in the mazurka that Denisov's low stature was not noticeable and that he looked the dashing hero he felt himself to be" (One, four, XII). Tolstoj also knew how to describe Denisov as a partisan leader, and here he availed himself of Davydov's descriptions of himself. In *War and Peace* Denisov's face is "grown thin" and "covered with a thick, short, black beard." He wears a Cossack coat and "a holy image of Nikolaj, the wonder-worker, on his breast." (Four, three, IV and VIII). In "Partisan's Diary" Davydov reports several close escapes from death by peasant axe, from which he learned to adapt himself to local dress and customs: "I donned a peasant caftan, began growing a beard, and instead of the Order of St. Anne hung an image of St. Nikolaj, the wonder-worker, and began speaking completely in the language of the people" (II, 42-43).

Like Denisov, Davydov was an outspoken man frequently in trouble with the authorities. He believed that he should have achieved the highest rank and command of an army. Instead, he was denied commands and promotions until needed in the six wars in which he fought. He left the army twice, and the last years of his life were characterized by bitter complaints against the government and merciless delight in the latest Petersburg scandals. Tolstoj corresponded with Davydov's son D. D. Davydov, from whom he obtained significant materials and a family view of General Davydov's bitterness about his career.[8] At the end of *War and Peace* Tolstoj describes a conversation in which "Denisov, who was dissatisfied with the government on account of his own disappointments in the service, heard with glee all the follies, as he considered them that were going on now in St. Petersburg, and made his comments on Pierre's words in harsh and cutting phrases" (Epilogue I, XIV). The first epilogue to *War and Peace* was intended to pave the way for its sequel, *The Decembrists*, and Denisov is shown to be a potential recruit for the Decembrist conspiracy when he makes his memorable pun on the German word *Bund* and the Russian word *bunt* 'revolt': "Everything's rotten and corrupt; I agree there; only your Tugenbund, I don't understand, but a *bunt* now, Je suis votre homme!" (Epilogue I, XIV.) Tolstoj correctly acknowledged Davydov's fame as a punster here, but so far as a readiness to join the Decembrist conspiracy, Denisov and Davydov are decisively not alike. Whatever his bitterness towards the government, Davydov was not a revolutionary, and not even very liberal. In "Various Anecdotes ..." he recounted the attempts of his cousin Vasilij Davydov to recruit him into the conspiracy and emphasized his own refusal to join a *Tugenbund*: "Why do you keep harping about a German *bunt*? Show me a Russian *bunt* and I'll up and pacify it" (*Zapiski*, 42).

Denisov appears prominently in *War and Peace* as the leader of a detachment of hussars and cossacks formed into an irregular partisan force to fight behind Napoleon's lines. Davydov, of course, was the founder of modern guerrilla warfare. He used this ancient mode of war in an entirely new way with great success and in defiance of the rules of war in force at the time. On the eve of the Battle of Borodino Fieldmarshal Kutuzov personally gave him command of a small party which was so successful in disrupting the French supply lines and so effective against larger enemy units that he became known abroad, even to Sir Walter Scott who once planned to write a novel about Davydov titled *The Black Captain*.[9] During the late summer and autumn of 1812 he led his steadily growing detachment in numerous raids on the French, building a virtual army of soldiers and peasants which alarmed Alexander I, eventually making his way to Poland and on to the capture of Dresden, always leading a vanguard of the Russian army, and finally leading a regular division first and triumphantly into the streets of Paris in 1814. Davydov knew that he was leading a people's war — this was what frightened Alexander and the high command — and he understood that this savage way of fighting was "not for kissing."[10] To Tolstoj, with his emphasis on heroes as a reflection of the will of the people and his contempt for the egoistic great men of history, Davydov was of understandable importance to *War and Peace*. Tolstoj spoke directly in his novel about Davydov as a man of authentic Russian instinct:

> Denis Davydov was the first to feel with his Russian instinct the value of this terrible cudgel which belabored the French, and asked no questions about the

etiquette of the military art; and to him belongs the credit of the first step towards the recognition of this method of warfare. The first detachment of irregulars — Davydov's — was formed on the 24th of August, and others soon followed. (Four, three, III.)

Tolstoj believed that "one of the most conspicuous and advantageous departures from the so-called rules of warfare is the independent action of men acting against men huddled in a mass. Such independent action is always seen in a war that assumes a national character .... War of this kind has been called partisan warfare on the supposition that this name defined its special significance." In Tolstoj's opinion, partisan warfare is "always successful, as history testifies." (Four, three, II.)

"Partisan's Diary" is a racy and pungent account of Davydov's adventures behind the French lines. Partisan warfare required ingenuity and boldness, and Davydov was always anxious about keeping his independence. Tolstoj begins his account of Denisov's partisan operations with a story of his outwitting of two rival partisan leaders eager to take command of his detachment:

> On the 22nd of October, Denisov, who was a leader of a band of irregulars, was eagerly engaged in a typical operation of this irregular warfare. From early morning he had been with his men, moving about the woods, watching a big convoy of cavalry baggage that had dropped behind the other French troops .... Not only Denisov and Doloxov (who was also a leader of a small band acting in the same district) were aware of the presence of this convoy. Some generals in command of some larger detachments, with staff-officers also, knew of this convoy, and, as Denisov said, their mouths were watering for it. Two of these generals — one a Pole, the other a German — had almost at the same time sent to Denisov an invitation to join their respective detachments in attacking the convoy. "No, friends, I wasn't born yesterday!" said Denisov, on reading these documents; and he wrote to the German that in spite of his ardent desire to serve under so brilliant and renowned a general, he must deprive himself of that happiness because he was already under the command of the Polish general. To the Pole he wrote the same thing, informing him that he was already serving under the command of the German. (Four, three, III.)

Tolstoj drew on an actual entry in "Partisan's Diary" for this account. On October 21 (not October 22) Davydov was presented with the same dilemma when he was invited by two rival commanders, General Ožarskij and Count Orlov-Denisov, to join them in an attack on a convoy of cavalry baggage. He sent identical messages to his rivals, assuring each that he was under the command of the other, thus forestalling their attempts to coopt him until he was able to get assurance of his independence from Kutuzov. (II, 87-88.)

Five days later, however, Davydov spotted a French division under the command of General Ogereau between Ljaxovo and Belkino. Realizing that it was too large for his own small detachment, he overcame his scruples and united with two other partisans — Figner and Seslavin — and invited Count Orlov-Denisov to assume command of a raid. The operation was successful and a great many Russian prisoners were liberated. (II, 97-101.) This is the origin of Denisov's partisan raid in partnership with the adventurer Doloxov, the raid in which Petja Rostov is killed (Four, three, III–XXII). Tolstoj's fictional treatment of the raid is factual in almost every detail to Davydov's account, the only exception being that in *War and Peace* the event is placed between Mikulino and Šamševo. Twenty sections of one part of the novel are thus indebted almost in total to Davydov as a source. Tolstoj's acount is accurate to its source even in the use of such details as partisan jargon. Where in an entry of September 3 Davydov reported that he was eager to attack a supply train, but, lest he blunder into a trap, had to capture a "tongue" (*jazyk*; II, 46), Tolstoj wrote: "There was only one thing that he still needed to know, and that was what troops these were; and for that object Denisov needed a 'tongue' (that is, some man belonging to that column of the enemy)" (Four, three, III). And as Dayvdov sent a daredevil out to capture a "tongue," so also Denisov sends out his own bravo for the same purpose.

As an interlude in the account of Denisov's raid, Tolstoj tells the story of the young French drummer-boy who is befriended by Petja Rostov. Petja is ashamed to show a kindness to a prisoner, but to his relief Denisov finds nothing to be ashamed of: "Yes, poor little fellow .... Fetch him in here. His name is Vincent Bosse. Fetch him in." (Four, three, VII.) According to Tolstoj, Vincent Bosse is called Vesennij by the Cossacks and Visenja by the Russian soldiers and peasants. In real life the boy was named Vincent Bode, and Davydov called him Vikentij. In an entry for October 9 he wrote that the fifteen-year-old Vikentij Bode caused his heart to "beat with pity." "How could I abandon this unfortunate to the chance circumstances of the hunger, cold, and shelterless expanses while I had the means of his salvation at hand?" Vincent Bode remained with Davydov all the way to Paris, "healthy, happy, and almost grown up, where I delivered him personally to his aged father." (II, 81-82.)

Partisan warfare was not, however, a compassionate mode of the military art. In "Partisan's Diary" Davydov makes it seem exciting, adventurous, even comical at times, but Tolstoj knew better and likened it to dogs falling on a wounded animal. The only incidents of sadism Davydov reports are the actions of the partisan leader A. S. Figner, in an entry for October 26:

> I had long heard about the barbaric deeds of Figner, but was unable to believe that his cruelty went to the point of murdering disarmed enemies .... It seemed that any evil feeling whatsoever, even less a feeling of vengeance, was unable to

find place in the hearts of our soldiers …. Scarcely did he hear about my prisoners than he hurried to me with a request to let them be torn to pieces by some sort of new Cossacks who were still not, in his opinion, honed to a proper pitch of ferocity. I can't describe what I felt at these words — Figner's handsome features and the kind, pleasant expression of his eyes, so it seemed, spoke to the contrary.

Davydov and Figner argued bitterly about the proper way to treat prisoners:

"Perhaps you do not shoot prisoners?" "Yes," I said, "I shot two traitors to the fatherland, one of whom was a robber of a temple of God." "Then you have shot prisoners," he said. "Never," I replied, "go and ask, even in secret, among my Cossacks." "Well, we'll go on together," he said, "and you'll soon drop these prejudices." "If my honor as a soldier and my compassion are indeed prejudices," I said, "then I will die with them…." (II, 95-96.)

At the end of the raid, on October 28, as the cursing prisoners are led past the two partisan leaders, they are silenced by Figner's menacing words, "Filez, filez!" (II, 101).

The counterpart of Figner in *War and Peace* is the sadistic Doloxov. The character of Doloxov is based for the most part on Fedor Tolstoj, Davydov's close friend and Tolstoj's uncle, but it is Davydov's relationship with Figner that is relevant to the character of Doloxov in the sections of *War and Peace* dealing with partisan warfare (Zajdenšnur, 138; Rozova, 126). The argument between Denisov and Doloxov over treatment of prisoners is a memorable incident in the novel:

"What do I do with them? I take a receipt for them, and then send them off!" cried Denisov, suddenly flushing. "And I make bold to say that I haven't a single man's life on my conscience. Is there any difference in your sending thirty, or even three hundred men, under escort to the town rather than stain — I say so bluntly — one's honor as a soldier?" "But for me and you, brother, it's high time to drop such delicacy," Doloxov went on, apparently deriving peculiar gratification from talking on a subject irritating to Denisov. "Why, we all know how much your receipts are worth. You send off a hundred men and thirty reach the town. They die of hunger or are killed along the way. So isn't it just as well to make short work of them?" (Four, three, VIII.)

And at the end of the raid Tolstoj added a subtle detail from "Partisan's Diary": "'Filez, filez!' said Doloxov, who had picked up the expression from the French; and when he met the eyes of the passing prisoners, his eyes gleamed with a cruel light" (Four, three XV). Even the detail of the receipts for prisoners is taken from "Partisan's Diary": "I always turned over prisoners under receipt" (II, 45). And just as Doloxov visits the French camp in a French uniform on the eve of the raid, so also Figner habitually spied on the French in this dangerous manner: "As a matter of fact, on another occasion he appeared dressed in a French uniform in the middle of the enemy camp and surveyed its disposition. This was repeated more than once." (II, 95.)

Tolstoj especially liked the anecdotal quality of Davydov's writings. Davydov was one of the finest conversationalists of his time — Puškin considered him and Prince Vjazemskij the best story-tellers and punsters in Russian society — and his prose works are filled with fascinating anecdotes about persons and events. A chief theme of *War and Peace* is the wisdom of the Commander-in Chief, Prince M. I. Kutuzov, who knows that the best way to fight the French is not to fight at all, but rather let frost and distance take their toll. A key motif of this theme is the conflict between Kutuzov and the militant General A. P. Ermolov: the young general constantly pressures Kutuzov to join battle, and, conversely, whenever Kutuzov resolves to fight, Ermolov sabotages his plans. This conflict is always dramatized in anecdotal incidents — subtly indirect confrontations, usually in the presence of the other officers of Kutuzov's suite. Thus, when Ermolov reports to Kutuzov that it will be impossible to stop the Grande Armée at Fili, after the battle of Borodino, Tolstoj uses an anecdote to convey the situation. When Ermolov suggests that battle is not possible:

> Kutuzov looked at him in wonder, and made him repeat the words he had just uttered. When he had done so, he put out his hand to him. "Give me your hand," he said; and turning it so as to feel the pulse, he said: "You are not feeling well, darling. Think what you are saying." (Three, three, III.)

Just prior to the Battle at Taturino, Ermolov attends an all-night party in order to avoid Kutuzov's command to alert the army. When Kutuzov awakens to find his troops unprepared, he is at first outraged, but for political reasons accepts the inevitable and allows the insubordination to pass:

> Kutuzov took a sidelong glance behind him at Ermolov, to whom he had not spoken since the previous day. "Here they are begging to advance, proposing all sorts of projects, and as soon as you get to work, there's nothing ready and the enemy, forewarned, takes his measures." Ermolov half closed his eyes and faintly smiled, as he heard these words. He knew the storm had blown over him, and that Kutuzov would not go beyond this hint. "That's his little joke at my expense," said Ermolov, softly poking Raevskij, near him, with his knee. (Four, two, VII.)

Soon after this, Ermolov cannot resist poking fun in return at Kutuzov for the unexpected reversal of their roles: "The time has not passed, your highness, the enemy has not gone away. If you were to command an advance? Or else the guards won't have a sight of smoke." (Four, two, VII.)

Both of these incidents are based on anecdotes in "Partisan's Diary." In his account of Ermolov's actions at Fili, Davydov wrote:

> When Ermolov began heatedly demonstrating that it was impossible to consider a new battle, the prince, feeling his pulse, said to him: "Are you all right, darling?" "I am healthy enough," he replied, "to see the impossibility of a new battle." (II, 36.)

Davydov's account of Ermolov's insubordination at Tarutino is also similar to Tolstoj's:

> Kutuzov and his suite, in the ranks of which were Raevskij and Ermolov, stopped near the guards; at that moment the prince said: "Here they are begging to advance, proposing projects of all sorts, and as soon as you get to work, there's nothing been done and the enemy, warned in advance, having taken his measures, retreats in good time." Ermolov, understanding that these words referred to him, touched Raevskij's stirrup and said: "He is making merry at my expense." (II, 73.)

Ermolov soon became impatient with Kutuzov's reversion to slow pursuit of the enemy, and remarked:

> "The opportunity has not been lost, the enemy has not gone away; now, your highness, it is only fitting that we, for our part, advance in friendly fashion, because from here the guards can't even see the smoke." (II, 73.)

As can be seen, Tolstoj makes perceptible changes when he adapts Davydov's text to *War and Peace*. He adjusts the syntax of quoted phrases to make them more telling, he adds tones, mannerisms, and revealing little characteristics to his speakers. Tolstoj's changes are sometimes due to his use of other testimonies about incidents, sometimes he arbitrarily reinterprets statements for his own needs, sometimes he is even careless (Christian, 59-94). With Davydov, however, Tolstoj is true to the original even when making changes for his own stylistic effect, and this can be seen especially clearly in his use of Davydov's works for their authentic soldier's language and for the "spirit of the time." Davydov was useful to Tolstoj for his authentic attitude towards war, which he expressed in a fast, spicy style. Here perhaps more than in any other respect Davydov was able to "provide the tone of truth" that Tolstoj so highly valued. Davydov's military experience complemented Tolstoj's in many ways, most especially in a way of war and patriotism that Tolstoj could not have known in the pacification of the Causasus or the ignominious defeat of the Crimean War. Tolstoj found Davydov's account of the Treaty of Tilsit, in the work titled "Tilsit in 1807," to be a good source of Russian patriotic attitudes, and he used Davydov's own attitude in his depictions of young Nikolaj Rostov during his first encounter with the reality of war. Rostov's impression of the aftermath of the Battle of Pratzen Hill, for example, is reminiscent of Davydov's account of his first view of war at the Battle of Morungen in 1805, in "A Meeting with Kamenskij." Thus, where Davydov confessed to a feeling of fear at the sight of "turned-up bodies with open glazed eyes, still gazing, so it seemed, at the sky ... scattered about like vessels of precious drink smashed by a violent hand ..." (I, 121), Rostov is terrified by a scene where "all over the field, like ridges of dung on well-kept ploughland lay the heaps of dead and wounded, a dozen or fifteen bodies to every three acres" (One, three, XVIII).[11] Rostov and Davydov also share a love of Alexander I in their youth. Tolstoj devotes considerable attention to Rostov's attitudes and his desire to sacrifice himself for his tsar:

> Rostov was standing near the trumpeters, and with his keen eyes he recognized the Tsar from a distance and watched him approaching. When the Tsar was only twenty paces away, and Nikolaj saw clearly in every detail the handsome, young, and happy face, he experienced a feeling of tenderness and ecstasy such as he had never known before. Everything in the Tsar — every feature, every movement — seemed to him full of charm. (One, three, VIII.)

Davydov experienced much the same feeling when he saw Alexander up close:

> Oh! How clearly — despite my youth — how clearly my soul understood the deep, but mute grief of this pure father of his people, this man of most virtuous life! With what tear-filled eyes, but also with what ecstasy I looked upon the Monarch who preserved complete outward calm, all the dignity of his high order in the face of, as it seemed, unavoidable and final ruin! (I, 307-8.)

For all his love of the tsar, Rostov is unable to reconcile himself to the treaty with Napoleon, and in this he represented for Tolstoj the attitude of the entire Russian army. According to Tolstoj:

> Rostov, like the whole army indeed, was far from having passed through that revolution of feeling in regard to Napoleon and the French — transforming them from foes into friends — that had taken place at headquarters and in Boris. In the army everyone was still feeling the same mingled hatred, fear, and contempt for Bonaparte and the French. (Two, two, XIX.)

Again Davydov's feelings at Tilsit are similar to Rostov's:

> The society of the French was of little use to us; not one of us sought either friendship or acquaintance with any of them, despite their efforts — as the result of a secret order by Napoleon — to attract us with every kind of affability and courtesy. For affability and courtesy we repaid affability and courtesy — and that was that. (I, 310.)

Finally, Tolstoj found many of Davydov's descriptions of places useful to *War and Peace*. Here one could point to almost any description in Davydov's works, from Austria in 1805 to Smolensk and Moscow in 1812, and back across the River Niemen to Europe. Not simply in physical descriptions, which were available to Tolstoj in many accounts, but in specific details and unmistakably Davydovian language. Borodino, Fili, Tarutino, the river Berezova — the tone of Davydov's truth can be found in Tolstoj's descriptions of the events at all these places and others. Especially similar in details are Davydov's description in "Partisan's Diary" of the field of Borodino on the eve of battle (II, 32-33) and Tolstoj's description of the same scene (Three, two, XXI). Even the inexperienced Pierre Bezuxov's impression of the scene corresponds in details to Davydov's expert description. Tolstoj was aware that Borodino was Davydov's estate, and he wrote that "some ten thousands of men lay sacrificed on the fields and meadows belonging to the Davydov family" (Three, two, XXXIX). Davydov's description of the meeting of the two emperors at Tilsit is also an unmistakable source of Tolstoj's treatment. Thus, where Boris Drubeckoj, Rostov's childhood friend, sees the raft on the river with the monograms of the two monarchs, watches Napoleon ride through his guards along the further bank, notes Alexander's pensive face as he sits silent in an inn on the bank of the River Niemen, and witnesses the event where Napoleon reaches the raft first and helps Alexander from his boat, Davydov saw Napoleon galloping at full speed through the ranks of his Old Guard, watched Alexander sit at a table in the inn, and noted that "Napoleon's boat reached the pavilion a bit sooner, so that he gained several seconds in which, leaping from the boat, to cross the pavilion with several quick steps and greet our Emperor as he stepped from his own boat." Davydov also describes the pavilion, with its large letters N and A, and both Davydov and Tolstoj conclude their descriptions by noting how the two emperors disappear inside the pavilion. (Two, two, XIX; I, 304-8.) Tolstoj knew that Davydov was an inveterate taker of notes, and it is curious that he adds to his description the remark that "Boris made it his habit to keep an attentive watch on what was passing round him, and to note it all down."

As for Tolstoj's differences with Davydov, he does not at any time openly refute Davydov in *War and Peace*, as he so often disputes the opinions of his other sources. Instead, he either ignores Davydov's inconvenient opinions or refutes them without identifying Davydov as his opponent. He especially ignores the fact that Davydov thoroughly disapproved of Kutuzov's policy of retreat and avoidance of battle in 1812. Tolstoj, of course, approved Kutuzov's policy, and he saw this acceptance of the inevitability of war and history as the best proof of Kutuzov's wisdom as a leader of the Russian nation in a time of great crisis. Here Tolstoj failed to appreciate Davydov's natural Russian instinct, or found it inapplicable to his view of history. The differences between the two men in this all-important aspect of *War and Peace* are centered on two historical figures, General A. P. Ermolov and General D. S. Doxturov. To Tolstoj, Doxturov was a quiet, unassuming man whom he admired and perceived as a crucial figure of several decisive military events. To Davydov, Doxturov was indecisive and lacked good judgment. And where Davydov admired Ermolov, who was his cousin and whom he praised as a bold officer who frequently saved the day in opposition to Kutuzov's reluctance to fight, Tolstoj treated Ermolov as a vain seeker of glory who lacked Kutuzov's wisdom and instinct for the will of the Russian army and people. Davydov collected numerous materials for a biography of Ermolov, and when he gave up his plans for this project he added them to "Partisan's Diary," largely as footnotes, or left them as a collection to be published in the 1863 *Memoirs*. Tolstoj used these materials extensively in *War and Peace*, but he completely reinterpreted them in a way that can be seen as a debate with Davydov.

At the beginning of his treatment of Napoleon's abandonment of Moscow, Tolstoj takes time to praise Doxturov as "that modest little general whom no one has depicted to us making plans of campaign, dashing at the head of regiments, dropping crosses about batteries, or doing anything of the kind ...." In Tolstoj's opinion, "people looked on and spoke of Doxturov as lacking in decision and penetration, though all through the Russian wars with the French ... we always find him in command where the position is particularly difficult." In proof of his contention, Tolstoj recounts Doxturov's actions at Austerlitz, Smolensk, Borodino, Fominskoe, and Malej Jaroslavec, always stressing that Doxturov won the battles and others took the credit. (Four, two, XV.) Where history has credited Ermolov's swift actions for forcing Napoleon to retreat along the same wasted route along which he invaded Russia, Tolstoj believed that Doxturov was the man really responsible for this brilliant maneuver. His sarcastic references to those who make plans, lead regiments, and drop crosses about batteries are aimed directly at Ermolov, one of whose celebrated acts was to throw crosses at the heaps of corpses below the notorious Raevskij Redoubt — an event reported by both Tolstoj and Davydov.

Davydov, who was the person who looked on and spoke of Doxturov as "a far from penetrating general" (II, 75), also devotes attention to the officer, usually in context with his accounts about Ermolov. Doxturov's name appears throughout "Partisan's Diary" in reports of the battles at Smolensk, Borodino, Fominskoe, and Malej Jaroslavec. Tolstoj was particularly attentive to Davydov's account of the actions of Ermolov and Doxturov at Fominskoe. According to both Davydov and Tolstoj, Doxturov was sent in early October to attack Broussier's division at Fominskoe. On October 10, on the advice of Ermolov, he stopped at Aristovo while, unknown to the Russians, the entire Grande Armée joined Broussier at Fominskoe and prepared to march along a well-provisioned route to Smolensk. Fortunately, on October 11 the partisan leader Seslavin spotted the French army and rushed to Aristovo to warn Ermolov and Doxturov. At this point, Tolstoj and Davydov seriously diverge in their accounts. According to Tolstoj, Ermolov panicked and wanted to call the Russian army to immediate battle. Doxturov, who according to Tolstoj was more attuned to Kutuzov's sense of the inevitability of history, insisted that Kutuzov be informed first. (Three, two, XV.) According to Davydov, who certainly never considered attacking French troops on impulse a futile exercise, Doxturov feared to anger Kutuzov by calling out the army without his knowledge. Ermolov, being a more decisive and penetrating general, thereupon took full responsibility and ordered the army out in Kutuzov's name. In Davydov's opinion, this saved the day and enabled the Russians to gain victory at Fominskoe. (II, 74-75.) Tolstoj, of course, believed that the action was futile. Unlike Kutuzov and Doxturov, Ermolov did not understand that history, not individual initiative, decided that Napoleon would have to retreat along the wasted route back to Europe.

At no point in his interpretation of the roles of Kutuzov, Doxturov, and Ermolov — an interpretation that is crucial to his interpretation of war and history as a whole — does Tolstoj reveal that he is engaging in a debate with Davydov. To identify his opponent would weaken his reliance on Davydov as a figure of incontestably Russian greatness, of course; and it might have damaged Davydov's greatest value to *War and Peace*, Tolstoj's dependence on him as an example of the authentic Russian instinct he so greatly valued. But despite this respect for Davydov, Tolstoj had his own strong opinions and he remained unabashedly arbitrary in his use of historical materials. There is thus a consistency to his duality: he accepted Davydov's testimonies with, for him, exceptional lack of criticism, and in those instances where Davydov's views did not accord with his needs, he refuted him anonymously. This is clearly a deliberate tactic to which Tolstoj gave serious thought in the writing of *War and Peace*. In effect, Tolstoj had his cake and ate it too: he sustained Davydov's great value to his novel without compromising it.

The question of Davydov as a prototype for the character of Vas'ka Denisov is another problem entirely. As has been stated, the problem here is not the usual problem of the difference between real life and fiction, but that regardless of Denisov's similarity to Davydov he is an entirely different personality. Denisov looks like Davydov. He shares Davydov's mannerisms even to their identical speech defect, both men being asthmatics. He speaks

Davydov's words, performs his military feats, expresses his opinions. And yet he is almost the antithesis of Denis Davydov. Denisov is certainly not a poet, nor even the least bit poetic, for example, and where Davydov was one of the most brilliant men of his time, sophisticated and articulate, an aggressive seeker of attention and cultivator of his image as the partisan poet, Denisov is a modest man, even a plodder, a limited man of unimaginative intellect who makes his way doggedly through the intricacies of Russian society and army politics. Denisov is a fine squadron and company commander, but he could never rise to Davydov's high rank of lieutenant general. He is not without social polish, and he is an ingenious partisan leader, but he is too rough and honest to be compared to the really quite crafty and devious Davydov. Thus, where Denisov is bested in his argument with Doloxov about the treatment of prisoners, Davydov presents himself in "Partisan's Diary" as Figner's superior in debate. And where Denisov's honor is outraged by Doloxov's sadistic behavior, Davydov, for all his professed disapproval, takes keen delight in recounting the details of Figner's vicious treatment of unarmed French prisoners. (II, 96-97.)[12] Tolstoj used the facts and words of Davydov's life in his creation of the character of Denisov, but he created an entirely different personality for *War and Peace*.

Moreover, it was not as a prototype for Denisov that Davydov exerted his greatest influence on *War and Peace*, but as a source of historical authenticity. What Tolstoj found most useful in Davydov was his writings, the unmistakable realness of his accounts of the Napoleonic wars — their details, their mood of time and place, their record of a man who witnessed and participated in all of it and recounted it in a lively, credible style, their reproductions of the words of historical personages spoken not in the grand phrases of memoirs, but in the everyday language of military life. Tolstoj looked to Davydov for sharp insights and his reader's eye usually halted on the anecdotal. He changed Davydov's style into his own, preferring always the perceptive and pungent phrase or the authentic word. He was, as always, selective in content, fully using what he agreed with and rejecting what he did not agree with. Tolstoj admired Davydov as he admired few other men, and in the poet-hussar's writings he found what he needed to substantiate and heighten his opinions about war as the will of peoples, and thus as the will of God, and he used both the man and his historical accounts to the fullest possible effect in the writing of *War and Peace*. But he had his own aesthetic needs and his own philosophical views which were more important to him than his source.

University of Illinois at Chicago

NOTES

1. See E. E. Zajdenšnur, "Istorija pisanija i pečatanija 'Vojny i mira'," in L. N. Tolstoj, *Polnoe sobranie sočinenij*, 16 (Moscow: Goslit, 1955), 138.

2. *Sočinenija v trex tomax*, 4th ed. (Moscow: D. D. Davydov, 1860); *Razbor trex statej, pomeščennyx v "Zapiskax" Napoleona* (Moscow, 1825).

3. I have here cited *Sočinenija v trex tomax* (St. Petersburg, 1895). According to V. N. Orlov, "Sud'ba literaturnogo nasledstva Denisa Davydova," *Literaturnoe nasledstvo*, 19-21 (1935), 298-99, the texts of the 1860 and 1896 editions are identical.

4. The most complete edition is *Sočinenija*, ed. V. N. Orlov (Moscow: GIXL, 1962). I have not cited this edition because it is printed from the original manuscripts and is thus significantly different from the 1860 text used by Tolstoj.

5. *Zapiski* (London: S. Tchorzewski, 1863).

6. See for example Z. G. Rozova, "Dnevnik partizana D. Davydova kak material dlja 'Vojny i mira' L. Tolstogo," *Trudy Kafedry russkoj literatury L'vovskogo universiteta*, 1 (1958), 123-30, and R. F. Christian, *Tolstoy's "War and Peace": A Study* (Oxford: Clarendon Press, 1962), 65.

7. I have used the Constance Garnett translation modified against the original Russian text to ensure that it matches correctly the materials taken from Davydov's texts.

8. See D. D. Davydov, "Izvestie o žizni D. V. Davydova," *Sočinenija v trex tomax*, 1869, 91-119, and V. D. Davydov, "Zametki o 'Zapiskax' moego otca — starika D. V. Davydova," *Russkaja starina*, 1872, No. 9, 399-402.

9. Davydov's nephew studied in Scotland where he met Scott and initiated a correspondence between him and Davydov. See Gleb Struve, "Scott Letters Discovered in Russia," *The Bulletin of the John Rylands Library*, 27 (1944), and "Russian Friends and Correspondents of Sir Walter Scott," *Comparative Literature*, 2 (1950), 307-26.

10. For a study of Davydov's life and works see V. N. Orlov, *Puti i sud'by* (Moscow–Leningrad: Sov. pisatel', 1963), 61-101, and its variant as the introduction to the 1962 edition.

11. Note the similes of the two writers. Where Davydov, the notorious drinker, thinks of "vessels of precious drink," Tolstoj thinks of ... dung.

12. There is no reason to believe that Davydov was not honorable in his treatment of the French in 1812. But although he does mention a few incidents of brutal behavior on the part of his Cossacks, and he approves the summary execution of French soldiers by enraged peasants, he avoids mention of sadism except in the case of Figner or passes over unpleasant incidents with humorous remarks. Moreover, Davydov was accused of sadistic treatment of Polish soldiers and even civilians in the pacification of the Polish Rebellion of 1830-31, and his attempts to gloss over certain events in his two memoirs on the Rebellion are somehow unconvincing. In any case, the shooting of prisoners is a common amusement in war, and neither the real Figner nor the fictional Doloxov are anomalies.

THE DEATH OF IVAN IL'IČ — CHAPTER ONE

Gary R. Jahn

Every passing year brings fresh proof of the continuing vitality of Tolstoj's short novel *The Death of Ivan Il'ič* (*Smert' Ivana Il'iča*, 1886). Indeed, the untimely death of Tolstoj's hero seems almost to have been compensated by the longevity of the story memorializing him. Among the numerous disputes generated by this "most simple and ordinary story" is the problem of the author's placement of the matter related in the first chapter. Since the remainder of the work contains not a single departure from strict chronological order in its account of the protagonist's life and death, some have found it strange that the story's chronologically final chapter should have been placed first.

The question evoked by the narrative displacement of the account in chapter one of the public announcement of Ivan's demise, its effect on his judicial colleagues and family, and Petr Ivanovič's attendance at the requiem for his deceased friend has been stated by C. J. G. Turner: "Why is this chapter there at all, and why is it placed at the beginning of the story rather than at the end?"[1] According to Turner, the first chapter, as we have it, is a relic of an earlier, eventually discarded, plan for telling the story. Even so, he continues, it manages to retain a reasonably justifiable function in the final text: "The chronological displacement of this chapter enables it to suggest, by its structural position at the beginning of the story, the social milieu in which Ivan Ilyich was to make his career and at the same time, by its chronological position at the end of the story, the fact that the milieu was unchanged when his career came to an end." (121.)

G. Schaarschmidt, however, maintains that Turner's opinion does insufficient justice to the structural integrity of the story's final version.[2] He identifies a tension between inert habit and dawning awareness as the thematic dominant of the story, and he maintains that this tension is revealed even in the pattern of the story's organization. He divides the text into three parts: 1) chapter one; 2) chapters two and three; 3) chapters four through twelve. (358-60.) A gradual shift from "awareness" to "habit" is evident in the first section, the second section is dominated by "habit," while the third presents a gradual shift from "habit" to "awareness" (365). The extra-chronological positioning of the first chapter thus results in an organization which is analogous to a mirror image: awareness to habit – habit – habit to awareness. This symmetry is not possible on the basis of a purely chronological organization, and Schaarschmidt justifiably concludes that "to say that chapter one could be transposed so easily to the end [as Turner does] is to ignore that so doing creates a narrative hiatus between the end of chapter twelve and the beginning of chapter one, and the required adjustments would change the meaning of the story." (365-66).

Schaarschmidt has succeeded in demonstrating that the placement of chapter one has a more than fortuitous importance for our appreciation of the story, and he makes a good case that Turner did not pursue the question of the first chapter far enough. On the other hand, it may be that Schaarschmidt has himself pursued it too far. His imaginative and linguistically complex analysis has located the function of chapter one within a pattern of organization which exists (granting that it does exist) at a very deep and not easily visible level of the text.[3] He has, in fact, looked so deeply into the text that he seems to have neglected certain functions of chapter one which are more readily apparent. These are best seen in terms of the particular artistic problems which Tolstoj faced in devising a chapter which, whatever other functions it may serve, is basically introductory in nature. It is useful to discuss the implications of chapter one considered as an introduction to the theme, the organizational structure, and the system of images of the subsequent text. The goal is to provide another, hopefully more comprehensive, answer to Turner's excellent question: "Why is this chapter there ...?"

The title of the work makes it clear that two factors will be mainly involved: death and Ivan Il'ič. Both make their first appearance in the story in a newspaper announcement, that is, an object brought to the attention of the public at large, which comes to the particular notice of a group of Ivan Il'ič's fellow judges during an interval in their work. Both the man and his death are in this way connected immediately to the motif of judgment. The "judicial" responsibility of rendering judgment on Ivan's death, suggested by the connection between the judges and the news, is, however, only partially carried out. In this respect it is significant that the desultory conversation of the judges prior to their becoming aware that Ivan Il'ič has died concerns a question of "jurisdiction," but it is the finality of the announcement and the propriety of its conventional verbal formulas and customary sentiments which seems most effectively to absolve them from dealing with the essence of Ivan's death. The larger significance of the case of Ivan Il'ič, it seems, is unappealably "closed" by the heavy black border of the funeral notice.[4]

Ignoring the essential meaning of Ivan's demise, his colleagues concern themselves with its incidental concomitants: changes in official position and the like. Petr Ivanovič, however, feels obliged, as Ivan's oldest and closest friend, to pay a visit of condolence and respect to the bereaved. By attending the requiem and viewing the corpse Petr Ivanovič enters into a more immediate confrontation with death than was provided by the newspaper announcement. When he regards the severe countenance of his deceased associate, he comes face to face with death. The discomfort which Petr Ivanovič experiences is ultimately neutralized, however, by his ability simply to walk away from the bier. Furthermore, death is, although more palpably present than before, still contained: on this occasion by the edge of the coffin (*podstilka groba*), recalling the black border of the funeral announcement; and the chanting of the clerics, reminiscent of the stylized language of the printed notice. The saving grace of conventional conduct also helps to alleviate Petr Ivanovič's perplexity: "Petr Ivanovič entered ... confused as to what he was supposed to do. One thing he knew: it never hurt to cross oneself on these occasions." (63.)

Despite the various factors which shelter Petr Ivanovič from the reality of death, the dead face of Ivan Il'ič produces a feeling of "dis-ease" in him: "Something made him feel uncomfortable, and for that reason Petr Ivanovič once more hurriedly crossed himself and, as it seemed to him, too hurriedly, not in conformity with the proprieties, turned away and went to the door." (64.) The effect of Ivan Il'ič's dead face is immediately counterbalanced by the gay and imperturbable countenance of Švarc: "A single glance at the playful, well-fleshed, and elegant figure of Švarc refreshed Petr Ivanovič. Petr Ivanovič understood that he, Švarc, stood above all this and refused to give way to depressing impressions." (64.)

Petr Ivanovič's attitude at the requiem is ambivalent. He experiences discomfort followed by relief. These conflicting emotions are dramatically expressed by the juxtaposition of the images of Ivan Il'ič and Švarc. Ivan's face is sunken, solemn, and severe, and it gives the impression of being concerned with serious matters and the performance of inescapable responsibilities ("That which had to be done had been done," 64); it is a reminder to the living of the reality of death, and causes Petr Ivanovič's discomfort. Švarc's face, on the contrary, is playful and his concern is for that evening's game of *vint*; his "well-fleshed" figure brims with life, and "just looking at him" is enough to restore Petr Ivanovič's habitual sense of contentment (64). These overt comparisons suggest one more: a contrast between darkness in Švarc (his black garments, the significance of his name) and a presumed light in the dead Ivan.

Thus, an important thematic function of the first chapter is to provide an introductory account of the various attitudes toward the fact of Ivan's death among those to whose notice the fact comes. There is a gradual focusing apparent in the organization of this account, ranging from the breadth of the public at large and the opinions of Ivan's former colleagues with their superficially polite but essentially callous indifference to his passing, through the similar attitude of Ivan's wife and family, the playful solemnity of Švarc, and the severe countenance of the deceased himself. Each of these attitudes is reflected to the reader through Petr Ivanovič; ultimately, they are reduced to the competing sensations of discomfort and contentment which he himself experiences.

As for the structural implications of the first chapter, it is evident that it provides a framework for the gradual reduction of attitudes toward Ivan's death from their general dimensions to the particular form they take within Petr Ivanovič. A second function is to provide the framework for a concurrent broadening of the image of Ivan Il'ič himself, the other element of concern in the story's title. He is at first only a name in a frame (in the death notice), but he grows to become a face in a coffin and an object of discussion among those who knew him. To the face, then, is added an environment: his dead face communicates a "reproach and reminder to the living" (64). This second structural dimension is also conveyed through the medium of Petr Ivanovič. It is he who discovers the announcement in the newspaper, views the corpse, and is involved in all the conversations with Ivan's acquaintances and family which are reported. The two structural dimensions within the first chapter co-operate to produce a tension between what we see *through* Petr Ivanovič and what we see *in* him. The former is an ever broadening view of Ivan Il'ič from a printed name to a physical body to the human environment of which he was a part. The latter is an ever narrowing view of the impression created by Ivan's death from the universal joy that "it was he and not I who died" (62), to the calculating self-interest of his colleagues and family, to the personal obligations of his friends, and culminating in the ambivalence experienced by his closest friend, Petr Ivanovič himself.

On one hand the structure of the first chapter suggests that a continuing increase in the fullness and complexity of the representation of Ivan will follow, and it does. To the name and the face are added, in the course of the subsequent chapters, a past, a present, a mind, feelings, and ultimately a soul. On the other hand, chapter one offers a gradual focusing of the various attitudes toward death which culminates in an unresolved question about the meaning of Ivan's demise. The two faces of Ivan and Švarc, as mirrored in the perplexed mind of Petr Ivanovič, dramatically express the opposing sides in this implied debate. It is suggested that there is a need to choose between these mutually exclusive attitudes toward death, thus returning to the motif of death and judgment with which the chapter began.[5] Since the particular death at issue is that of Ivan Il'ič, it follows that the resolution of the question depends on the acquisition of further information about him, an acquisition which the gradual enlargement of Ivan's image in chapter one has also prepared us to expect.

Petr Ivanovič is central to both of the structural functions of the first chapter, but in the sequel he all but disappears. Perhaps this is merely the result of an abandoned structural plan (Petr Ivanovič was originally conceived as the narrator of the story). If so, it is remarkably fortuitous that his sudden disappearance leaves a gap of the right proportions to accomodate the reader who has just, by seeing through the eyes and coming to know the mind of Petr Ivanovič, been inspired with an unresolved affective tension in the face of death and the implicit desire to resolve it. It is perhaps not simply coincidence that Petr Ivanovič himself was first presented as a reader (of the newspaper). It is, at least, certain to be the reader of the story who will from chapter two on observe the increasingly full delineation of Ivan Il'ič, and it is also the reader who will continue Petr Ivanovič's abandoned internal struggle to find the proper attitude toward death. The profound irony of the narrator's tone in chapter one makes at least one thing absolutely clear: Petr Ivanovič's ultimate disregard of his internal dilemma is not a satisfactory solution of it.

A characteristic feature of the further development of the portrait of Ivan Il'ič, on the basis of which the reader is invited to render judgment, is the frequent recurrence of episodes, details, and metaphors which are closely associated with the motif of enclosure and delimitation suggested in chapter one by the references to the black border of the death notice and the edge of Ivan's coffin. The importance of these two original images of confinement for the text as a whole can scarcely be overestimated, for chapters two through twelve contain an entire network of references which seem to arise from them. (The emphasis in the following examples is mine, GRJ.)

We are told that although Ivan, as a young man, was more unpredictable than his stodgy elder brother, his behavior always remained "within certain *limits*" (*v izvestnyx predelax*, 70). We learn that the quality which above all others enabled him to succeed in his work was his capacity to reduce even the most complex matters to the *confines* of a correctly drawn document. This ability derives from his mastery of "the device of *putting aside from himself* all considerations not directly relevant to the official aspect of the case" (*priem otstranenija ot sebja vsex obstojatel'stv, ne kasajuščixsja služby*, 72). He applies this method with equal severity to the nagging complexities of his married life, once it becomes clear to him that a "*definite* relationship" (*opredelennoe otnošenie*, 74) is as needful at home as at work. Not surprisingly, the *otstranenie* characteristic of his official position is mirrored by domestic "*aliena-tion*" (*otčuždenie*, 75).

The effect of the network of *barriers* which Ivan had gradually erected around himself is exacerbated by the onset and progress of his illness. As his sufferings increase he *withdraws* more and more from the life of those around

him. He ceases to participate in his favorite amusements and is portrayed as
overhearing others at play from "*behind the door*" of an adjacent *room* (91). He
confines himself more and more to his study until he seems permanently
installed there, lying upon the sofa with *his face turned to the back*. As his
sufferings increase, Ivan seeks to protect himself from them. When his resolve
simply to ignore his pain proved unworkable, he sought "other *screens*"
(*drugie širmy*, 94) behind which to take shelter. He realizes that he has become
a "*constraint*" (*stesnenie*, 95) on the freedom of others and that they have
begun to *block him out* of their lives. Eventually, he experiences an "*isolation* as
complete as though he were *at the bottom of the sea* or *in the earth*" (*odi-
nočestvo, polnee kotorogo ne moglo byt' nigde: ni na dne morja, ni v zemle*, 108).

All of these examples, and their number could easily be multiplied, are
reflections of the original images of confinement, constraint, and enclosure
which are presented in chapter one. The later examples grow from the black
border of the death notice and the framing effect of Ivan's coffin as from a
seed. Yet, at the same time, these original images are paradoxically also the
final fruit of the organism of metaphor and incident which the story contains.
The text, in this sense, turns out to be an account of how it happened that Ivan
Il'ič changed from a normal, ordinary, living man into something that could
be conveniently fitted into the tiny frame of a funeral notice.

The "problem of chapter one" is to be solved, therefore, by regarding it as
an introduction which, besides affording an opportunity for the traditional
presentation of the central characters and situation, is rich in implications for
the theme, structure, and dominant images of the subsequent text. Themati-
cally, it establishes the contrasting postures of decorous indifference and
spiritual unease as irreducible polarities in an implied debate about the
appropriate attitude to the protagonist's death. Structurally, it creates an
expectation of the more complete portrait of Ivan and his life which is supplied
in chapters two through twelve. In accomplishing this, it incorporates one of
the story's central images: that of the enclosing or bordering effect of the black
frame of Ivan's death notice and the edge of his coffin. These early expressions
of the forces which confine and crush the protagonist are extensively developed in chapters two through twelve and are ultimately reincarnated in the
image of the black bag in chapter nine and echoed again in chapter twelve
when "that which had been oppressing him and wouldn't depart (*ne vyxodilo*)
suddenly was departing all at once, *from two sides, from ten sides, from all
sides*" (113; emphasis mine, GRJ). Finally, it may be suggested that chapter
one performs the hortatory function of inviting the reader to assume the role
of observer and judge so conveniently abandoned at the end of the chapter by
Petr Ivanovič's hasty departure for an evening of cards. Thus, the reader is

subtly instructed as to the approach to be adopted toward what follows; deciding the significance of the death of Ivan Il'ič has become the duty of the reader himself.

University of Minnesota

NOTES

1.   C. J. G. Turner, "The Language of Fiction: Word-Clusters in Tolstoy's 'The Death of Ivan Ilyich,'" *Modern Language Journal*, 65 (1970), 120.

2.   Gunter Schaarschmidt, "Theme and Discourse Structure in 'The Death of Ivan Il'ich,'" *Canadian Slavonic Papers*, 21 (1979), 356-66.

3.   I present an alternative to Schaarschmidt's scheme of the story's organization in a paper, "Tension and Resolution in the Structure of *The Death of Ivan Il'ič*," *Canadian Slavonic Papers*, 24 (1982), 229-38.

4.   The highly conventionalized (and typical) text of the notice and the specific allusion to its surrounding black border are as follows: "V černom obodke bylo napečatano: 'Praskov'ja Fedorovna Golovina s duševnym priskorbiem izveščaet rodnyx i znakomyx o končine vozljublennogo supruga svoego, člena Sudebnoj palaty, Ivana Il'iča Golovina, posledovavšej 4-go fevralja sego 1882 goda. Vynos tela v pjatnicu, v 1 čas popoludni.'" L. N. Tolstoj, *Polnoe sobranie sočinenij* (90 vols.; Moscow: GIXL, 1928-58), XXVI, 61.

5.   The call to judgment is implicit in the final lines of chapter one. Petr Ivanovič "did not once look at the corpse" during the requiem and "to the very end of it did not give way to its enervating influences." There follows a brief exchange between Petr Ivanovič and Gerasim: "'Well, brother Gerasim ... it's too bad, isn't it?' 'It's God's will. We'll all come to it.'" Petr Ivanovič manages to ignore even so direct a hint as this, however, and departs in high spirits, thinking of a game of cards and enjoying the "fresh air" after "the smell of incense, the corpse, and carbolic acid" (68).

POLISH THEMES IN THE POETRY OF NEKRASOV

Sigmund S. Birkenmayer

The poet Nikolaj Nekrasov's attitude toward Poland and the Poles, and the reflection of that attitude in his poetry, are of considerable interest to literary critics in both Poland and Russia. The same can be said about the influence of Polish Romantic literature on Nekrasov's poems, in which we often find themes that can be regarded as Polish. In recent years, several Polish literary critics have made a study of these themes, dividing them in terms of the influence of Nekrasov's mother on his attitude toward the Polish struggle for independence, and the poet's attitude toward the anti-Russian insurrection of January 1863 in Poland.[1]

N. A. Nekrasov was born on 28 November 1821 in the town of Nemirov in southwestern Russia. His father was a Russian army officer, while his mother (née Zakrzewska) came from a family of Polish landowners in Podolia (a province of Poland prior to 1795). It was she, not her husband, who played a major role in the formation of the poet's character. P. I. Lebedev-Poljanskij, in his biographical sketch of Nekrasov, gives this account of the romance between the poet's Polish mother and Russian father:

> Aleksej Sergeevič often went on official business to Kiev, Odessa, Warsaw, and other places. During one of his official missions he became acquainted with the family of the Polish magnate Zakrzewski and fell in love with his daughter Elena Andreevna. How an intelligent, well-educated, beautiful, and refined Polish aristocratic young lady could have allowed herself to be captivated by a half-literate, coarse Russian officer, is difficult to understand. But she also fell in love with him, and, despite her parents' entreaties and active opposition, eloped secretly with him.[2]

The marriage ceremony of Aleksej Sergeevič Nekrasov and Elena Andreevna Zakrevskaja took place on 17 November 1817 in the town of Juzvin in southwestern Russia. The couple had three sons, of whom Nikolaj was the oldest. In 1823, when the future poet was not yet three years old, his father retired from the army and settled on his family estate of Grešnevo, in Yaroslavl province (northeast of Moscow). It was there that Nikolaj spent his childhood.

Nekrasov was not brought up in what could be called a happy family atmosphere. The father was a petty and ignorant despot, self-indulgent but at the same time unforgiving or even cruel to others. He treated his family and serfs with equal brutality. The mother, on the contrary, was a cultured and well educated woman. She had graduated from a women's boarding school in southwestern Russia, and knew both Russian and Polish (having studied these languages there). She also loved and appreciated music, and was fond of reading. The incompatibility of Nekrasov's parents became evident to him at a very early age. He became extremely attached and fiercely loyal to his mother, and he began to violently dislike or even hate his father. It was with her that he spent long hours reading or conversing, and it was she who awakened in him a love for beauty and an interest in poetry. To her he dedicated his first poem, written at the age of seven:

> Любезна маменька, примите
> Сей слабый труд
> И разсмотрите,
> Годится ли куда-нибудь.[3]

(Accept, the dearest of mothers, / This feeble work / And, prithee, tell me / If it is any good at all.)

In this poem, composed for his mother's nameday, young Nikolaj may have tried to express both his devotion and his gratitude to her who, by reading good literature to him, had given him his first lessons in literary taste. As some of the poet's biographers conjecture, his early readings must have included the works of contemporary Russian and Polish poets (particularly the Romantics, like Puškin and Mickiewicz).

The strong influence of Nekrasov's mother on her son's spiritual, intellectual, and moral development has been recognized by most critics. She died in 1841, when the poet was twenty years old. It is a matter of conjecture whether, during her lifetime, he fully realized her importance in the formation of his character. Be that as it may, much of the idealism that pervades his poetry can be traced directly to the influence of his mother. Her romanticism, her compassion for those suffering, were the traits which Nekrasov inherited from her and which he embodied in his poetry.

But was his mother Polish? In my book on Nekrasov, published in 1968, I answered this question affirmatively, on the basis of biographical data including Nekrasov's reminiscences of what his mother supposedly had told him.[4] However, in 1971, two articles by Polish critics, Bazyli Białokozowicz and Andrzej Cesarz, appeared in *Przegląd humanistyczny*, each containing new evidence supposedly disproving the Polish origin of Nekrasov's mother. Both critics attempted to present the controversial question as objectively and impartially as possible, arriving in different ways at similar conclusions. Some of their observations have a direct bearing on my arguments in this article:

> The problem of the Polish origin of Nekrasov's mother should not ... be examined from the viewpoint of national chauvinism. (Cesarz, 157.)

A. L. Grigor'ev reminds us that Nekrasov for some time regarded his mother as Polish ... about which he had written in his unfinished poem [*Mat'* — S.B.] and in his autobiography. (Cesarz, 161.)[5]

One should also mention — as Grigor'ev does — Dmitrij Čiževskij's article in German. He allows for the fact that Nekrasov's mother could have come from a Ukrainian family raised in the sphere of Polish culture. (Cesarz, 163.)[6]

Even if we accept the version that the Zakrzewski landowner family from Podolia, into which the poet's mother was born, was a Ukrainian-Polish, Ukrainian, or even Russian family, there is not the slightest doubt that it remained in the sphere of the influence of Polish traditions. (Białokozowicz, 103.)

Both critics reach similar conclusions, namely, that the problem of the national origin of Nekrasov's mother is perhaps less important than Nekrasov's human and artistic concern for Poland and the Poles. Though not without some reservations, I would tend to agree with their conclusions.

Extensive references to Nekrasov's mother are found in his "Iz poèmy *Mat'*: Otryvki" ("Excerpts from the Poem 'Mother'"), published in his last collection of poems (1877). In it, she is portrayed as her son remembers her: a loving parent, a gentle teacher, a shining example of Christian virtues to be admired and imitated.[7] This lyrical Introduction (I) is followed by Part II, in which the poet goes back in his memory to his childhood and evokes long forgotten sights and events on his family estate. Then he recalls a letter he found among his mother's papers, and again recollections begin to crowd his mind. In his imagination, he goes into the garden half expecting his mother to appear — and suddenly he sees her walking in the moonlight, a letter in her hand:

> Она идет; то медленны, то скоры
> Ее шаги, письмо в ее руке ...
> Она идет ... Внимательные взоры
> По нем скользят в тревоге и тоске.
>
> (II, 418)

(She comes; now slow, now quick are / Her steps, a letter in her hand ... / She comes ... Her pensive eyes / Glance over it with sadness and fear.)

Here follows Part III which opens with an apparently authentic letter written to Elena Andreevna (Nekrasov's mother) by her Polish mother. The letter is permeated by a mother's grief over her daughter running away and becoming "a slave to a hated Muscovite"; it ends with a final plea for Elena to return to Poland — a plea which, as we already know, went unheeded. Another fragment follows, in which Nekrasov leafs through the books that his mother brought with her "from a faraway land" (most probably, Poland). He reads the remarks that she penciled in the margins, and comments with deep conviction: "A searching, penetrating mind lived here." (II, 420.) Suddenly he feels compelled to read the fateful letter once more — and, as he does, a poetic image of his mother again appears before his eyes:

> И снова плакал я, и думал над письмом,
> И вновь его прочел внимательно с начала,
> И кроткая душа, терзаемая в нем,
> Впервые предо мной в красе своей предстала ...
> (II, 420.)

(Again I wept, and mused over the letter, / And read again attentively — / And the meek soul, tormented in it, / In all its beauty first appeared to me ...)

Reading the letter, the poet expresses a Romantic belief that his mother will remain with him, at least in spirit: "I nerazlučnoju ostalas' ty s tex por / O mat'-stradalica! s tvoim pečal'nym synom" ("From that time on, you never have departed, / O my suffering mother, from your grieving son"; II, 420). Then Nekrasov's thoughts turn once more to his early childhood, when his mother was "a nurse and guardian angel" to him. He speaks with compassion of the suffering which her decision to leave her country and marry a stranger brought upon her:

> В ином краю, не менее несчастном,
> Но менее суровом рождена,
> На севере угрюмом и ненастном
> В осьмнадцать лет уж ты была одна.
> Тот разлюбил, кому судьба вручила,
> С кем в чуждый край доверчиво пошла ...
> (II, 421.)

(Born in another land no less unhappy / But less austere, you were alone / In the forbidding, sullen North, / A girl of eighteen years. / He ceased to love you, with whom your fate was bound, / With whom you, trustingly, went to a foreign country.)

He recalls another incident from his childhood, that of his mother playing the piano in one of her sad moods. However, she tried to appear "poised and cheerful" to others, including her son. (II, 421.) And when comparing her lot with that of the Russian people, she thought that hers was perhaps the less unfortunate:

> "Несчастна я, терзаемая другом,
> Но пред тобой, о женщина-раба!
> Перед рабом, согнувшимся над плугом,
> Моя судьба — завидная судьба!
> Несчастна ты, о родина! я знаю:

> Весь край в крови, весь заревом обьят ...
> Но край, где я люблю и умираю,
> Несчастнее, несчастнее стократ!"
>   (II, 421.)

("I am unhappy, tormented by a friend, / But when I see you, O woman slave, / And your slave husband bent over his plow — / Then my own fate is to be envied! / Unhappy is my native land! I know: / The country's bathed in blood and all ablaze ... / But my new country, where I live and die, / Is still unhappier — yea, a hundredfold!"

Orłowski (who believes that Nekrasov's mother was Polish) comments thus on the above passage: "And so, the poet here speaks clearly about an unhappy country, about the lack of freedom, and the terror reigning in the Russian-occupied part of Poland. Such a view of Poland's fate was in total agreement with the poet's previously expressed position on this matter." (Orłowski, 172.) In the last section of the poem, Nekrasov portrays his mother as a woman endowed with great spiritual strength. He speaks with admiration of her loving and kind attitude toward the peasants. Then, in the closing stanzas of the poem, he openly acknowledges his mother's influence on his mature attitudes:

> И если я наполнил жизнь борьбою
> За идеал добра и красоты,
> И носит песнь, слагаемая мною,
> Живой любви глубокие черты —
> О мать моя, подвигнут я тобою!
> Во мне спасла живую душу ты!
>   (II, 423.)

(And if I filled my life with struggle / For the ideal of good and beauty, / And if the song which I am composing / Bears all the marks of living love — / By you, my mother, I was raised up! / By you my soul was saved!)

"Iz poèmy *Mat'*: Otryvki" was written less than a year before Nekrasov's death. It expresses his strong belief that finally he has been able to render his mother a tribute that can only come from a grateful and loving son. References to his mother's supposed Polish origin and to the country of her birth are interspersed throughout the poem, as though the poet, in the last years of his life, wanted to emphasize that he had never forgotten his debt of gratitude to his Polish-born mother.

Nekrasov's attitude toward Poland and the Poles in general, and toward the January 1863 insurrection in particular, is also an important theme of his poetry. Both Russian and Polish literary critics assert, on the basis of available evidence, that the poet sympathized deeply with the Polish movement of national liberation and even knew some of its leaders personally.[8] In the 1860's Nekrasov's interest in the Polish question intensified. Unlike Herzen, whose political activity abroad was not hampered by the censorship, Nekrasov was unable to express his views on Poland publicly for fear of jeopardizing his journal *Sovremennik* (*The Contemporary*) which under his editorship had often incurred the wrath of the Tsarist government by publishing liberal and even radical articles. However, Nekrasov's official attitude of non-involvement in Polish matters did not signify his approval of the Tsarist policy regarding Poland. Eloquent proof of his real attitude toward the Polish question is his refusal to publish in *Sovremennik*, at the time of the 1863 insurrection, Ja. Polonskij's anti-Polish drama *Razlad* (*Discord*), in which the author accused the Poles of sowing discord among fraternal Slavic nations through their anti-Tsarist uprising (Orłowski, 168). This officially endorsed view was evidently not shared by Nekrasov, whose attitude toward the Polish cause was sympathetic and understanding.

Most Russian and Polish literary critics agree that Nekrasov indeed had a sympathetic and compassionate attitude toward the Polish national aspirations in the second half of the nineteenth century. The political situation in Russia at the time made it impossible (or even dangerous) for the poet to express his views on the Polish question; he did, however, make indirect references to it in his poems. Direct and interesting information about Nekrasov's real attitude toward Poland is found in Henryk Kwiatkowski's reminiscences. Kwiatkowski, a Polish writer and critic, visited Nekrasov in late 1877, a few months before the poet's death. During the visit, Nekrasov gave Kwiatkowski his photograph, on the back of which he had written a short poem reading as follows:

> Благословляю, юноша, тебя!
> Трудись, мой друг, всех люби, всех прощай ...
> Верь, как и я, что взойдет вновь заря
> И счастлив будет вновь твой край ...
> Сей семена любви, правды, мира,
> И время лишь оправиться нам дай —
> Сойдемся вновь в день общаго пира,
> И счастлив будет вновь твой край ...[9]

(I bless you, o youth! / Toil, o my friend, love and forgive everybody, / Believe, as I do, that a day will break again / And your country will again be happy ... / Sow seeds of love, truth, and peace, / And only give us time to improve ourselves — / We'll be together again on a feast-day for all, / And your country will again be happy ...)

Some Polish and Russian critics doubt the veracity of Kwiatkowski's account and regard the above poem as his fabrication.[10] However, Kwiatkowski's account vividly illustrates Nekrasov's general attitude toward Poland and the Poles.

After the ruthless suppression (ordered by the Tsar and carried out by Count Murav'ev) of the January 1863 uprising in Poland and Lithuania, Nekrasov wrote a poem entitled "Iz avtobiografii general-lejtenanta Fedora Illarionoviča Rudometova 2-go" ("From the Autobiography of Lieutenant General Fedor Illarionovich Rudometov II"). In it, he portrayed a faithful servant of the Tsarist regime who had distinguished himself by cruelly suppressing an insurrection against the Russians in "a vast country" (a veiled reference to Russian-occupied Poland and Lithuania).

> Потом, когда обширный край
> Мне вверили по праву,
> Девиз: "Блюди — и усмиряй!"
> Я оправдал на славу ...
>
> (II, 447.)

(Later, when a vast country / Was entrusted to me by right, / The motto "Guard — and pacify!" / I justified gloriously ...)

This portrayal of "Lieutenant General Rudometov" bears close resemblance to Count Murav'ev, known as "the Hangman" (vešatel') because of his cruel suppression of the 1863 uprising. Such is the opinion of V. Evgen'ev-Maksimov, one of Nekrasov' modern biographers (Orłowski, 170). Another biographer, K. I. Čukovskij, believes that the poem about Rudometov is an excellent example of what he regards as Nekrasov's use of Aesopian language.[11] The poet's indignation at the Tsarist oppression of the Poles, and his contempt for the Tsarist government, are demonstrated covertly but forcefully in this poem, written in the fateful year 1863.

Nekrasov, with his innate sensitivity to human suffering, could not remain indifferent to the fate of the Polish insurgents of 1863 who, as they were being deported to Siberia, aroused his compassion. In the poem "Blagodarenie Gospodinu Bogu" (Thanks to God Our Lord"), written in the same year, he describes a fleeting but poignant scene involving one of the (mostly young) Polish patriots:

> Скоро попались нам пешие ссыльные,
> С гиком ямщик налетел,
> В тряской телеге два путника пыльные
> Скачут ... Едва разглядел ...
>
> Подле лица — молодого, прекрасного —
> С саблей усач ...
> Брат, удаляемый с поста опасного,
> Есть ли там смена? Прощай!
>
> (II, 160.)

(Soon we encountered exiles on foot. / Yelling, the coachman drove upon them; / In a ramshackle cart two dusty travelers / Were dashing by ... I barely made them out ...

Next to a face — a young, handsome face — / A fierce-looking soldier, armed with a saber ... / Brother, being taken from a dangerous outpost, / Have you someone to replace you there? Farewell!)

These Polish deportees are also mentioned in Nekrasov's narrative and epic poem, *Komu na Rusi žit' xorošo?* (*Who is Happy in Russia?*), written in the years 1865-76. In Part I of the poem in the chapter entitled "Pomeščik" ("The Landowner"), a displaced Russian nobleman gives this description of post-reform Russia (following the abolition of serfdom in 1861) and post-insurrection Poland:

> ... Куда
> Ни едешь, попадаются
> Одни крестьяне пьяные,
> Акцизные чиновники,
> Поляки пересыльные ...
>
> (III, 232.)

(... Wherever / You go, you encounter / Only drunken peasants, / Tax office collectors, / And Polish deportees ...)

In his satirical poem "Kreščenskie morozy" ("Epiphany Frost"), written in 1865, Nekrasov inserted the following lines into his description of the feasting and carousing of the Petersburg rich amidst the starvation and misery of the city's poor and hungry:

> Никакие известия из Вильно,
> Никакие статьи из Москвы
> Нас теперь не волнуют так сильно,
> Как подобные слухи ...
>
> (II, 213.)

(No sort of news from Vilna, / No sort of articles from Moscow, / Now upset us as much / As do similar rumors.)

It is a well-known fact that in 1863, under the heading "Iz Vil'no" ("From Vilna"), official Russian newspapers published Murav'ev's reports on the progress of his ruthless pacification of Poland and Lithuania; and "Stat'i iz Moskvy" ("Articles from Moscow") were none other but M. Katkov's anti-Polish articles published in *Moskovskie vedomosti* (*Moscow News*), in which that journalist demanded that both the Polish insurrection and the Russian revolutionary movement be suppressed without mercy. (Orłowski, 170.)

Białokozowicz begins his discussion of Nekrasov's real versus his poetic attitude toward Poland and the Russian oppression of the Polish nation: "The attitude of Nikolaj Nekrasov himself ... toward Polish matters and problems was a very complex one. His mother was an educated and refined Polish woman, and so already in his childhood the future poet came in contact with Polish culture ...." (103.) Later in his discussion, Białokozowicz states with apparent conviction: "A. L. Grigor'ev quite justifiably believes that we must consider the objective expression of the image of a suffering mother and take into account the unquestionable fact that 'in this [female] character, the idea of Polish-Russian friendship ... was beautifully and poetically expressed ...." (103-04.) Białokozowicz, by quoting Grigor'ev, obviously wants to erase any impression that he lacks objectivity in his own evaluation of the impact of the "Polishness" of Nekrasov's mother on the poet's attitude toward Poland and the Poles. But many of his arguments are faulty, and it is difficult to agree with his ideologically biased statement that "Nekrasov's friendly attitude toward Poland, the Poles, and their national liberation struggle, is related to his revolutionary convictions" (105). On the other hand, I would be inclined to agree with the conclusions of both Cesarz and Orłowski: "His spontaneous nature reacted vigorously to all social injustice, and his sympathies for the martyred Polish nation often found expression in his poems ..." (Cesarz, 175). And: "It is beyond doubt that the poet viewed the Poles through a prism of virtues and values ascribed to his mother. This is a fact that attests favorably to his attitude toward the Polish nation. This attitude was not expressed [by him] openly and directly under the conditions of censorship at the time." (Orłowski, 172.)

The complexity of Nekrasov's attitude toward Poland, her people, and her problems was caused by several factors: his emotional and psychological attitude toward his mother; the political climate of his time; and his idealistic and poetic concepts. It is appropriate to discuss these factors in conclusion.

Nekrasov's mother occupies a prominent place in his recollections and his poetry. Her love for him was the only bright reminiscence of his otherwise unhappy childhood. She was his friend and teacher in these early years of his life, reading Mickiewicz's and Puškin's poems to him and encouraging him to write poetry. She opened his eyes to human suffering around him and, by her own example, taught him to love his fellow human beings and feel compassion for them. Her romanticism and idealism, her capacity for both tenderness and passion, were the traits which Nekrasov inherited from her and, later on, embodied in his poetry. As some critics surmise, it was only after her death that the poet began to realize how much she had loved him and what she had done for him. Normal human feelings like guilt and remorse undoubtedly contributed to his poetic idealization of his mother throughout the remainder of his life. To her he dedicated many of his lyrics — "Nesčastnye" ("The Unfortunates"), "Rycar' na čas" ("A Knight for an Hour"), "Iz poèmy *Mat'*: Otryvki" ("From the Poem *Mother*: Excerpts"), and "Bajuški-baju" ("Lullaby").

The strong influence of Nekrasov's mother on her son's spiritual, intellectual, and moral development has been recognized by most critics, with the exception of Corbet, who believes that her direct impact on her son's personality was not great and that a sentimental remorse outweighed filial trust and love in the lifelong and quite remarkable enshrinement of the poet's mother to be found in his works.[12] Nevertheless, there is enough evidence to support a belief that Nekrasov's mother fostered his idealism, introduced him at an early age to the spell of the written word, and, through her own example, taught him compassion and on whom to bestow it.

Russia's political climate of the years 1846-66 (the twenty years during which Nekrasov was the editor of *Sovremennik*) was not favorable to any progressive ideas, be they liberal or radical. A. M. Garkavi emphasizes that a study of the poet's struggle against Tsarist censorship is of primary importance for our understanding of the conditions under which he lived and wrote.[13] Likewise, Białokozowicz and Orłowski point out that because of the censorship Nekrasov was unable to express publicly his real attitude toward the Polish question, while at the same time refusing to publish an anti-Polish drama in his *Sovremennik*. (Białokozowicz, 103; Orłowski, 168). His cautious, politically inhibited attitude toward Poland and the Poles was transformed into a poetic attitude, and he was quite successful in getting the latter attitude past the censorship into his poetry. Proof of this are the poems "Iz avtobiografii ... Rudometova," "Blagodarenie Gospodinu Bogu" (both of which were written in 1863), "Kreščenskie morozy" (1865), the reference to Polish deportees of 1863 in Part I of *Komu na Rusi žit' xorošo* (written probably in 1865), and "Iz poèmy *Mat'*: Otryvki" (written and published in 1877).

Nekrasov's idealistic and poetic concepts of human beings in general and the Polish nation in particular were inherited from his mother. He himself acknowledged this in his autobiographical poems "Rycar' na čas" (1860) and "Iz poèmy *Mat'*: Otryvki" (1877). In his home library he had Russian translations of *Grażyna* and *Konrad Wallenrod,* two long narrative poems by Mickiewicz which exemplify the Polish Romantic poet's idealistic concepts of Polish patriotism. A. N. Pypin, a contemporary of Nekrasov, noted in his diary: "When he [Nekrasov] became acquainted with Mickiewicz's works he understood what role could be played in society by poetry."[14] Undoubtedly, Mickiewicz's idealistic and poetic concepts of mankind and of the Polish nation were absorbed through Nekrasov's reading of the poetry of the Polish Romantics, particularly Mickiewicz and Słowacki, to whose works his mother had introduced him at an early age.

The inescapable conclusion is that Nekrasov's political attitude toward the Polish people and their national aspirations was strongly affected by his emotional and psychological attitudes toward his mother. It was this poetic and subjective attitude — his political attitude interpreted into art — that he was able to get past the censors into his poetry, particularly in the years immediately following the January 1863 Polish insurrection against Russia.

The Pennsylvania State University

NOTES

1. Bazyli Białokozowicz, "Polska i Polacy w poezji rosyjskiej doby powstania styczniowego," *Przegląd humanistyczny,* 3 (1971), 83-108; Andrzej Cesarz, "Matka Niekrasowa," *Przegląd humanistyczny,* 6 (1971), 153-79; Jan Orłowski, "Polacy w poezji Niekrasowa," *Przegląd humanistyczny,* 2 (1971), 167-72.

2. P. I. Lebedev-Poljanskij, *N. A. Nekrasov: Kritiko-biografičeskij očerk* (Moscow: Goslit, 1921), 7.

3. Quoted from M. M. Stasjulevič, "Biografičeskij očerk," in *Stixotvorenija N. A. Nekrasova: Polnoe sobranie v odnom tome,* 2nd ed. (St. Petersburg: M. M. Stasjulevič, 1882), vii.

4. Sigmund S. Birkenmayer, *Nikolaj Nekrasov: His Life and Poetic Art* (The Hague: Mouton, 1968), 13-15.

5. A. L. Grigor'ev, "Nekrasov za rubežom: Itogi i problemy izučenija Nekrasova v sovremennom zarubežnom literaturovedenii," *Russkaja literatura,* 4 (1967), 227.

6. D. Čyževśkyj, "Zu den polnisch russischen literarischen Beziehungen, 3: Die Mutter N. A. Nekrasovs," *Zeitschrift für slavische Philologie,* 23 (1955), 271-74.

7. N. A. Nekrasov, "Iz poèmy *Mat':* Otryvki," *Polnoe sobranie sočinenij i pisem* (12 vols.; Moscow: Goslit, 1948–53), II, 415. All translations are mine.

8. See Ju. Levin and G. Rabinovič, "Nekrasov i pervyj russkij perevod *Mazepy* Slovackogo," *Nekrasovskij sbornik, III* (Moscow: AN SSSR, 1960), 180; A. Kušakov, "O 'pol'skoj teme' v russkoj demokratičeskoj poèzii 60-x godov XIX veka," *Učenye zapiski Orlovskogo gosudarstvennogo pedagogičeskogo instituta,* 15 (1957), 101-32; Białokozowicz, 83, 105; Cesarz, 155-56, 158, 166, 170; Orłowski, 167-68, 169.

9. Henryk Kwiatkowski, "Przyczynek do wspomnień o Niekrasowie," *Kraj,* 49 (1883), 19-20.

10. V. Evgen'ev-Maksimov, *Žizn' i dejatel'nost' N. A. Nekrasova, I* (Moscow: Goslit, 1947), 74; Grigor'ev, 227; Cesarz, 166.

11. K. I. Čukovskij, "'Èzopova reč'' v tvorčestve N. A. Nekrasova," *Nekrasovskij sbornik, I* (Moscow: AN SSSR, 1951), 12.

12. Charles Corbet, *Nekrasov, l'homme et le poète* (Paris: Institut d'Études Slaves de l'Université de Paris, 1948), 12 ff.

13. A. M. Garkavi, "Nekrasov i cenzura," *Nekrasovskij sbornik, II* (Moscow: AN SSSR, 1956), 445.

14. A. N. Pypin, "O N. A. Nekrasove: Iz zapisnoj knižki," *Sovremennik,* 1 (1913), 223.

CRIME AND PUNISHMENT IN ČEXOV

Leonard A. Polakiewicz

The issue of crime and punishment is a major theme in Čexov's works, dating from his formative period, as in "The Trial" ("Sud," 1881), "A Case from a Lawyer's Practice" ("Slučaj iz sudebnoj praktiki," 1883), "Drama at the Hunt" ("Drama na oxote," 1884-85); from his middle period when he produced such works as "The Bet" ("Pari," 1888), "Thieves ("Vory," 1890), and "Peasant Women" ("Baby," 1891); or from the period of his artistic maturity such as "In Exile" ("V ssylke," 1892), "Murder" ("Ubijstvo," 1895), and "In the Ravine" ("V ovrage," 1900).

Čexov portrays crime in its seemingly infinite varieties including counterfeiting ("In the Ravine"), embezzlement ("The Confession" ["Ispoved', 1883]), ordinary theft ("The Thief" ["Vor," 1883]), assault and battery ("Sorrow" ["Gore," 1885]), and murder ("In Court" ["V sude," 1886]). Punishment, historically the inevitable response to crime, also appears in such a multiplicity of forms as flogging ("Murder"), and banishment to Siberia or penal servitude ("In Exile"). The subject of capital punishment surfaces in such stories as "The Bet," while factual accounts of executions are documented in *Island of Sakhalin* (1891-95). The subject is of particular interest in Čexov's "The Bet" and "The Head Gardener's Story" ("Rasskaz staršego sadovnika," 1894). The former focuses on the theme of life imprisonment without reference to a specific crime; the latter focuses on murder, the most serious of crimes, and upon the most severe punishment, the death penalty.[1] An attempt will be made to determine whether these works argue in favor of or against either life imprisonment or capital punishment.

"The Bet" and "The Head Gardener's Story" are philosophical works. The first was written two years preceding and the second four years following Čexov's publicized trip to the penal colony on the island of Sakhalin (1890). This experience generated his sociological study *Island of Sakhalin* which, together with two fictional works, Dostoevskij's *Notes from the House of the Dead* and Tolstoj's *Resurrection*, constitute a significant contribution to Russia's corpus of penological literature. It should be noted that "The Bet" and "The Head Gardener's Story" have thematic links with *Island of Sakhalin*, particularly with the latter's twenty-first chapter entitled "The Morality of the Exile Population — Crimes — Investigation and Trial — Punishment — Birch Rods and Lashes — The Death Penalty." In fact, there is every reason to believe that the writing of this chapter provided the thematic germ for "The Head Gardener's Story."[2]

Although the death penalty for non-political crimes was abolished in Russia as early as 1753 during the reign of Empress Elizabeth, it continued to be a feature of Russian criminal justice and was as controversial an issue during Čexov's time as it is in the United States today. Life imprisonment, on the other hand, was long established and less controversial. Čexov's first open treatment of the theme of life imprisonment appears in "The Bet" and develops from an initial debate over the ultimate punishment. An old banker recalls how fifteen years before, at a party of his, some "clever" and "intellectual" men became engaged in a heated discussion about capital punishment. The majority of the guests condemned it on the grounds that is was outdated, immoral, and unsuitable for Christian states. As a substitute form of punishment, they favored life imprisonment. Their host, without taking a stand either for or against capital punishment, argued only that from the moral standpoint, captial punishment is more moral and more humane than life imprisonment since the former kills a man instantly, while the latter kills him slowly.

Čexov's personal viewpoint is best expressed by another guest who claims that both forms of punishment are immoral, "for they both have the same objective — to take away life. The State is not God. It has not the right to take away what it cannot restore when it wants to." (VII, 203-4.) This view is in complete harmony with Čexov's great respect for human life, a respect reflected, for example, in a revealing letter written to A. S. Suvorin shortly before Čexov's departure for Sakhalin. In this letter (9 March 1890) the author expresses his thoughts about the lives of prisoners on Sakhalin of which he learned from books:

> We have sent *millions* of people to rot in prison, we have let them rot casually, barbarously, without giving it a thought, we have driven people in chains for thousands of miles through the cold, infected them with syphilis, made them depraved, multiplied criminals, and we have thrust the blame for all this on red-nosed jail-keepers. Today all of educated Europe knows it is not the fault of jailers, but rather of all of us. (XV, 30.)

Given the fact that many of the prisoners on Sakhalin were sentenced to life imprisonment, these words indicate, albeit obliquely, Čexov's attitude toward that form of punishment. A year after his return from the penal colony, in a letter to the same addressee (13 May 1891), Čexov openly attacked incarceration for life and resolved to oppose it in his penological study: "I will fight chiefly against life imprisonment in which I see the cause of all evil, and against the present laws concerning exiles which are terribly outdated and contradictory." (XV, 201.)

The final view voiced in "The Bet" is that of a lawyer who, though agreeing that the death sentence and the life sentence are equally immoral, claims that if forced to choose between them, he would certainly choose the second, for in his mind, "to live anyhow is better than not at all" (VII, 204). A "wild and senseless" bet takes place where money is staked against a man's freedom. The frivolous, wealthy, and spoiled banker wagers two million rubles that the lawyer will be unable to withstand five years of voluntary confinement; the impetuous, inexperienced, and greedy lawyer proudly accepts the challenge and even volunteers to triple the period of his confinement. In the end of the frame of the story, on the eve of the expiration of the fifteen-year term, the financially ruined banker contemplates the murder of his "prisoner" to avoid the disgrace of bankruptcy.[3] His idea to shift the blame for the intended murder of his prisoner (who reads Shakespeare, among other writers) mirrors the actions of Macbeth as he prepares to murder his king. The banker is ultimately spared the murder when the lawyer's pride and *Übermensch* complex lead him to abandon his "cell" five hours prior to the fixed time, thereby voiding the bet and renouncing the money. The reader realizes with the conclusion of the story that neither man has learned anything positive from his experience; neither man has really changed. The banker's ruling obsession is still money, while the lawyer's pride reaches diabolical proportions in his virulent renunciations. In essence, both men remain morally blind.

During his confinement the lawyer has become intimate with most of the collected knowledge of mankind but, without contact with people, his initial loneliness is transformed over the years into a hatred of Man and of Life. He has become a sort of malevolent God who passes a damning judgment on the human race: "You have taken lies for truth, and hideousness for beauty." (VII, 208.) The lawyer could just as well be speaking about himself. He has exchanged his life — the opportunity to work for the good of mankind, to defend the accused and perhaps save many from prison — for the promise of money. Despite his reading, he has not learned to swallow his pride, abandon the absurd bet, and rejoin society. He passes judgment on mankind, but he offers nothing in return. At the end of the story he is almost dead, both physically and spiritually.

The banker is no better off. Though free to associate with people, he seems as bound and isolated by the bet as the lawyer. The bet preoccupies him so that he wastes his fortune and becomes a slave to the money he is left with. The two million that he does not deem worth the price of a life at the outset, he is willing to kill for at the end. Neither man has really known freedom, love, or truth, and for this reason Čexov holds them both up to scorn. For the view which pervades Čexov's works is that "to live anyhow" is never a worthy substitute for living decently.

Ironically, both men in "The Bet" display an initial belief in the sanctity of life and in the immorality of denying a man his freedom, but both wind up accomplices in the very act they have condemned as immoral. Assuming the role of God, each imprisons the other through the bet, so that finally neither the jailer nor the prisoner is free.

It is also ironic that the lawyer, who intially asserts that "to live anyhow is better than not at all" abandons this contention in the final analysis when he rejects life, saying it is not worth living at all. In his note of renunciation, the lawyer declares: "I despise freedom, and life, and health .... I despise wisdom and all the blessings of this world." (VII, 208-9.) Yet what else is there in life? His note of renunciation suggests the reason for his failure — rather than growing in understanding and tolerance of humanity, the lawyer has come to despise it. His intelligence and insight into man's follies and shortcomings have not been tempered by love and compassion. Instead, he has become an embittered cynic. We realize how much his views are at variance with Čexov's as we recall Čexov's words to A. N. Pleščeev: "My holy of holies is the human body, health, intelligence, talent, inspiration, love and absolute freedom — freedom from violence and falsehood no matter how the last two manifest themselves." (XIV, 251.)

The final irony of "The Bet" is that the issue of which is more tolerable, capital punishment or life imprisonment — the question that precipitated the insane wager — is never settled, because it was an absurd and vain effort from the start. Neither the lawyer nor the banker gain wisdom from the fifteen-year exercise, so the lawyer's imprisonment was for nothing. The bet led only to isolation, the devaluation of life, and a general contempt for humanity. Although two men, rather than the state, were responsible for the imprisonment, the act is no less immoral and the effect no less devastating than that experienced by the Sakhalin prisoners Čexov described in his letter. Diabolical pride led the banker and the lawyer to play God with life, usurping a right which, as one guest pointed out, belongs to God alone. They should have heeded this guest who also cautioned them that no man has "the right to take away what he cannot restore" (VII, 204).

A more universal Čexovian theme in "The Bet" appears to be that man has a choice between other-imposed or self-imposed prisons, whether physical or intellectual, on the one hand, and absolute freedom achieved not by avoiding human contact or by experiencing life vicariously through books, but by living a complete and decent life on the other.

From the banker's garden, which turned out for the lawyer not to be an Eden but a hell of isolation from mankind and from the meaning of life, we are taken to another garden in the frame part of "The Head Gardener's Story" where the question of crime and punishment (and, ultimately, of crime without punishment) is raised again.

It appears that in addition to Čexov's earlier mentioned work on the twenty-first chapter of *Island of Sakhalin*, another event served as an impetus for the writing of "The Head Gardener's Story." In March 1894, Čexov met several times with the critic, publicist, and jurist L. E. Obolenskij. During their last visit, they discussed the death penalty; in particular, whether it was possible to demonstrate its harmfulness for the state itself from a purely utilitarian point of view.[4] In a follow-up letter of 31 March 1894, Obolenskij observed that utilitarian arguments against the death penalty appear weak when compared to the state's arguments in its defense, therefore, it becomes necessary to appeal to man's emotions, to his sympathy, altruism, moral instinct or moral feelings, for "it is precisely these feelings which cry out within us against the death penalty. We must nourish and act upon them so as to make it impossible for the death penalty to exist. This can be done only by the clergy and *artists*." (Italics Obolenskij's; see Dolotova, 36.) In "The Head Gardener's Story," a suspected murderer is at first condemned to death but then acquitted. Obolenskij's thoughts are reflected, in part, in the gardener's view of the acquittal: "The sentence of acquittal may bring harm to inhabitants of the town, but on the other hand, think of the beneficial influence upon them of faith in man." (VIII, 386.) These words appear to reconcile utilitarian goals with the norms of social morality. Obolenskij maintained that " the death penalty, whatever the form, is murder, and it undermines respect for life which also exists in the soul of a criminal as a motive contra crime." Lastly, the critic suggested to Čexov: "If I were a great artist like yourself, Anton Pavlovič, I ... would take the most *loathsome* criminal who had committed the most heinous crime and I would depict the moments of his spiritual state (as well as the spiritual state *of all* executioners and witnesses of the execution) so that people would become horrified by their own crime because execution is a more serious crime than a whole series of murders committed by the most inveterate murderer." (See Dolotova, 36-37.) Čexov largely heeded this advice. The criminal in "The Head Gardener's Story," notorious for his vicious life and convicted of many crimes, commits a "heinous crime" by killing a saintly doctor.

It is worth noting parenthetically that Obolenskij's equation of the execution by the state with murder is also the basic tenet of the famous eighteenth-century Italian, Cezáre Beccaria, with whose monumental reform work in the field of criminal jurisprudence, *Essay on Crimes and Punishments* (published, 1764), Čexov was well acquainted.[5] Beccaria's fundamental position was that there should be no capital punishment because it is unjust and not based on law. He defined laws as the sum of the smallest portions of the private liberty of each individual; laws represent the general will which is the aggregate of the wills of collective individuals. Yet, he pointed out, no one has ever given to others the right to take life, for if this were so, such a permission could not be reconciled with the maxim which tells us that a man has no right to kill himself. Only if man had that right could he give it to another. Therefore, since no right exists which could authorize the punishment by death, such punishment is "a war of a whole nation against a citizen whose destruction they consider as necessary or useful to the general good." Beccaria warns of the death penalty's pernicious effect on society, for "laws which are intended to moderate the ferocity of mankind, should not increase it by examples of barbarity." His final point is that "men have discovered a sentiment which tells them, that they are not lawfully in the power of any one, but of that necessity only which with its iron sceptre rules the universe."[6]

The guest in "The Bet" who argued that the death penalty is immoral because it takes away life, and "the State is not God ... it has not the right to take away what it cannot restore when it wants to" (VII, 204), clearly echoes Beccaria's last observation. In "The Head Gardener's Story," the exponent of the humanitarian views of Beccaria and Obolenskij is Mixail Karlovič, the gardener; although, to be sure, he expresses them in an extreme if not distorted form.[7]

The head gardener is introduced by narrator one in the idyllic garden setting of the frame part of the story. The theme of rebirth and life is suggested by the beautiful spring morning, while the birds and "flowers brought out into the open air and basking in the sunshine" (VIII, 382), suggest freedom; both themes are important in the legend and its frame.

In its broadest sense, "The Head Gardener's Story" contains the theme of the eternal polemic between those who take an optimistic view of the basic decency of man and those who hold, pessimistically, that man is by nature a degenerate and vicious creature. More specifically, the story presents two conflicting opinions on the efficacy of the legal system: the landowner and the merchant advocate strict adherence to the letter of the law in order to combat man's natural corruption, while the gardener, with his unlimited faith in humanity, effectively advocates doing away with law courts altogether. Both points of view, being extreme, are unrealistic and untenable. The reader realizes that ultimately a middle ground must be sought between blind faith in man's capacity to be virtuous and unconditional condemnation of man's folly.

The narrator of the frame of the story (Čexov's persona) represents this open-minded middle ground. He is a participant, albeit a silent one, in the conversation of the landowner and the merchant, and he listens without protest to their assertion that judicial leniency in the prosecution of crime leads to the "demoralization of the masses" and a rise in arson, burglary, and murder. Specifically, they object to the courts' indulgent attitude toward crime as evidenced by the frequent acquittal of criminals, especially "on grounds of abnormality and aberration" (VIII, 383). These sentiments prompt Mixail Karlovič to voice a diametrically opposed view. He maintains that he is delighted by verdicts of not guilty, and that he does not feel they pose a threat either to morality or to justice, adding:

> Even when my conscience tells me the jury have made a mistake in acquitting the criminal, even then I am triumphant. Judge for yourselves, gentlemen; if the judges and the jury have more faith *in man* than in evidence, material proofs, and speeches for prosecution, is not that faith *in man* in itself higher than any ordinary considerations? Such faith is only attainable by those few who understand and feel Christ. (VIII, 383.)

To demonstrate the primacy of "faith in man" over "material proofs" of human depravity and evil, Mixail Karlovič (narrator two) tells a "very charming legend" which was told to him, in Swedish, by his grandmother. The legend (most likely created by Čexov himself) provides a somewhat hagiographical account of a doctor's life.[8] He appears in town seemingly from nowhere. His name is never established. After his death, the judge refers to him only as Dr. So-and-so (*Doktor Takoj-to*). The gardener notes that although the doctor was knowledgeable, uncommunicative, morose, and lived as moderately as a monk, he had an unlimited capacity to love, for in his breast there "beat an angel's heart" (VIII, 384). The Christ-like doctor loved the townspeople as his children and was ready to lay down his life for them. When his patients died, he attended their funerals and wept for them. Like Čexov, the doctor was consumptive and took no fees for his services. "His saintliness (*svjatost'*)," we are told, "guarded him from evil" (VIII, 385). Other hagiographical details speak of his nights spent in contemplation; note the robbers not only respected him, but even fed him and, as in the case of St. Francis of Assisi, "even horses, cows, and dogs recognized him and showed their joy when they saw him" (VIII, 385). The doctor trusted everyone completely and was confident that there was no thief who could bring himself to do him wrong. One day, however, he was found dead, lying in a ravine, covered with blood; but even in death he remained true to his faith in the goodness of man, for "his pale face wore an expression of amazement. Yes, not horror, but amazement was the emotion that had been fixed upon his face when he saw the murderer before him." (VIII, 385.)

The doctor not only lived by love, but also infected everyone else with his love to the extent that the judges and the jury freed his murderer, despite the overwhelming evidence against him. Rejecting the verdict of guilty and the assigned sentence of death, the judge explained his decision, saying: "I cannot admit the thought there exists a man who would dare to murder our friend the doctor! A man could not sink so low!" (VIII, 386.)

After narrating this legend with its vivid and dramatic illustration of man's faith in man, the gardener provides an explication of his thoughts on the tale's moral in the same didactic tone evident in the preface to his tale:

> The murderer was set free ... and for such faith in humanity, God forgave the sins of all the inhabitants of that town. He rejoices when people believe that man is His image and semblance, and grieves if, forgetful of human dignity, they judge worse of men than of dogs. The sentence of acquittal may bring harm to the inhabitants of the town, but on the other hand, think of the beneficial influence upon them of that faith in man — a faith which does not remain dead, you know; it raises up generous feelings in us, and always impels us to love and respect every man. Every man. And that is important. (VIII, 386.)

These words bring to mind Čexov's comment to Suvorin of 18 October 1888 in which he also emphasized the importance of loving every man:

> If Jesus Christ had been more radical and had said, 'Love your enemies as yourself,' he would not have said what he wished. Neighbors — it is a general conception, but enemies — a particular matter. The trouble is not that we hate enemies, of whom we have few, but that we do not love sufficiently our neighbors, of whom we have many, many. (XIV, 199.)

It needs to be mentioned that the original, unexpurgated text of the story contained two additional lines in the gardener's preface which read: "It is not hard to believe in God. The Inquisitors, Biron, and Arakčeev believed in God. No, you should believe in man." (XVI, 197.) It is understandable that Čexov complained to I. I. Gorbunov-Posadov that the censor deleted these words, for they reflect his personal beliefs; his faith in man. (See XVI, 197.)

The most reliable interpretation of the story, however, requires, because of its narrative structure, that "The Head Gardener's Story" be evaluated in light of its teller. A close look at the description of Mixail Karlovič provided by the narrator of the frame part of the story suggests that the gardener is perhaps neither a fountain of wisdom nor a model of the generous human compassion he preaches in his tale. Although the narrator refers to Mixail Karlovič's "faith in man" as a "fine thought," he allows us to view the gardener from a perspective that pointedly reveals the folly of an indiscriminate social application of Christian forgiveness and love.

That Mixail Karlovič lacks the experience of life that would give authority to his defense of human goodness and judicial leniency is suggested both by his occupation and his leisure reading. In the idyllic garden of the count's greenhouse, Mixail Karlovič is able to maintain ideal notions of life that would probably wither upon transplantation to the real world where human temperaments are as various as the range in temperatures. Čexov was not particularly fond of Ibsen. He criticized him for lack of objectivity and a simplistic view of life.[9] The gardener's love for the Norwegian dramatist underscores the idealism fostered by his rather utopian environment. His conceptions of justice are derived not so much from direct contact with life as from literature and folk legends that simplify moral and ethical realities.

The contrast between Mixail Karlovič's affirmation of "love and respect for every man" and his own "dignified and haughty" demeanor further undercuts the moral authority of the story. He has appropriated the title of "head gardener" (unnecessary since "there were no under gardeners;" VIII, 382), he has a distaste for the "coarseness of the Russian language" (VIII, 383), and he strikes an attitude of superiority toward both the workers he superintends and the landowners he speaks with. Such behavior points not to a magnanimous "love and respect for every man," but to a quite regal desire for self-exaltation and individual distinction that assumes some men are more entitled to love and respect than others. In light of this, his statement that the faith he speaks of and claims to have "is only attainable by those few who understand Christ" (VIII, 383), is particularly revealing. That his doctrine of faith in man does not survive the test of application in his own life seriously impairs the credibility of the wider application of his "fine thought" in his story of the acquitted murderer. The narrator notes that despite Mixail Karlovič's Russian-Swedish heritage, he is "looked upon by everyone as a German." The confusion of ethnic backgrounds is significant. If German scientism ignores man's spiritual essence and attempts to reduce all of life to physical facts, the gardener, ironically, though taken for a German, errs in the opposite direction by summarily dismissing factual evidence as irrelevant. He advances his opinions with the same conclusive absolutism and intolerance of contradiction that marks the scientific periodical debates of "the bloody Germans" in "A Boring Story." After he finishes his legend, the gardener refuses to hear any objections from the landowner. The opening line of Mixail Karlovič's narrative indicates that the problem with all theories of man whether derived from scientific experiments or inherited faith is that they fail to leave room for infinite exceptions. While he talks with assurance and conviction of Man in the abstract, when he comes down to the individual case of his tale he cannot even remember the doctor's name. He assures his listeners that "it does not matter" whether the doctor's name is Thompson or Wilson, yet his lapse matters quite critically. In his absorption with *Man*, Mixail Karlovič discounts *man*, and his failure to appreciate the human variety which requires that each case be individualized, clearly identifies the gardener with Čexov's prototypical advocates of general, inflexible laws, Sergeant Prišibeev ("Unter Prišibeev," 1885) and Belikov ("The Man in a Case," 1898). Applied as indiscriminately as Sergeant Prišibeev's all-inclusive "articles of the law," the gardener's religious "faith in man" is as dangerous to society as the denial of man's capacity for self-government implicit in the Sergeant's codes. The spokesman for Priši-beev's "code of laws" in "The Head Gardener's Story" is the landowner who concludes his diatribe against leniency in the courts with a citation from Shakespeare: "... in our evil and corrupt age virtue must ask forgiveness of vice" (VIII, 383).[10] The quote is an important point of reference for the story that follows, for Shakespeare's vision of the moral complexity of vice and virtue equally discredits an "indulgent attitude" based on excessive faith in man and the authoritarian "sense of justice" the landowner prescribes for his "evil and corrupt age."

"The Head Gardener's Story" is undercut not only by contradictions between teller and tale, but also by inherent contradictions within the "legend" itself. For example, the gardener's description of the doctor as a "morose and unsociable" man who chooses to live the life of a hermit in aloof independence from the town challenges, somewhat, his account of the unqualified love that existed between the townspeople and the doctor.

It should be noted that after the murderer was found, the townspeople cautioned the authorities to "take care that a mistake is not made, it does happen, you know, that evidence tells a lie" (VIII, 386).[11] The motif of miscarriage of justice is present in many of Čexov's works. Judicial error is at the heart of stories such as "In Court" where, on the basis of circumstantial evidence and because of careless investigatory procedures, Xarlamov is wrongly accused of murdering his wife. In "Peasant Women" the religious hypocrite, Matvej, frames Mašen'ka for a murder she probably did not commit, while in "The Shooting Party," Kamyšev, the investigating magistrate turns out to be the murderer and escapes punishment whereas Urbenin, who is innocent, is convicted of murder. At times, judicial error is treated humorously as in "The Swedish Match" ("Švedskaja spička," 1883) where arrests are made of those suspected of murdering a retired officer until it is discovered that the officer is alive, the prisoner of love of the wife of the chief of police. The most famous and serious expression of concern in Čexov's works about judicial error is voiced by the paranoid Ivan Dmitrič Gromov in "Ward No. 6" ("Palata No. 6," 1892):

> Legal procedures being what they are today, a miscarriage of justice is not only quite possible but would be nothing to wonder at .... Only one thing is needed to make a judge deprive an innocent man of all his rights and sentence him to hard labor: time ... Is it not absurd even to think of justice when society regards every kind of violence as both rational and expedient, while every act of clemency, such as a verdict of acquittal provokes an outburst of dissatisfaction and feelings of revenge? (VIII, 113.)

In "The Head Gardener's Story" the landowner is clearly the exponent of "every kind of violence as both rational and expedient."

Could it possibly be that the truth is that the doctor in the legend was not murdered but fell by accident and perhaps the alleged murderer had merely found the body in the ravine and robbed it? Čexov, it seems, has removed all possibility of a simple solution and made vivid the horror of a wrong accusation. In the final analysis, it appears that in "The Head Gardener's Story" a judicial error has been made in the opposite direction as the apparent murderer is set free.[12]

The story could easily be interpreted as Tolstojan, for it embodies two of his five main precepts, notably, "Love all people alike," and "Do not resist evil by violence." The doctor's exemplary life and the gardener's special emphasis that "he loved everyone" (VIII, 384) and the release of the murderer, offer one of the most vivid embodiments of these precepts in Čexov's works.[13] In light of the personality of the teller of the legend, however, we see that the treatment of these themes is satirical.[14] "The Head Gardener's Story," unlike Tolstoj's *Narodnye rasskazy* (*Stories for the People*), contains not a religious message but a message to believe in man, who, in the words of Dr. Svistickij from "Perpetuum Mobile" (1884), is "the crown of creation" (III, 25).

The focus upon the issue of crime and punishment in both "The Bet" and "The Head Gardener's Story" offers evidence of Čexov's deep commitment to humanitarian concerns. In "The Head Gardener's Story" the argument against the death penalty is presented obliquely as faith in man spares the murderer from execution. As always with Čexov, we realize that the issue may be argued either way but ultimately a middle ground must be sought. If it is immoral to set a murderer free, it is equally immoral to put him to death. The story appears to suggest that in dealing with the issue of crime and punishment, men should be guided by both reason and faith in man, for they are not mutually exclusive.

University of Minnesota

NOTES

1. Despite their artistic and philosophical merit, "The Bet" and "The Head Gardener's Story" have not received due attention. Major studies on Čexov in English, for example, Karl D. Kramer, *The Chameleon and the Dream: The Image of Reality in Čexov's Stories*, (The Hague: Mouton, 1970); Beverly Hahn, *Chekhov: A Study of the Major Stories and Plays* (Cambridge: Univ. Press, 1977); Donald Rayfield, *Chekhov: The Evolution of His Art* (New York: Barnes and Noble, 1975), and Thomas Winner, *Chekhov and His Prose* (New York: Holt, Rinehart and Winston, 1966), mention only their titles, while most Soviet critics, for example, Zinovij S.

Papernyj, *A. P. Čexov: Očerk tvorčestva* (Moscow: Sov. pisatel', 1960), 121-23, Vladimir Ja. Lakšin, *Tolstoj i Čexov* (Moscow: Sov. pisatel' 1963), 28, Aleksandr P. Čudakov, *Poètika Čexova* (Moscow: Nauka, 1971), 94, 105, 265, Kornej Čukovskij, *O Čexove* (Moscow: GIXL, 1967), 22, and G. Berdnikov, *A. P. Čexov: Idejnye i tvorčeskie iskanija* (Moscow: GIXL, 1961), 222-23, provide only cursory comments. A somewhat lengthier treatment of "The Head Gardener's Story," focusing mainly on its genesis, is provided by L. M. Dolotova, "Motiv i proizvedenie ('Rasskaz staršego sadovnika', 'Ubijstvo')," in *V tvorčeskoj laboratorii Čexova*, ed. L. D. Opul'skaja, et al. (Moscow: Nauka, 1974), 35-53.

2. Events surrounding the publication of "The Head Gardener's Story," 25 December 1894, in *Russkie vedomosti*, suggest that the tale was written during November-December of that year. Chapters I-XIX of *Island of Sakhalin* were published between December 1891 and July 1894. Although Chapter XXI had also been completed by this time, it was banned by the censor and did not appear until 1895 when the entire twenty-three chapters were published in book form. During the second half of 1894 and the beginning of 1895, Čexov was preparing the final draft of this book. (See letters of 13 November 1894 to V. A. Gol'cev [XVI, 182-83] and 9 April 1895 to V. M. Lavrov [XVI, 226-27; 238], in *Polnoe sobranie sočinenij i pisem A. P. Čexova*, ed. S. D. Baluxatyj et al. [20 vols.; Moscow: Ogiz, 1944-51].) This activity overlaps the period of writing "The Head Gardener's Story." All translations from Čexov's letters and works in this paper are mine from this edition.

3. It appears that Čexov based the detail of the banker's thoughts of killing the lawyer because he could not pay up on a well publicized event in the life of Karl Xristoforovič Landsbery who was tried in 1879 for killing an old acquaintance because he could not pay him a debt of five thousand rubles. (See Dolotova, 44.) During his stay on Sakhalin, Čexov made Landsbery's acquaintance and even dined at his house. (See *Island of Sakhalin*, X, 25.)

4. See: N. I. Gitovič, *Letopis' žizni i tvorčestva A. P. Čexova* (Moscow: GIXL, 1955), 360-61.

5. Čexov owned a Russian translation of Beccaria's book entitled *Rassuždenie o prestuplenijax i nakazanijax*. Perev. s ital. na franc. Andreem Morelletom, a s onogo na rossijskij Dmitriem Jazykovym (St. Petersburg, 1803). See "Raboty, imevšiesja v biblioteke A. P. Čexova," A. P. Čexov, *Polnoe sobranie sočinenij i pisem*, ed. H. F. Bel'čikov et al. (30 vols.; Moscow: Nauka, 1974–), XIX-XV, 895.

6. Cesare Bonesane, Marchese di Beccaria, "Of the Punishment of Death," Chapter XXVIII, *An Essay on Crimes and Punishments* by the Marquis Beccaria of Milan with a Commentary by M. de Voltaire (Edinburgh: Alexander Donaldson, 1778), 104-5, 111-12.

7. Interestingly enough, Obolenskij and Mixail Karlovič are marked by the common trait of being eccentric. Although Čexov considered the critic to be an intelligent and interesting individual, he remarked to Suvorin that Obolenskij "gives the impression of a man who was trained, trained, and overtrained. He constantly uses emotional phrases." (See letter of 10 April 1894 to A. S. Suvorin, XVI, 140.) In a letter of 12 April 1894 to V. A. Gol'cev, Čexov again stressed this point, saying that "Obolenskij has been devoured by emotions" (XVI, 141).

8. During the early part of 1894, Čexov made the following entry in his *Notebooks*: "Murder. A corpse in the ravine. The young investigator is inexperienced. A small town. He searches for the murderer a long time but does not find him." Several details from this entry appear in the story, which suggests that Čexov created the "legend" himself. Apparently Čexov was in the mood to write "legends" that year for, in addition to "The Head Gardener's Story," he created "The Black Monk" and "The Student."

9. These impressions of Čexov about Ibsen were recorded by Ol'ga Knipper. See David Magarshack, *Chekhov: A Life* (Westport, Conn.: Greenwood Press, 1970), 351. Constantin Stanislavski, *My Life in Art* (New York: World Publishing, 1968), 345, also recalls Čexov's critical attitude toward Ibsen: "Chekhov did not like Ibsen as a dramatist, although he placed Ibsen's talents very high." It is interesting to note that while in Sakhalin, Čexov met a zealous, rather intolerant Dr. Boris Aleksandrovič Perlin who was at odds with the authorities because of his protests against local conditions. With his gray whiskers, the doctor appeared to Čexov to resemble Ibsen (*Island of Sakhalin*, X, 25). The doctor, it appears, was the prototype for Mixail Karlovič.

10. The quote is of Hamlet's words (III, 4).

11. It should be noted that "The Head Gardener's Story" anticipates Čexov's personal stand and his pronouncements on the famous Dreyfus case which also was tried and decided largely on circumstantial evidence.

12. On 22 November 1894 Čexov served on the jury in the Serpuxov court. He informed Suvorin on 27 November that he was favorably impressed with the way the jury system worked in Russia (XVI, 187). This was an obvious retreat from his previous position and appears to have influenced his portrayal of the court in "The Head Gardener's Story" in a positive light.

13. Despite the fact that many aspects of Tolstoj's teaching had little appeal to Čexov, as late as 28 January 1900 he wrote to M. O. Menšikov: "I love no man as I do Tolstoj; I am an unbeliever, but among all faiths, I consider that of Tolstoj nearest my heart and most suited to my nature." (XVIII, 312.) Precisely because Tolstoj's faith was nearest to Čexov's nature, it is understandable that in December of 1894, less than ten months after having stated to Suvorin that he had rejected Tolstoj's philosophy (letter of 27 March 1894 to A. S. Suvorin, XVI, 132-33), Čexov could still write the Tolstojan "The Head Gardener's Story." It is not surprising, therefore, that I. I. Gorbunov-Posadov, a close friend and follower of Tolstoj and editor of the Tolstojan publishing house *The Intermediary* (*Posrednik*), expressed enthusiasm for the story and offered to publish it in a popular edition. See letter of 25 December 1894 to Čexov, VIII, 567.

14. A satirical treatment of Tolstoj's precepts is not unusual for Čexov. As Josephine Newcombe, "Was Čexov a Tolstoyan?" *Slavic and East European Journal*, 18 (1974), 144-47, successfully demonstrates, even of the stories Čexov created during 1886–88, when Tolstoj's philosophy impressed him the most, not one of them ends on a note in full accordance with Tolstoj's theories. "The Bet" itself is a satirical treatment of Tolstoj's ideas of asceticism.

PART II

MODERNISM

FUNCTIONS OF THE FAIRY TALE IN SOLOGUB'S PROSE

Pierre R. Hart

In their attempts to devise vehicles appropriate to a new artistic vision, Russia's Symbolists turned to genres which had been relatively neglected during the protracted reign of the Realist novel. Lyric verse, emphasizing unmediated, subjective experience and favoring spatial rather than temporal form, reasserted itself as the preferred means of verbal expression, and it exerted considerable influence upon prose composition. The first decade of the twentieth century saw a variety of experiments with fiction, many of which approximated poetry in their concern with rhythmical, repetitive phrasing, and deliberate word play.[1] Sophisticated and self-reflective though this type of writing may have been, it shared certain "primitivist" assumptions with the visual and plastic art works of the same era. Reacting to the cultural accretions which had come to burden artistic practice, these authors presumed that both aesthetic and philosophical purposes could better be served by modeling their works after the ostensibly simpler products of earlier ages and less tutored peoples.[2] Russia's rich tradition of oral literature provided a natural base of reference, and the fairy tale in particular commanded attention for both its structural and stylistic features. An examination of this traditional genre's contribution to the short fiction of Fedor Sologub reveals several ways in which the primitivist impulse served the author's particular dualistic vision.

Almost a century earlier, the German Romantics had recognized the potential of the *Märchen* for communicating an order of experience not immediately accessible to the senses. They were the first to create a literary equivalent in which they sought to suggest a relationship between the world of appearances and that ineffable realm of essences which lay beyond it. Among the Russian writers, Gogol''s use of the *Kunstmärchen* in his Petersburg tales successfully completed an adaptive process initiated in his *Evenings on a Farm near Dikan'ka*. If we compare these urban accounts of the fantastic with the original folk genre, several distinct changes are apparent. Rather than the fairy tale's universality of place, the setting has become fixed in both time and location; rather than an external focus on events in their formal relationship, there is a pronounced shift toward the description of individual responses to such events; and rather than reassuring the reader that logic and coherency have been restored to the world, Gogol' leaves him to ponder an ambiguous future.[3] Moreover, the primacy of verbal play, noted by many critics as the distinguishing feature of Gogol''s prose, may itself be construed as a transmutation of that oral tradition in which the narrator made his contribution to the basic text through verbal gestures. As is true of his subject matter, Gogol''s style confounds the reader's expectations of traditional narrative, employing analogous devices to totally unexpected ends.

The several distinguishing features of Gogol''s Petersburg tales confirm André Jolles' definition of the relationship between the traditional fairy tale and its literary counterpart. In his elaboration of a literary typology based on the mimetic principle, Jolles postulates that the simple form is informed by an "ethic of occurrences" (*Ethik des Geschehens*) which does not so much specify man's conduct as it does the proper course of events.[4] Although an author such as Gogol' typically fails to satisfy these expectations in his works, it is almost always the case that the true fairy tale does so.[5] In those rare instances where the ethic of occurrences is violated, an *Antimärchen* results "in which the naively, in the original Schillerean sense, immoral world, the world of the tragic, is realized" (Jolles, 242). If, as Bruno Bettelheim contends, the true fairy tale is future oriented, facilitating the child's psychological development, the infrequency of the *Antimärchen* as a traditional form is understandable.[6] Its internal ambiguities and consequent failure to provide the requisite reassurances to the listener or reader can only serve to impede maturational processes. The social utility of such inventions, however, may be of less interest to the individual writer than are representations of his particular experiences and sensations. In the peculiar realm of the *Kunstmärchen*, the subjective impulse regularly leads to a new ordering principle devoid of any ethic of occurrences. All of those attributes noted in the Petersburg tales, such as the specificity of time and place, reinforce the impression of unique rather than universal experience, thereby strengthening their association with the world of tragic reality.[7]

The Symbolists' enthusiastic acceptance of Gogol''s fiction is well documented and it was largely the primitivist sensibility, broadly defined as "the absence ... of a firm and rational distinction between the inner world of feeling and the external order of existence" which they presumed to share with him.[8] As the heirs of Romanticism, these authors sought to expand upon its conceptions in an age which had all but lost the mythic mentality. To the degree that they were able to invoke the world of the *Märchen* itself, they were successful in their search for unity. More commonly, however, they had to concede the primacy of external reality which proved so unyielding to the would-be unifier. Sologub's prose offers a case in point. Although his novel, *The Created Legend* (*Tvorimaja legenda*, 1907–14), begins with the assertion of the artist's mythopoeic talents, a more pessimistic vision prevails in much of his fiction. The short story "In Bondage" ("V Plenu," 1905) juxtaposes the conventions of realistic prose and the *Märchen* in a particularly inventive confirmation of the latter view.[9]

As a short story, the work depicts a young boy's fantasy response to the restrictions imposed upon his activities. His imagined plight, prompted by a comparison between his own uneventful life and that of three other young boys, is of little consequence, save for the fact that it inspires the latter to disrupt an adult dinner party with a shower of arrows and curses. At the story's conclusion, Paka's situation has not changed; he remains subject to a degree of parental supervision that appears appropriate to his tender age. These same events, viewed in the context of the fairy tale, assume very different dimensions and suggest a more sober conclusion. A young prince, who formerly enjoyed an idyllic existence with his real mother, finds himself the captive of a wicked fairy. To secure his release, he enlists the aid of "the free hunters" (*volnye oxotniki*) who obtain a magic agent which "no witch can withstand." Despite their best efforts, however, the hunters fail in their mission and the young prince is left to suffer at the hands of the wicked fairy.

Paka, the story's main character, is one of a lengthy series of Sologub's child heroes who are confronted by an alien world. Their common response to what they perceive as incomprehensible or threatening is a retreat into fantasies of their own invention.[10] To the degree that we regard "In Bondage" as a psychological short story in which Paka is the source of pure fantasy, we recognize both the motivation and ultimate insufficiency of his response. At the age of seven he longs both for the security and attention that a doting parent might provide and for the degree of freedom necessary to explore a range of new experiences outside the family domain. His dilemma consists in being denied these conditions; his socialite mother does not provide the measure of personal concern which the boy expects nor does she permit him to roam at will.

Somehow, Paka must explain his discontent, if only for his own satisfaction, and he does so with the aid of fantasy. It is important to note that he himself is the author, and thus exercises total control over both its substance and interpretation. This places Paka in a different relationship to the fairy tale than is commonly the case. A child typically comes to the story in its fixed form, that is, it has an independent source in traditional oral culture and even though the child may not be consciously searching for solutions the work affords him the opportunity to profit from its richly suggestive contents. As Bettelheim remarks: "This is where the fairy tale provides what the child needs most; it begins exactly where the child is emotionally, shows him where he has to go, and how to do it." (122.) As this statement suggests, the fairy tale is not a refuge but a constructive force which enables the child to cope with perplexing problems in the process of maturing.

Quite another effect results if the story, in its entirety, is taken as an example of the *Kunstmärchen*, duplicating to some degree the characteristics of the fairy tale. Under this assumption, Paka is not the creator of a fantasy but a participant in a world controlled by evil forces. Although the initial descriptions of events and characters militate against such an interpretation, with the narrator maintaining an independent stance and stressing the differences between the real and imagined worlds, this distinction is gradually lost in the course of the narration. When, at the story's conclusion, the narrator gloomily remarks, "everything is fettered, link by link, bewitched forever, in captivity," we are left with little choice but to accept Paka's interpretation as the definitive one.

The several stages through which the narrator progresses to a realization of the truth in fantasy can be readily identified. Emphasis on Paka's distress and his thought processes prompt the reader to think in terms of childish imagination. Left to himself, the boy begins to compare his lot with that of the other vacationing boys: "The demon of comparison is a very petty demon but one of the most dangerous. And his seductions are for the little and weak one, irresistible." (IV, 239.) Invocation of "petty demon of comparison" introduces the notion of supernatural forces but, at least for the moment, their effect is localized rather than universal. Further suggestion of the idiosyncratic nature of the boy's vision derives from the description of the sun's effect: "The burning sun enveloped him in its heat and clouded his thoughts. Strange dreams swarmed in Paka's head ...." (IV, 240.)[11] By virtue of their strangeness, his thoughts appear to be discounted as accurate reflections of events.

Even Paka betrays an uncertainly about the validity of his ideas at the outset. In describing his situation to the other boys, he must account for the nominal presence of a female parent while protecting the image of an idealized mother. If, as he asserts, a wicked fairy has truly replaced his mother, we might expect that all traces of the latter would have vanished. Such is the assumption of the three brothers to whom Paka describes his predicament; they are quick to elaborate upon the conventions of the fairy tale, one of them referring to the woman as a "wicked witch." Yet this characterization exceeds the limits that Paka has subconsciously imposed, and he corrects the reference in terms that suggest his persisting awareness of the young woman as his actual mother: "She is a very well-bred fairy and never forgets herself." (IV, 247.)

In the final analysis, the young boy's perception of his situation is less important than the narrator's, and the clues to the latter's confirmation of the truth of the fairy tale need to be specified. His initially "realistic" descriptive terminology is gradually replaced by that which Paka has devised to reflect his interpretation of things. The turning point, at which the narrator signals his readiness to accept the fantasy in its totality, occurs when he describes a meeting between Paka and the wicked fairy/mother. The very structure of the descriptive statement makes the differences in perception clear, and it is equally apparent that the child's view prevails: "Paka announced that he had to go to his mama. And he went — to the wicked fairy." (IV, 257.) Subsequent references to the woman as the wicked fairy strengthen this characterization, as does the slightly sinister description of her physical attributes: "The wicked fairy was alone ... She was young, beautiful. Dark hair, languid movements. Dark burning eyes." (IV, 257.)

Paka's behavior in the woman's presence further encourages our identification of her with the wicked fairy. Although he forgets himself once and addresses her as "mama," his conduct and remarks are otherwise consistent with the notion that he is indeed pleading with his captor. The distance which he believes to separate them is reflected in his persistent use of the polite form of address, contrary to normal familial practice. In the course of their conversation, direct reference to the fairy tale's influence is made, the wicked fairy accusing Paka of being a "little fantast" (*malen'kij fantazer*) who has overindulged in his reading of such stories. Any lingering doubts about the relationship of the fairy tale to this story are dispelled by Paka's reflection upon this accusation. Observing that the woman herself reads "long fairy tales in French," he concludes: "Apparently even in fairy tales not everything is a fairy tale but there is also some truth ...." (IV, 261.)

Vladimir Propp's investigation of the morphology of the fairy tale has demonstrated that it invariably contains a limited set of events, which are presented in a constant order, that its characters are readily recognizable as belonging to particular types with prescribed activities, and that the narrative progression is from a description of basic harm or lack, through several intermediate situations to a final statement of resolution.[12] "In Bondage" reflects, through a variety of details, its dependency upon, and deliberate departure from these traditional features. Using Propp's terminology, we can categorize Paka as the victim-hero, essentially passive in nature and with a limited range of functions. Given his relative youth and inexperience, his role is appropriate in terms of the realistic short story and fairy tale alike. His passivity has particular consequences with respect to the fairy tale's conventions, however, for the actions which a more decisive hero would take to eliminate the basic harm must here be assigned to others. Helper figures most frequently assume such duties and the "free hunters" serve in that relationship to Paka. It is they who first encourage the boy in his interpretation of reality, it is they who suggest the magic agent for securing his release from enchantment, and finally, it is their failure which proves the absence of an ethic of occurrences, bringing the account to its pessimistic conclusion.

Inasmuch as helper figures are expressions of the hero's own unrealized strengths and capabilities in the fairy tale, their inadequacies might also be construed as comments on the hero's weakness. At least superficially, the three brothers embody the qualities which Paka would like to have. They express their independence by building forest hideouts, fishing, and going barefooted, all pleasures which are denied to Paka. Yet theirs is an illusory strength, naively assumed and ultimately disproved. Viewed realistically, they are simply inexperienced but enthusiastic boys who become caught up in an adventure which is partly of their own invention. When their father sternly reproaches them for the ill-fated attempt to free Paka, they admit, for the moment, to having been deluded. But they revert to their function as fairy tale figures when, at the story's conclusion, they attempt to use still other "winged words." The insufficiency of words in confrontation with evil, fully understandable in the context of the realistic short story, produces a disquieting effect as an element of the fairy tale.

Once Paka has persuaded the free hunters that the situation is as he perceives it to be, the narrative focus shifts to them. Their faith in the veracity of his account parallels their confidence in the "winged words" as an effective means of lifting the magic spell. Indeed, such an attitude is consonant with the terms of the fairy tale in which verbal formulae are often literally realized, effecting an immediate change of state in the person or object. In the present case, the "winged words" are presumed capable of releasing Paka from his enchantment although it remains unclear whether they are intended literally. There is a curious relationship between the expression and the intimacy which Paka wishes to maintain with the wicked fairy/mother. Euphemistically referred to as "recalling one's mother" (*pro mat' vspomnit'*), the phrase itself implies sexual intimacy of a type which a young boy could only entertain subconsciously. By their very refusal to repeat the expression to Paka, the free hunters reveal their awareness of its true significance, yet they use it in the most determined fashion, inscribing the words on their arrows.

The free hunters' attack simultaneously marks the narrative climax and the conclusive violation of the fairy tale's spirit. As each of the arrows lands, the narrator describes the accompanying cry, not with the vocabulary of fantasy, but in clearly realistic terms: "A child's voice shouted out some obscene words," "another child's voice was heard shouting out an obscenity," "a third ringing voice shouted out hideous words." (IV, 262.) The particular descriptive phrases, *ploščadnaja bran', gadost', bezobraznye slova*, leave no doubt as to the real, morally repugnant nature of the expressions.

We might, however, contend that the initial failure is itself a part of the fairy tale's formula and that this incident can therefore be discounted as having particular meaning. Indeed, we learn that as the train bearing Paka and the wicked fairy departs, the brothers test the power of new "winged words" which they have just acquired. But the third, traditionally successful attempt goes unrealized and we are forced back to an evaluation of the initial attack as central to the story's outcome. Words, the narrator tells us in his concluding, despairing remarks, are both "powerless and poor." It is apparent that the story, having posed the type of problem which might readily be solved if the laws of the fairy tale were fully operative, is so constructed as to admit only of defeat.

To define the work as an *Antimärchen*, which recognized tragic reality as its ultimate base, is not to explain the particular reason for its ending. The most obvious explanation would appear to depend upon the significance of the "winged words." If their sexual message is taken seriously, it is clear that Paka's liberation cannot be effected in that manner. Yet, in the final analysis, his situation admits of no solution, whatever the formulation. As the narrator remarks, "In vain do free hunters search for those who are wise and knowledgeable" (IV, 28). What is at issue, then, is the very essence of the fairy tale, namely "the confidence that we are secure in a world not destitute of sense, that we can adapt ourselves to it and act and live even if we cannot view or comprehend the world as a whole" (Bettelheim, 47). Even that more realistic possibility, that Paka might surrender his infantile attachments naturally over time, has been denied, with the result that everything appears fixed in a kind of limbo.

The narrator's admission of the impotence of words directly challenges one of the fairy tale's conventions, but of equal importance is its implication for the craft of Sologub's fiction. Despite the proclamation of the artist's creative powers at the beginning of *The Created Legend*, Sologub does not indulge in the type of elaborate verbal constructions that would underscore the primacy of language in its artistic function. Stylistically, he continues in the tradition of the nineteenth-century Realists, his economies of description insuring that the reader's attention remain fixed on events and characters rather than the manner of their portrayal. The almost telegraphic depiction of the evil fairy, previously cited, is one example of his spare technique: "Temnye volosy, tomnye dviženija. Žgučij vzor černyx glaz." (IV, 256.) Such sobriety of depiction confirms the conclusion to the story itself: it is impossible to transform the fundamental design of the world through verbal intervention. Once that design has been discovered, the artist can do little more than report it. As one of the more pessimistic "seers" among the Symbolists, Sologub detected an underlying reality that was essentially evil.

Although certain features of "In Bondage" suggest a union of fairy tale and short story, there is no explicit equation of the two. Another of Sologub's works, "Turandina" (1912), deliberately superimposes a fairy tale upon the realm of the everyday, with equally ambiguous results. The hero of this story is not a naive child but rather, a promising young lawyer who has successfully defended several persons who might otherwise have been judged guilty. Yet he is possessed of the escapist tendencies which typify Sologub's characters; surveying an ostensibly good and beautiful landscape, he is saddened by what appears to be a correlation between the visual impression of the scene and the potential for evil in the world: "It was as if someone evil and insidious were seeking to seduce him by revealing all the beauty of nature in such entrancing form." (XIV, 95.) Bulanin regards this beauty as a deceptive veil which some temptress has cast to conceal the evils of nature and he looks to the fairy tale as an alternative which, even though temporary, might relieve him of the press of the physical world. Unlike Paka, who fashions a fairy tale from the particulars of his own life, he recalls a particular story and wills the forest enchantress Turandina into existence. Why he is motivated by this story is not totally clear; his relationship with the women of this world appears less than satisfactory, and the promise of Turandina's innocent affection might thus hold particular appeal.

The moment of realization deserves particular mention, for it captures all the ambiguity of Sologub's interpretation of the fairy tale. On the one hand, there is the momentary expression of omnipotence while, on the other, there is the question of its consequences: "As though becoming one with the great universal Will, he spoke with great power and authority as only once in his life is a man given power to do." (XIV, 97.) Wish fulfillment is a commonplace within the fairy tale, and even when individual wishes are ill-advised, the ethic of occurrences insures that they are effectively related to the entire story. In this instance, the wish seemingly occurs within the context of mundane reality and serves to introduce the fairy tale proper. Yet the act requires supernatural intervention, thereby obliterating the distinction between the two spheres. Whatever the forces which govern the whole of existence, they momentarily coincide with Bulanin's personal impulses. Depending upon their inherent nature, what has been willed might either be for better or for worse.

The ensuing description of Turandina as a physical being conveys that combination of the angelic and demonic which can be found in many of Sologub's portraits of young women. Despite the initial emphasis upon her external beauty, the portrayal concludes in a manner which suggests a more profoundly evil essence: "She would have seemed like an angel from heaven had not her heavy black eyebrows met and so disclosed her witchery." (XIV, 98.) There is little about Turandina's conduct or words to confirm the sugges- tion of her demonic origins. She professes to tell the truth and declares that she has come to Bulanin as one who, in his practice of the law, defends truth. The single detail to imply that she might well represent evil attempting to further insinuate itself in the world, concerns her magical bag. Upon command, it provides anything which might be of use in the life of man. Bulanin is tempted with the power of the bag on three separate occasions. He does not succumb to temptation on either of the first two, altruistically using it to provide Turandina's clothing and passport. It is only at his relative's urging that he finally comes to regard it as an inexhaustible source of money which can be his for the asking. Even at that point, however, there is nothing to explicitly confirm the suspicion that the young lawyer has finally sold himself to the devil.

Quite unlike the conclusion to "In Bondage," the final chapter of "Turandina" would appear to confirm the formulaic happy ending. Two details argue against such a conclusion. As mysteriously as she earlier appeared, Turandina departs to be reunited with her father. The fairy tale, so the narrator informs us, has ended, and reality reaffirms itself. Yet she leaves two children behind, the older of whom remains in mysterious communication with his mother. It might be argued that Turandina has successfully completed her mission, insuring the continued presence of evil in the person of her seven-year-old son.

Viewed in terms of its overall structure, "Turandina" confirms the basic *Antimärchen* design of "In Bondage." Its conclusion may be less obviously pessimistic but, asuming that Bulanin has indeed willed evil into the world, there has been a reversal of the traditional liquidation of harm. Instead of recognizing his error and resisting the further expansion of this power, the hero actually insures its continuation by fathering the two children. And, what is perhaps most disquieting is the thoroughly uncritical manner in which Turandina is accepted by the members of society. Apart from an occasional mention of her mysterious origins, there is no question raised concerning her character or influence upon others. Even the narrator refrains from reminding his reader of that sinister element included in his initial description of the woman.

Sologub's willful inversion of traditional forms is consistent with his conception of the world. Like many of his contemporaries, he objected to representations of reality which dealt only in the superficialities of the realm of the senses. To the degree that he accepted the conventions of the fairy tale, he confirmed the primitivist assumption that traditional modes of expression more fully reflected the whole of human experience. What ultimately distinguished Sologub's decadence, however, was his rejection of the basic laws governing such forms. Rather than the *Märchen*'s life-affirming impulse, his Manichean vision dictated its opposite, with the cheerless prospect of enduring evil left for the reader's contemplation.

Louisiana State University

NOTES

1. Patricia Carden, "Ornamentalism and Modernism," in *Russian Modernism*, ed. George Gibian and H. W. Tjalsma (Ithaca: Cornell Univ. Press, 1976), 49-64, provides a useful summary of the stylistic features common in ornamental prose.

2. Robert Goldwater, *Primitivism in Modern Art* (New York: Vintage, 1967), 251, aptly summarizes the motivation for emulating the art of primitive cultures: "It is the assumption that the further one goes back — historically, psychologically or aesthetically — the simpler things become; and that because they are simpler they are more profound, more important, and more valuable."

3. James Holquist, "The Devil in Mufti: The *Märchenwelt* in Gogol's Short Stories," *PMLA*, 82, (1967), 353-62.

4. André Jolles, *Einfache Formen*, (Tubingen: Max Niemeyer, 1972), 241, remarks: "So können wir sagen, daß in dem Märchen eine Form vorliegt, in der das Geschehen, der Lauf der Dinge so geordnet sind, daß sie den Anforderungen der naiven Moral völlig entsprechen, also nach unserem absoluten Gefühlsurteil 'gut' und 'gerecht' sind."

5. For an application of Jolles' notions to Gogol''s story "Vij," see F. C. Driessen, *Gogol as a Short Story Writer* (The Hague: Mouton, 1965), 140-51.

6. Bruno Bettelheim, *The Uses of Enchantment* (New York: Alfred Knopf, 1977), 9-11.

7. Jolles, *Einfache Formen*, 244, remarking upon the disruptive influence of historical detail within the confines of the simple form, contends: "Historische Örtlichkeit, historische Zeit nähern sich den unmoralischen Wirklichkeit, brechen die Macht des selbstverständlich und notwendig Wunderbaren." The relationship of the fantastic to the reality of Petersburg, then, is quite different from that to be found in the ahistoric world of the true fairy tale.

8. Michael Bell, *Primitivism* (London: Methuen, 1973), 7-8.

9. Fedor Sologub, *Sobranie sočinenij* (18 vols.; St. Petersburg: Sirin, 1913–14), IV.

10. For an extensive analysis of one such story, see Carola Hansson, *Fedor Sologub as a Short Story Writer* (Stockholm: Almqvist and Wiksell 1975), 24-62.

11. Andreas Leitner, *Die Erzählungen Fedor Sologubs* (Munich: Otto Sagner, 1976), 196, observes that the sun is often a negative element in Sologub's work, causing unrest and distress. Although the bright light of day may sometimes dispel illusions, it also works in the opposite manner, casting an unreal glow over an otherwise sordid world.

12. V. Ja. Propp, *Morfologija skazki* (Leningrad, 1928), provides the structural concepts for this analysis. Although Propp correctly notes that the term "folktale" (*skazka*) embraces a number of forms in addition to the fairy tale, I have found the latter term more appropriate for the purposes of this discussion.

FAIRY TALE MOTIFS IN SOLOGUB'S "DREAM ON THE ROCKS"

Linda J. Ivanits

Although Sologub's contemporaries regarded his short stories highly, both Soviet and Western scholars have until recently neglected this aspect of his work. In the past decade, however, new editions of his stories and several critical studies have appeared in the West. All these studies agree that Sologub's stories, like the rest of his fiction, turn on the juxtaposition of the vulgar world of everyday reality to a vision of an ideal realm of pristine tranquility and beauty.[1] No doubt the most familiar example of this dualism occurs in *The Petty Demon* (*Melkij bes*) in the contrast between the banal, dirty world of Peredonov and the world of exotic beauty and sensuality which Ljudmila attempts to create. Often in Sologub's works the other, non-earthly world seems to reflect the mythic concept of the world at the time of its creation — a sort of Golden Age or Paradise before the Fall. In *The Created Legend* (*Tvorimaja legenda*) Trirodov and Elizaveta escape for a time to the wondrous land of Ojle where they are "innocent, like children" and speak "in a new and sweet dialect, like the language of the first-created paradise."[2] Many of the protagonists of Sologub's short stories cope with earthly existence by transforming it in their imaginations to a wondrous other-world. In "Lohengrin" Mašen'ka Pestrjakova imagines that her ordinary bookbinder fiancé is in truth Wagner's mythical knight (XIV, 19-47); Elena Nikolaevna of "The Crowned One" is able to accept her husband's death by believing that she is really a forest princess ("Venčannaja," XIV, 251-59), and the elderly protagonist of "The Hoop" recovers the world of childhood and his happiness when he plays with a hoop ("Obruč," IV, 99-105).

Frequently in Sologub's short stories the juxtaposition between the two worlds is presented through fairy-tale patterns and motifs. In such stories, the mythic world of first creation takes the form of a magic kingdom in which a beautiful princess dwells. In "Turandina" the lawyer Petr Bulanin is married for a time to an unearthly beauty who claims to be a princess banished from her kingdom (XIV, 91-110); the child Paka of "In Captivity" imagines that an evil fairy has cast a spell on him, driven him from his princely home, and is now posing as his mother, while his real mother still resides in the enchanted kingdom ("V plenu," IV, 151-70); young Gotik of "Two Gotiks" believes that at night while his diurnal self sleeps, his nocturnal self ventures into the magic castle of the beautiful Princess Selenita ("Dva Gotika," VII, 65-89). As the last two examples suggest, fairy-tale patterns often clothe the presentation of a child's search for identity in Sologub's fiction. In addition, this search is frequently accompanied by the motif of the displacement of a good mother by an evil one or a stepmother, as in the folk tale of "Vasilisa the Beautiful." Vasilisa's wicked stepmother dispatches her to Baba Jaga for light and, with the help of a magic doll which her real mother had given her before dying, Vasilisa completes the tasks set to her by the witch, returns home with light, and, eventually, marries the son of the tsar.

In Sologub's early story "The White Mama," Leša, a lost child, tells the protagonist Saksaulov that his "white mama" has been taken away in a coffin and he now lives with his "black mama." Saksaulov interprets this to mean that Leša lives with a stepmother, and, upon further investigation, he learns that this stepmother attempted to get rid of the child by banishing him to a park bench far from home. The story ends with the unconvincing suggestion that they "lived happily ever after." Saksaulov adopts Leša and marries a girl whose identity seems to merge both with that of the "white mama" and with Tamara, Saksaulov's ethereal first fiancée who had died five years previously. ("Belaja mama," III, 145-60.)[3]

Highly representative of the stories which build on fairy-tale patterns, and yet artistically more satisfying and complex than "The White Mama," is the story "Dream on the Rocks" ("Mečta na kamnjax," XIV, 51-66). The meaning of the fairy tale in Sologub's stories is especially clear in this story, and we can appreciate here the pattern of the fairy tale (or "magic" tale) in the sense that V. Ja. Propp described it:

> The magic tale begins with the infliction of some sort of loss or injury (enchantment, banishment, and so forth) or with the desire to have something (the tsar sends his son for the fire-bird) and develops through the departure of the hero from home, a meeting with a donor, who gives him a magic agent or helper through the aid of which the object of the search is found. Further, the tale gives a duel with the antagonist (the most important form of which is a fight with a dragon), a return, and pursuit ....[4]

In "Dream on the Rocks" the twelve-year-old protagonist Griška lives with his mother Annuška, who since her husband's death has been forced to work as a cook to support herself and her son. Annuška is often cross with Griška, and life around him in the stuffy kitchen and dirty courtyard is dreary and ugly. But Griška escapes from this ugliness by dreaming. He yields to reveries about a distant magic kingdom where he, as hero, fights giants in defense of the weak and where the beautiful Princess Turandina lives. Griška cannot believe that he is only a servant's son condemned to live forever in the unsightly, stifling city and to be shunned by upper-class boys. He imagines that Turandina cast a spell on him and caused him to abandon his fairy-tale homeland and forget his true identity. He feels that "Griška" is not his real name and that it will one day peel off him "like a badly glued label on a wine bottle" (XIV, 57). One day he is jolted from his dreams of Turandina by his mother, who sends him after pastries for unexpected guests of the mistress. On the way home, again lost in thoughts of Turandina, Griška bumps into a stranger and drops the pastries. He is coarsely abused by passers-by and, while gathering his lemon biscuits from the dirty sidewalk, he concludes that Turandina is just as evil as the people in the city, for she has cast him into a terrible sleep from which he will never awaken to learn his true identity. (XIV, 64-65.)

In "Dream on the Rocks" Griška, like the hero of the fairy tale, enters another world (through his fantasies) to find the object of his quest (his true name). But, while this story contains many of the appropriate personages and evokes the quest pattern, there are some crucial differences between it and the fairy tale. Bruno Bettelheim and others maintain that the distinction between the real world and the fantasy world in fairy tales is clear. The pattern is one of departure from this world, entry into a supernatural realm, often by crossing a boundary (a fiery river, a dense forest, a tunnel in the earth), and then, when the object of the quest has been obtained, return to this world.[5] On reading the fairy tale, a child is not inclined to confuse the two worlds. Nor is there any ambiguity in the personages of the magic tale. In the division of the mother figure, for example, one becomes all good, the other all bad (Bettelheim, 69, 9, and elsewhere). In "Dream on the Rocks" the quest is unsuccessful (Griška does not find his true name), the boundaries between the two worlds are blurred, and the mother figures — Annuška as "bad" mother, Turandina as "good" — are ambivalent.

From Griška's perspective, and in contrast to the fairy tale, the here-and-now is posited as the "unreal" world (it is the world to which he, like the protagonists of most of the other tales mentioned above, has been banished and in which he is held captive), and the magic kingdom is posited as home — the world to which he desires to return. The narrator's nostalgic lyrical preface to "Dream on the Rocks" seems to support this reversal of realities:

> Year after year passes, centuries pass, and still not revealed to man is the mystery of his soul. Man asks, experiences, but does not find an answer. Wise people, such as children, do not know. And not even everyone is able to ask: Who am I?
>
> (XIV, 51.)

But in the story itself, the situation is more complicated than a simple reversal of values assigned to the two worlds. In fact, there is a suggestion that there may be no essential difference between these worlds, for the ugly here-and-now slips imperceptibly into the distant magic kingdom and vice-versa. Griška is suddenly jolted from his dreams back to the kitchen when his mother calls, and he is similarly jolted from one world to the other when he drops the pastries. This lack of stability in the two worlds is especially evident in the ambivalence of the mother figures. However coarse and angry Annuška may seem, there are moments of tenderness between her and Griška (XIV, 57). Turandina, on the other hand, is not only beautiful, but cruel (XIV, 63).

The body of the story, unlike the lyrical preface, seems to contain a certain narrative irony in the tendency to perceive one's immediate situation or what is nearby as ugly and what is distant as beautiful and good. One is reminded that in the land of Ojle following the Goddess "Lirika" Elizaveta and Trirodov encountered the Goddess "Irony," who removed the shrouds one by one from their wondrous vision of the world. "A great sorrow was revealed, the inescapable contradiction of every world, the fatal identity of perfect opposites" (XX, 46). So too in "Dream on the Rocks" the initial lyrical nostalgia for the other world yields to doubt about the nature of this world. Possibly the very acknowledgement of a dichotomy between the vulgar here-and-now and a beautiful, remote land of perfection contains the seeds of destruction of this other realm, which is in constant danger of slipping into its opposite. It is significant that Griška's accident occurs in part because he must venture to a faraway bakery rather than the one across the street. His mistress believes that everything in the distant bakery is wonderful and tasty, while everything in the local one is foul (XIV, 61). This journey to the distant bakery for pastries contains a mocking echo of Griška's more essential quest — into the world of his imagination to discover his true self.

"Dream on the Rocks" is the story of a child's search for identity in a world where the distinction between illusion and reality is unclear. But in contrast to some of the other stories of this type where the theme of sexual maturation is only latent ("Two Gotiks," "In Captivity"), "Dream on the Rocks" deals explicitly with the child's sexual awakening. Griška experiences incomprehensible, agitated feelings during the love scenes in the novels which Annuška likes him to read to her (XIV, 55). In his dreams he pictures beautiful, tender, but at times cruel women and well proportioned pages. These women, he thinks, "promise all the joy and all the pain which it is possible for one person to give another" (XIV, 56). Griška casts himself in the role of a page vis-à-vis Turandina, and he imagines himself kneeling before her listening to the painful story of how she playfully cast a spell on him (XIV, 59-60). He also imagines himself as a sick child lying in a luxurious, soft bed under satin covers (unlike his hard bed and torn quilt near the stuffy kitchen) while he is attended by his beautiful princess-mother, whose identity seems to be an extension of Turandina's (XIV, 63).

Griška's agitated emotions and Turandina's sadistic pleasure at hurting him are reminiscent of the relationship between fourteen-year-old Saša

Pyl'nikov and Ljudmila Rutilova of *The Petty Demon*. Ljudmila also makes Saša kneel before her during their erotic games; and she enjoys pinching his cheeks until red spots appear (VI, 212, 216). Both Griška and Saša are unsure about the precise nature of their relationship with the older woman. Griška is both son and page to his princess, and Saša thinks at one point how nice it would be to have Ljudmila for a sister so that he could address her intimately as "dearest Ljudmiločka" (VI, 205). *The Petty Demon* contains suggestions that Ljudmila, like Turandina, is to be envisioned as a fairy-tale beauty.[6]

Saša's relationship with Ljudmila can be understood as a sort of rite of puberty, for through it he is initiated into the realm of sexual agitation and, simultaneously, into the sordid affairs of the everyday world (especially at the masquerade, VI, 348-68). This initiation is corruptive, for by the end of the novel Saša has learned to lie convincingly (VI, 369). Griška's accident also symbolizes an initiation of sorts. His passage from childhood to early manhood (signaled by the onset of sexual turbulence) is accompanied by a loss of faith in his ideal world. He now perceives that Turandina is evil and he abandons hope of finding his true identity (XIV, 65). This collapse of his ideal realm of dream on the dirty pavement of the city is foreshadowed in the very title of the story.[7] It is now too that Griška perceives the external world not only as ugly and vulgar, but also as populated by demonic forces. He thinks that the people around him are fantastic creatures who wish to carry him off (XIV, 64).

There are indications that Griška's belief that he is surrounded by hostile supernatural forces is correct. Nor is this the first time that such forces are mentioned in the story. In Turandina's eyes glow unkind little sparks, like those of "a young witch who has not yet tired of casting spells" (XIV, 60). (In *The Petty Demon* Ljudmila is also compared to a witch, VI, 181.) Turandina seems to collaborate with Annuška in sending Griška on his fatal mission. She tells him to hasten to Annuška, and Annuška, in turn, dispatches him to the bakery with the words, "The devil brought guests to the mistress at the wrong time" (XIV, 62). Perhaps the humming of the spinning wheel in Griška's first vision of Turandina portends the fatal control which these evil forces — especially the "beautiful, young witch" — will exercise over his life.

Thus, Sologub's story "Dream on the Rocks," while seeming initially to be the tale of a young dreamer and his casual accident, has, upon closer inspection, far broader implications. It is a story of growing up in which the rite of maturation involves the collapse of a vision of an ideal realm and the initiation into the mystery that the world is controlled by hostile forces. Since Sologub develops this theme with recourse to fairy-tale patterns and motifs, we might attempt a tentative appraisal of the theme of maturation in "Dream on the

Rocks" against a psychological understanding of the meaning of the fairy tale. Joseph Campbell, viewing the fairy tale as one of the endless variants of the monomyth, understands it as the representation of an inward journey towards selfhood: "The adventure of the hero follows the pattern of separation from the world, penetration to some source of power, and a life-enhancing return." Campbell stresses the significance of the hero's return, which has a regenerative effect on all of society. He also notes that the monomyth turns on the paradox that the sacred exists in the midst of the profane and that the two worlds, though separate, are at the same time one.[8]

Now in Sologub's tale the relationship between the sacred and the profane is skewed in such a way that there can be no true integration. Any intermingling of the profane or everyday life with the sacred or ideal realm is disastrous to the ideal, which is vulgarized. (The beautiful princess Turandina slips into the witch Turandina.) Yet, at the same time, the vision of the lyrical preface supports the existence of an ideal realm, though, evidentally, one which is totally removed from life on earth. Moreover, "Dream on the Rocks," like many of Sologub's other short stories, ends with a lyrical exodus which reaffirms the nostalgia for this other realm:

> Who am I, sent into the world by an unknown will for an unknown purpose? If I am a slave, whence comes my power to judge and condemn, and whence my haughty intentions? If I am more than a slave, then why does the world around me, ugly and false, lie in evil? Who am I? (XIV, 65.)

Thus, we are left with an unresolved tension between the two visions, lyrical and ironic; yet, we suspect that all does not bode well for Griška. In "Dream on the Rocks" true maturation in the sense that Campbell suggests is impossible, for growth is presented as a Fall from the Golden Age of childhood where the vision of the ideal is still untainted. Perhaps this is one of the reasons so many of Sologub's readers sense that his art is pessimistic and life-denying.[9] It might be reiterated that "Dream on the Rocks" is representative of many other stories. It is likely that close examinations would reveal that the ideal realm in most of Sologub's better stories is equally unstable and capable of containing hostile, demonic forces. Such studies are particularly warranted today in view of assertions that from the time of the writing of *The Created Legend*, Sologub manifests a genuine faith in the possibility of transforming life and his vision becomes more optimistic. "Dream on the Rocks" dates from this period, yet it can hardly be termed "optimistic."[10]

The Pennsylvania State University

NOTES

1. See Carola Hansson, *Fedor Sologub as a Short-Story Writer: Stylistic Analyses* (Stockholm: Almquist and Wiksell, 1975), 25-81, 80-84, and elsewhere, and Stanley J. Rabinowitz, *Sologub's Literary Children: Keys to a Symbolist's Prose* (Columbus, Ohio: Slavica, 1980), 23-70. Other recent articles on Sologub's short stories are Murl G. Barker, "Reality and Escape: Sologub's 'The Wall and the Shadows'," *Slavic and East European Journal*, 16 (1972), 419-26, and Patricia Pollack Brodsky, "Fertile Fields and Poisoned Gardens: Sologub's Debt to Hoffmann, Pushkin, and Hawthorne," *Essays in Literature* (Western Illinois University), 1 (1974), 96-108. Recent editions of Sologub's short stories are F. K. Sologub (Teternikov), *The Kiss of the Unborn and Other Stories*, tr. Murl Barker (Knoxville: Univ. of Tenn. Press, 1977) and *Rasskazy*, ed. and introd. Evelyn Bristol (Berkeley, Cal.: Berkeley Slavic Specialities, 1980).

2. F. K. Sologub (pseud. of Teternikov), *Sobranie sočinenij* (20 Vols.; St. Petersburg: Šipovnik-Sirin, 1909-1914), XX, 45. All further references to Sologub's works will be to this edition. Translations are mine. For a good discussion of sacred time in myths see Mircea Eliade, *The Sacred and the Profane: The Nature of Religion*, tr. William R. Trask (New York and London: Harcourt, Brace, Jovanovich, 1959), 68-113. Rabinowitz, 58 and elsewhere, mentions the significance of mythic time in Sologub, but does not elaborate on this subject.

3. K. Čukovskij, "Nav'i čary Melkogo Besa," in *O Fedore Sologube: Kritika, stat'i i zametki* ed. A. Čebotarevskaja (St. Petersburg: Šipovnik, 1911), 35-40, discusses the pervasiveness of the theme of "white mama versus black mama" in Sologub. For the story of Vasilisa the Beautiful see Aleksandr Afanas'ev, *Russian Fairy Tales*, tr. Norbert Guterman; comm. Roman Jakobson (New York: Pantheon, 1973), 439-47.

4. V. Ja. Propp, *Istoričeskie korni volšebnoj skazki* (Leningrad: Univ. Press, 1946), 7. Propp explains that this definition of the magic tale is a summary of his findings on his *Morfologija skazki* (Moscow: Nauka, 1969). It might be noted that Sologub entitled some of his very short prose pieces "little fairy tales" (*skazočki*). These *skazočki*, interestingly, are almost totally lacking in the motifs of the magic tale. For a discussion of them see Rabinowitz, 132-52.

5. Bruno Bettelheim, *The Uses of Enchantment: The Meaning and Importance of Fairy Tales* (New York: Alfred A. Knopf, 1976), 62-63. For a discussion of the boundaries, see Propp, *Istoričeskie korni*, 197-259.

6. For a discussion of the characterizations of Ljudmila and Saša see Linda J. Ivanits, "The Grotesque in Fedor Sologub's Novel *The Petty Demon*," in *Russian and Slavic Literature*, ed. R. Freeborn et al. (Cambridge, Mass.: Slavica, 1976), 149-55. The relationship between Griška and Turandina is also reminiscent of that between the page Astol'f and Queen Ortruda in *The Created Legend*. See, for example, Sologub, XIX, 215, 299-302.

7. Rabinowitz stresses the importance of the title "Dream on the Rocks" as an expression of Sologub's dualistic world view, 23-24.

8. Joseph Campbell, *The Hero with a Thousand Faces* (Princeton: Princeton Univ. Press, 1968), 35, 193, 217, and elsewhere.

9. See, for example, Renato Poggioli, *The Poets of Russia 1890-1930* (Cambridge, Mass.: Harvard Univ. Press, 1960), 109. Among Sologub's contemporaries see A. E. Red'ko, "Fedor Sologub v bytovyx proizvedenijax i v tvorimyx legendax," *Russkoe bogatstvo*, 2 (1909), 55-90; A. Dolinin, "Otrešennyj: K psixologii tvorčestva Fedora Sologuba," *Zavety*, 1913, 7, otd. 2, 55-85; and N. Pojarkov, "Poèt zla i d'javola," *Poèty našix dnej* (Moscow, 1907), 144-51.

10. For statements about optimism in Sologub see Rabinowitz, 124, 153-54, 161-62, and elsewhere. "Dream on the Rocks" first appeared in the newspaper *Reč'*, 1, 1912, Jan. 1.

THE RELIGIOUS COMPONENT OF RUSSIAN SYMBOLISM

David R. Schaffer

A major focus of the Russian Symbolists' own theoretical, artistic, and critical writings is the religious component of Russian Symbolism: a general Christian belief in another realm — an afterlife — at the center of which is a Good and Benevolent Supreme Being. This philosophy is not necessarily the product of any one, organized Christian religion; rather, it may incorporate elements not only of Russian Orthodoxy, but also of Roman Catholicism and the mystical religions of the East. It might best be described as a striving to recapture the very earliest forms of Christianity, before organized religions as we now know them came into being and their particular interpretations of Christianity diverged. The religious element, as will be demonstrated in this article, might provide one key to the distinction between Russian Symbolism and Russian Decadence.

The Russian Symbolists' and Decadents' contemporary critics lacked a perspective available only to later critics. Most post-1945 Western critics, in particular, while they have the advantage of this perspective, have often fallen into the habit of classifying the writers of these two movements solely on the basis of such non-thematic, general distinctions as "generations" (based on the authors' ages or the main period in which they published their works) or the place in which they lived ("Moscow" versus "Petersburg" writers). These distinctions often do not work, because there were important writers whose creative output spanned both "generations" or who lived in one city but published in the other. The issue has been made even more cloudy by terminological differences.[1] Even modern critics differ widely in their use of the terms Symbolist and Decadent, with some using either one term or the other exclusively to apply to both movements, and others speaking of a combined Decadent-Symbolist movement in an attempt to avoid the issue.

The religious element has long been noted by critics and scholars, many of whom consider it to be of major significance for Russian Symbolism (not Russian Decadence), and some of whom imply that it may be a criterion for distinguishing between Russian Symbolism and Russian Decadence.[2] Several of these critics have commented on an element of mysticism or religion in Russian Symbolism, but have not discussed the degree to which they are the product of a Christian outlook.[3] Most critics have not developed this idea significantly, often reverting to the argument that it is a mere matter of generations, and using this as their working definition.[4] It is only recently that scholars have begun to give renewed attention to the religious element.[5] Although the religious component is at least mentioned by almost all recent critics, none is willing to make it a primary criterion for distinguishing between Russian Symbolism and Decadence.

The religious element might be one key to distinguishing between Russian Symbolism and Russian Decadence on a thematic basis. There seems to be a definite tendency on the part of the Russian Decadents either not to have the religious element or to express an anti-Christian view, and an equally strong tendency on the part of the Russian Symbolists to reveal a Christian *Weltanschauung*. In several well-known poems by selected Russian Decadents and Russian Symbolists this theory seems to hold true. An examination and re-evaluation of those poems using the religious component as the main criterion will serve to test the viability of this theory.

Christian religious philosophy, and also a belief in Sophia — Holy Wisdom — will here be considered the basis of Russian Symbolism; Satanism, demonism, and other specifically anti-Christian views will be considered the basis of Russian Decadence. The existence of these two mutually exclusive philosophical views allows us to maintain, on a thematic basis, that there were two coexisting but separate literary movements in Russian literature.

Andrej Belyj's poem "To the Mother Country" ("Rodine," 1917) presents a picture of chaos. Russia immolates the poet-persona "in pillars of thundering fire." The poet-persona tells Russia that the descended Christ will come in fire to sweep away the disgraceful present world. The poem ends with the persona exhorting Russia, as the "Messiah of the coming era," to welcome this chaos. This poem, with its fire imagery and echoes from the Bible, provides a rather extreme example of the Apocalyptic theme in Russian Symbolism. Its underlying philosophy specifically includes Christ and both the Old and New Testaments (the pillar of fire and the Book of Revelation, respectively). There is one disclaimer, however, in that the course of events will lead to "the currents of cosmic days," a neutral phrase that does not limit the coming afterlife to being specifically Christian in quality.

Aleksandr Blok's poem "The Little Priest of the Bog" ("Bolotnyj popik," 1905) has as its setting a place where the snow has melted in an unnamed bog. It is sundown, after evening prayer, in the spring. The lack of specifics allows us to consider it a microcosm, in the center of which is the small figure of its priest. He is not necessarily of the Russian Orthodox faith: while he does wear a black cassock, his hat is of the Western sort, not of the brimless type worn by Russian Orthodox priests.

He prays silently, smiles, and bows down, as if performing a religious service. We are not given enough specific details to be able to say to which religion (if, indeed, to any) the service belongs. He is glad to pray for any creature of any faith, and prays "For the stem of a plant that is bent, / For the ailing paw of an animal, / And for the Pope of Rome." Thus he prays equally for all creatures — from the highest to the lowliest. He seems to be a priest of no particular, organized religion who professes a faith that is some form of universalism. The poem ends on a note of religious optimism when, in the last two lines, the persona tells the reader that he will be saved by this "black cassock" — obviously a synecdoche for the small priest and his universal type of faith. As a final comment on this poem, it is interesting to note that it is dated "17 April 1905. Easter." Thus the setting of springtime, presaging physical rebirth, is given the additional significance of being a time of spiritual rebirth: the Christian feast of Easter.

Much of Bloks' poetry is a reflection of his quest for Sophia. The poem "I Go into Dark Temples" ("Vxožu ja v tëmnye xramy," 1902) is an example of a poem inspired by this search. The persona goes to "dark temples," illuminated only by the flickering red light of the icon lamps, and waits for the Beautiful Lady. Although She never appears to him, and although he never hears Her breathing or hears Her speak, he does have a mental image of Her and has faith that She exists: "But I believe: Dear One — it is You." This poem's mood of reverie and expression of faith in Sophia project a generally religious atmosphere and show a philosophical belief that goes beyond the organized religions of its time. The concept of Sophia, given to Russian religious philosophy, of course, by Vladimir Solov'ev, is not a part of classical Russian Orthodoxy, but is unique to Russian Symbolism.

The persona of Valerij Brjusov's poem "I" ("Ja," 1899) wants to experience all of culture and every emotional state. Enjoying contradictions, he claims to love equally "all dreams, all speeches"; and he dedicates poetry "to all gods." What emerges is a picture of indifference: to love all gods means to love no single God. This view is similar to a pagan belief in many deities, which is in opposition to the Christian belief in one Supreme Being. In this respect the poem reflects a view closer to that of Russian Decadence.

Brjusov's poem "The Coming Huns" ("Grjaduščie gunny," 1904–05) depicts an Apocalyptic coming of a new barbaric horde from the East and the destruction in blood and fire of all of European (Western) knowledge and culture. Among the forms of destruction will be the burning of books and the desecration of places of religious worship. The poem ends with the persona greeting his annihilators "with a welcoming hymn."

This poem has been interpreted optimistically by such critics as Poggioli (100). But while there is a chance that fate will allow some knowledge to survive, there is an equal or greater chance that it will not. And while there are abundant references to destruction, there are none as to what civilization, if any, will be built in place of that destroyed. This total destruction reflects the

Russian Decadent view. Perhaps considerations of another realm, and of Good and Evil, are not an issue in this poem because there will be no subsequent culture and there will be no afterlife.

Fëdor Sologub's poem "Captive Animals" ("Plenennye zveri," 1905) depicts mankind as living in a wretched menagerie, caged in behind locked doors and deriving its sole satisfaction from howling. Mankind has long ceased to realize how bad its present living conditions are, and has also ceased longing for freedom. And so, mankind sits and howls, not daring to take any action to better the human condition.

Two elements of this poem are of particular interest: first, mankind "does not dare" to open the doors of its cage because it probably fears what may be on the outside. Not only is there another realm of existence, but that realm is something to be feared, is greater and more powerful than the realm of mankind, and keeps mankind in subjugation. Secondly, for Sologub's works in general a barking dog is often associated with evil. (See, for instance, his short story "The White Dog" ["Belaja sobaka," 1908].) The fact that mankind howls like canines brings to mind that in Goethe's *Faust* Mephistopheles first appears as a black poodle, and becomes a famulus to Faust. The poem "Captive Animals" may be saying that mankind is nothing more than the devil's servants.

Sologub's poem "When I was Sailing on a Stormy Sea" ("Kogda ja v burnom more plaval," 1902) shows the persona in a moment of crisis calling not upon God but upon the Devil (*D'javol*) for salvation. The Devil saves him from destruction, and the persona in exchange dedicates his remaining life to the Devil. One immediately thinks of Faust selling his soul to the devil. In this poem, however, the persona willingly remains true to his pact with the Devil.

There are references in this poem to black magic and to sin in the Christian concept. For example, the persona agrees to dedicate "the remains of my black days" to the Devil; and he speaks of his own "sinful body." And at the end of the poem the persona glorifies the Devil and says he will vilify the world and will tempt the rest of mankind ("I soblaznjaja soblaznju"). In other words, the persona will work to create a world of sin. This poem provides a clear example of the Russian Decadent philosophy.

Sologub's poem "The Devil's Swing" ("Čortovy kačeli," 1907) depicts a nameless persona — an everyman figure — riding on a swing (obviously, the course of life). It is a devil who moves the swing; the persona is powerless to affect either the swing's direction, height, or movement. The devil gives the swing a violent shove, it ascends to a great height, and the persona is tumbled off and apparently falls to his death.

Poggioli has commented that this "little, almost naive, parable clearly reveals Sologub's tendency to reduce diabolism to the level of devilry, to a mischief even more cruel than outright Satanism" (100). This statement is perhaps not strong enough. The devil in this poem is the petty, base Russian "čort," not Satan. But he is cruel and spiteful, delighting in the mischief he causes. In one place he "laughs," and in another he "guffaws with a snort"; and he sends the persona tumbling to his death. Mankind is at the mercy of forces he cannot control and that cause his destruction. These forces are personified by a devil. The essence of the other realm in this poem is Evil — seen as sadistic, mischievous cruelty.

Sologub is generally considered a Decadent by most critics, using a wide variety of criteria. Donchin, for example, calls him "the only real decadent of Russian poetry," and "this only pure Russian decadent" (26, 95). She also writes that "the apotheosis of evil and perversion is perhaps stronger in Sologub than in any other Russian writer. Again this may be a literary pose, an acknowledgement of the prevailing fashion, but with Sologub it is however so constant as to become second nature." (138.) Poggioli also concludes that whereas "the Satanism of many other Decadent poets, not excluding Bal'mont and Brjusov, is often hardly more than a pose ... Sologub's Satanism is ... a genuine reflection of his view of life" (109). For Sologub there was definitely another realm of existence beyond this one, and the ruler of that realm is Satan. His Satanism places him clearly among the Russian Decadents, in our definition; indeed, he may be called the archetypical Russian Decadent from this point of view.

We may now summarize instances in which our re-evaluation of the above works using the religious component as the main criterion would either agree with or differ from previous critical evaluations.

Belyj and Blok are universally considered Russian Symbolists. Sologub is universally considered a Russian Decadent.[6] Our new classification is in agreement with that of the above critics. One case in which our new classification differs from that of some of the above critics is that of Valerij Brjusov. Brjusov, although he called himself a Symbolist, was shown in the examples given to be more of a Russian Decadent. Of the critics cited, only Poggioli maintains this distinction (85, 96, 105, 142).

A special case is Zinaida Gippius. Because of her birthdate (1869), and because of the existence in some of her poetry of such elements as pessimism, despair, and death, Gippius has long been considered a Decadent. It is only recently that such critics as Temira Pachmuss and Olga Matich have suggested that she is actually more of a Russian Symbolist because of the religious element in her poetry.[7] Selected poems seem to support this argument. In the introduction to her first volume of poetry, Gippius stated that for her, poetry is one form of prayer — a form of communication with God.[8] Where

Sologub's persona calls upon the Devil in a time of dire need, the persona of Gippius' poem "Fear and Death" ("Strax i smert'," 1901) calls upon the Lord: "Oh my Lord and my God! Take pity on us, reassure us." And the persona wants to be "pure" before the Lord: "Give me strength before [Death], and purity before You." This obviously reflects both the Christian concept of the Lord God as the Supreme Being, and the Christian desire to be in a state of Grace at the time of death.

Other poems by Gippius reflect God as the Creator, and God specifically as the Holy Trinity. Indicative here are lines from her poem "Freedom" ("Svoboda," 1904):

> Tol'ko vzyvaju, imenen Syna,
> K Bogu, Tvorcu Bytija:
> Otče, vovek da budet edino
> Volja Tvoja i moja!

(I only appeal, in the name of the Son, / To God, the Creator of Existence: / Oh Father, may Your will and mine / Ever be one!)

The lack of full acceptance of God's will in this poem is counterbalanced by its complete acceptance in her poem "The Good Tidings" ("Blagaja vest'," 1904) describing the Annunciation and written from the point of view of Mary:

> Volja Gospoda — moja.
> Bud' že, kak Emu ugodnee ...
> Xočet On — xoču i ja.
> Pust' vojdët Ljubov' Gospodnjaja ...

(The will of the Lord — is mine. / May things be as He most chooses ... / Whatever He wishes — I also wish. / May the Lord's Love enter ...)

The increased emphasis on Love is a favorite theme of Gippius, and is often emphasized more strongly than in most of Christian tradition.

Gippius has several famous "devil" poems in which the persona has an encounter with the forces of Evil. One must consider here "Into a Line" ("V čertu," 1905), "To the Small Black One" ("Čërnen'komu," 1914), "The Little Devil" ("D'javolënok," 1906), "And What Afterwards?" ("A potom ...?," 1911), "The Hour of Victory" ("Čas pobedy," 1918), and "Indifference" ("Ravnodušie," 1938). In these poems the persona's attitude toward the evil being (it ranges from the coarse, petty "little devil" [d'javolënok] through "The Dark One" [Temnyj] and other devils of great power and philosophical importance) is predominantly that of fear, often mixed with loathing. It is only in the last of these poems, probably written much later than the others and at a time when Gippius herself was approaching the end of her life, that the persona becomes indifferent toward the Devil.

Gippius was perhaps the most religious of the Russian Symbolist poets. The dates of composition and publication dates of her poems about God and the devil attest to an almost constant and lifelong striving to probe the mysteries of Good and Evil, God and the Devil. The fact that Gippius was striving toward God and trying to resist the Devil places her poetry decidedly within Russian Symbolism as defined here, and makes her perhaps the most clear example of a Russian Symbolist by our new definition.

Gippius, who has even been called the "grandmother of Russian decadence,"[9] emerges in the poems cited here as much more a Russian Symbolist. This re-evaluation has only recently been argued in detail by Olga Matich. Earlier critics such as Donchin and Poggioli considered Gippius exclusively a Decadent, although Lo Gatto notes a certain "religious tendency" to some of her poetry. (See Donchin, 99; Poggioli, 111; Lo Gatto, 622.)

The religious component should be taken into consideration in the study of Russian Modernism. In previous studies of Russian Symbolism and Russian Decadence, critics all too often do not differentiate between an author's form (or style) and his content, to use an old dichotomy that is still useful here. An examination of the philosophical view and religious beliefs implicit in a work of literature may provide one element that may serve reliably as a criterion for a working definition of Russian Decadence and Russian Symbolism. Someone who was only or primarily interested in matters of pure aesthetics (Brjusov, for example) might best be considered outside of the philosophical considerations of Good and Evil and of God and the Devil.[10] Although our debt to him as an aesthetician must be acknowledged, we could consider him a European Symbolist, but not a Russian Symbolist by our new definition.

The prose genres of Russian Symbolism to date have still not been investigated as thoroughly as they could be, and definitely have not received the critical and scholarly attention they deserve. The religious component has been used for a re-evaluation of the short stories of Zinaida Gippius.[11] The prose of these and other Russian Symbolists and Decadents awaits a similar re-evaluation.

Laurel, Maryland

NOTES

1. For a valuable historical perspective and synopsis of the terms "Symbolist" and "Decadent" as used by various Russian writers of that period, see James West, *Russian Symbolism: A Study of Vyacheslav Ivanov and the Russian symbolist aesthetic* (London: Methuen, 1970), 108-21.

2. See, for example, D. S. Mirsky, *A History of Russian Literature*, ed. Francis J. Whitfield (2 vols.; New York: Alfred A. Knopf, 1966), II, 430 and chaps. 4, 5. (Mirsky is one of the earliest

major critics to have known most of the works of pre-Soviet Russian Modernism; the original two volumes of his *History* are based on writings available through 1925.) See also Leon Trotsky, *Literature and Revolution* (Ann Arbor: Univ. of Michigan Press, 1960), 234-35; Oleg A. Maslenikov, *The Frenzied Poets* (Berkeley: Univ. of California Press, 1952), iii, 14, 27-28, 65; Victor Erlich, *Russian Formalism*, 3rd ed. (The Hague: Mouton, 1969), 32, 35; Georgette Donchin, *The Influence of French Symbolism on Russian Poetry* (The Hague: Mouton, 1958), 26, 76; Renato Poggioli, *The Poets of Russia: 1890-1910* (Cambridge, Mass.: Harvard Univ. Press, 1960), 126, 134-35, 136 ff.; F. A. Stepun, *Mystische Weltschau: fünf Gestalten der russischen Symbolismus* (München, 1964); Ettore Lo Gatto, *Histoire de la littérature Russe* traduit de l'Italien par M. et A.-M. Cabrini (Paris: Desclée de Brouwer, 1965), 653, 657, 622, 635; Krystina Pomorska, *Russian Formalist Theory and its Poetic Ambiance* (The Hague: Mouton, 1968), 47; West, 2-3; Martin P. Rice, *Valery Brjusov and the Rise of Russian Symbolism* (Ann Arbor: Ardis, 1975), 67-68, 93.

3.   Trotsky, Erlich, and Stepun, for example, do not really discuss the Christian quality of the Russian Symbolists' mysticism and theurgy; and Lo Gatto has references to Christianity, but does not discuss the specifics of the religious beliefs or practices of the authors. West and Rice basically do not concern themselves with this issue, since their books are a study of aesthetics and a history of the movement, respectively.

4.   Mirsky, Donchin, Poggioli, Lo Gatto, Pomorska, and especially West and Rice seem in practice to use a generation distinction as their working distinction. West, 2-3, for example, refers to the "customary" generation distinction.

5.   In particular, see Temira Pachmuss, *Zinaida Hippius: An Intellectual Profile* (Carbondale and Edwardsville: Southern Illinois Univ. Press, 1971), 15; and Olga Matich, *Paradox in the Religious Poetry of Zinaida Gippius* (München: Wilhelm Fink, 1972), 10, 15.

6.   Donchin's reference to Sologub as a Symbolist (132) refers to writing technique, not to philosophical content.

7.   Pachmuss, 15, writes that Gippius' poetry "reveals … that antinomy between the poet's religious impulses and simultaneous blasphemy, and that bond between religion, poetry, and mystical sensuality which characterized Russian belles-lettres at the time." Pachmuss obviously refers here to the Symbolists, not the Decadents. (While Pachmuss uses Gippius' religious themes to suggest that Gippius was more of a Symbolist, she still does not develop and extend this idea to the point of defining Russian Symbolism in terms of the religious element.) Matich classifies Gippius the poet as a Russian symbolist, noting the religious themes of her poetry, but still relying heavily on a generation distinction: "… one should consider her together with the second generation symbolists, who in contrast with the decadents associate their art with religion rather than pure aestheticism" (15).

8.   Zinaida Nikolaevna Gippius, "Neobxodimoe o stixax," *Sobranie stixov 1889-1903 g.* (Moscow, 1904), i-vi.

9.   I. I. Baluev, "Gippius i 'dekadenty'," *Vozroždenie*, No. 194 (Feb., 1968), 98-102.

10.   As is well known, Brjusov wrote in 1910 that if poetry should not be made to serve civic themes, then neither should it be made to serve the aims of religion. See his essay "O 'reči rabskoj,' v zaščitu poèzii," *Apollon*, No. 9 (1910), otd. I, 31-34. This preference for pure aesthetics — art for art's sake, and not as an instrument of religious strivings — is reflected in his poetry. See, for example, the poem "To the Young Poet" ("Junomu poètu," 1896), in which the culminating precept given as advice to poets is: "… worship art, / Only it, wholeheartedly, without reserve."

11.   David Royal Schaffer, *The Short Stories of Zinaida Gippius: Decadent or Symbolist?* (Unpub. diss. Univ. of Wisconsin, 1979).

PART III

ART, POETICS, DRAMA

MAJAKOVSKIJ'S "STREET-" AND AN "ALOGICAL" CUBO-FUTURIST PAINTING BY MALEVIČ

Juliette Stapanian

Cubo-Futurism in Russian painting emerged alongside Cubism in France, Futurism in Italy, and Expressionism in Germany. A curious blend and variation of Cubist fragmentation and Futurist attention to movement, Cubo-Futurism provided a fertile point of departure for many experiments in early twentieth-century Russian painting. Kazimir Malevič, later known as the father of Suprematism, was among many major painters of the Russian avant-garde who explored Cubo-Futurism as an "intermediate category" in painting, in which Cubist composition based on contrasts of forms is joined by Futurist focus upon dynamic sensation.[1] Parallel concerns appeared in the literature of the time as well. In Russia a group of poets who became known as the Cubo-Futurists combined their interest in Cubist painting with their formulation of a literature of the "future."[2] Vladimir Majakovskij (1893–1930), trained as a painter before becoming a writer, appears a pivotal figure in this development. Yet, while scholars have frequently acknowledged the importance of the pictorial arts to Majakovskij's pre-revolutionary lyrics, these early works have generally been considered an opaque body of verse. One of Majakovskij's first published lyrics "Street-" (*Uličnoe*, 1913) has been described as "especially ambiguous and difficult."[3] Careful consideration of painterly techniques, however, offers substantial insights toward a literary interpretation of the lyric. At the same time artistic analogues aid in the elucidation of Majakovskij's poem, the composition of his lyric provides a model for understanding one of Malevič's own Cubo-Futurist "alogical" paintings of the period, his *Englishman in Moscow* (*Angličanin v Moskve*). Initially the individual images on this canvas appear to "not add up to a comprehensible totality."[4] Yet, as demonstrated in tandem with Majakovskij's poem, the composition of the painting is far from unique. The similarity of Malevič's painting to Majakovskij's poem — while essentially independent of the lyric — illustrates the extent of the interdisciplinary sensibility which prevailed during the period. Because Majakovskij's "Street-" seems to have been completed before Malevič's painting, a simple painting-to-poetry or unidirectional understanding of Cubo-Futurism must be rejected. Instead, analysis of "Street-" in the light of painterly analogues followed by a look at the picture *Englishman in Moscow* reveals a highly intricate interaction among the arts.

Majakovskij's "Street-" was first published in the almanac *Sadok sudej II* in 1913.[5] The lyric is divided into conventional verse lines, and is in fairly regular, iambic tetrameter. The rhyme scheme, too, is conventional except for two mosaic rhymes (*cvel' gde / sel'de, drob' ja / kop'ja*):

УЛИЧНОЕ	STREET-
В шатрах, истертых ликов цвель где,	In awnings/marquees, where (there is)
из ран лотков сочилась клюква,	the mold of rubbed-off faces,
а сквозь меня на лунном сельде	Cranberries oozed from wounds of
скакала крашеная буква.	hawkers' trays/gutters,
	and through me on a moon herring
	a painted letter was galloping.
Вбиваю гулко шага сваи,	I resonantly hammer-in the piles of (my)
бросаю в бубны улиц дробь я.	step/stride,
Ходьбой усталые трамваи	I throw a drumroll into the tambourines
скрестили блещущие копья.	of streets.
	Trams tired from walking
	have crossed (their) glistening spears.
Подняв пукой единый глаз,	Having raised with (its) hand/arm
кривая площадь кралась близко.	a single eye,
Смотрело небо в белый газ	The crooked/one-eyed square was stealing
лицом безглазым василиска.	near.
	The sky was looking into the white gas
	with the face of an eyeless basilisk.

While not unusual in its appearance on the printed page, the poem assaults poetic integrity at its very onset with the title "Street-," a neuter singular adjective in Russian. Simultaneous with the titular offering of an initial, but generalized locational framework for the poem — the street, the ambiguity arising from use of an isolated adjective normally accompanied by a noun taunts the reader with a seemingly partial introduction to the work. The lone adjective arouses certain grammatical expectations in the reader which propel him toward the text in search of a more complete semantic unit. In this respect, the single adjective could suggest a fragment of a specific verbal expression or epithet, such as "street traffic" (*uličnoe dviženie*), which is neuter in Russian. Use of the neuter singular adjective "street" in Russian may also signify an inanimate "street-thing" or a collectively shared "street" quality or position. Insofar as the poem is constructed from diverse pieces of urban images, the content of the lyric itself becomes the substantized adjective "street." In addition to its designation toward the street, the adjective *uličnoe* in Russian means "common" or "vulgar/cheap." From this perspective, the reader's entrance into the work of art passes through a distinctly anti-aesthetic or prosaic stance. This variation on the Futurists' notorious "slap" at refined art reverberates throughout the lyric.[6]

A "studied multiplicity of readings" often arises from use of fragmented images in Cubist paintings.[7] The artist's fractionation of conventional units or image frameworks followed by the shift or displacement of select consitutent elements throughout the canvas invites multiple interpretations of the resulting image combinations.[8] By this means an artist can maximize image associations with a minimum of depicted detail. While this aspect of a Cubist painting may obscure a reading of the picture in traditional terms, it is in essence central to the organization of the work.

Majakovskij similarly employs many disjointed images and poly-referential segments on his verbal canvas. By following various potential lines of meaning generated by these ambiguous word-images, the reader can discern definite frameworks throughout the text which comprise the image structure of the poem. This technique can be applied to an interpretation of the first line of the lyric. Here the expression *v šatrax* simultaneously evokes a variety of possible images, since *šater* can refer to a tent, booth, awning (marquee), a kind of hunting trap, and a type of church cupola. A semantic link among the various definitions lies in the basically pyramidal or conical outline of the referents, so that the expression *v šatrax* describes a collection of such geometric forms apparent in the urbanscape. These forms in turn serve as points of reference with which other images in the scene may be positioned. Although the chance for a single, focused image is displaced both by the plurality *v šatrax* and by multiple definitions of *šater*, the ambiguous image *v šatrax* represents a center of intersection for the major image planes of the poem. From the guidelines projected out of this "umbrella" term, four frameworks related to one of the different meanings of *šater* can be pieced together in the lyric — the street, the marketplace or bazaar, the ancient battle, and the mythic-religious. Because much of the complexity of the poem arises from extensive overlapping and exchange among the four planes, a brief sketch of their major markers in the poem provides a helpful overview of the composition.

The most general of the image-planes, suggested first by the title, incorporates details typical to an urban street scene. In this regard, the phrase *v šatrax* can be taken to mean "in church tops" or "in street awnings," while the subsequent image of "faces" (*likov*) may refer to people, *lotkov* to open gutters, and the "herring" and "painted letter" to street signs which appear in the line of vision. Within this generalized urban outline, a more specific image plane emerges — the "bazaar." Since *šater* can signify "booth," an appropriate interpretation of the word *lotkov* would be "hawker's trays." "Mold" (*cvel'*), "cranberries" (*kljukva*), "herring" (*sel'de*) as well as the "faces" of people and the "painted letter" of a seller's sign are all images common to a street market setting. Alternate meanings of poly-referential words simultaneously delineate the scene in terms of an ancient battle; in this framework, the phrase *v šatrax* can mean "in tents," a suitable definition of *likov* suggests "hosts," "wounds" (*ran*) imply a victim, and the "galloping" describes the movement of horses. The images of "spears" (*kop'ja*) and "drumroll/shot" (*drob'*) in stanza II further elaborate this battle-framework, which then culminates in the confrontation between the square and "basilisk" in stanza III. The other, and perhaps most subtle, image plane in the poem is suggested by the mythic-religious imagery of the work in conjunction with the criss-cross patterns rendered by the movement of images within the composition. Just as the phrase *v šatrax* can refer metonymically to churches, the word *likov* may be interpreted by its canonical meaning as "faces of icons," while the "cranberries in wounds of gutters/trays" and the crossed spears may be distorted variations of traditional crucifixion motifs. Because *nebo* can mean either "sky" or "heaven," the emergence of the basilisk (in Greek mythology, the king of serpents that could kill with a glance) at the end of the poem epitomizes the fluctuation between the sacred and profane throughout the lyric.

Multiple readings also surround the unusual image "mold of rubbed-off faces" in the first line of the poem. On one hand, this image is constructed by a mixture of stylistic types: *cvel'*, a dialect word for "mold," is combined with *lik*, an old or poetic form of the word "face" or "image" often with church-associated overtones. While "mold," as an indicator of decay, "visually" matches *lik*, as an antiquated verbal form for "face," the theme of decay reflects the temporal fabric of the lyric.[9] As mold forms an organic link between past and present, the motif "rubbed-off faces" implies a pre-history to the time of the poem (note the use of a past passive participle). Since *lik* can mean the face depicted on an icon, the "rubbed-off faces" may refer concretely to the appearance of age-worn or neglected religious pictures found in the churches suggested by the opening motif. Yet the word *lik* can also indicate a person, so that from the perspective of the street or bazaar, the image "rubbed-off faces" could describe the tired-out or blurred appearance of a crowd of people, or even a memory of people who had earlier been "in the tent-booths." In terms of a still greater projection backward into time, the image may represent the "faces" of the past, whose placement "in the tents" of yesteryear serves as the point of association with the image of people in shopping "tents" of the modern world. Despite the variety of plausible interpretations of the ambiguous combination *v šatrax/istertyx lik*, the phrase can be reduced to its basic, graphic elements — a location (*v šatrax*), an indication of outward appearance (*lik*), and a reference to a perceived change (*istertyx*). Not only does this use of perception anticipate the appearance of a first-person persona in line three, it is linked to the general shift of the human presence in the poem: while the image of people expected in connection with a street scene is first de-faced ("rubbed-off faces"), it is then displaced by the personified urban environment described in the lyric.

"Cranberries oozed from wounds of hawkers' trays/gutters // and through me on a moon herring, // a painted letter was galloping." This unusual array of images reflects some features common in Cubist painting. The most obvious of these is use of an isolated letter (the "painted letter") within a larger composition, a technique related to Cubist painters' interest in signboard and advertising art.[10] The specified interpenetration of objects ("through me") and the focus upon the visual topography of the cityscape also recall Cubist "vision." Use of descriptive verbs such as "ooze" and "galloping" echoes Futurist concentration on motion and the dynamic interrelationships among objects. Majakovskij's frequent use of locational and directional adverbs, prepositions, and prefixes indicates careful attention to the compositional placement of images relative to each other. Striking image shifts and visual puns are also used. Rather than ordinary cranberries in Majakovskij's poem, a shift brings cranberries oozing from "wounds" (an inverted metaphor complicated by the metonymical use of "berries" for their juice). Verbal play accompanies Majakovskij's manipulation of images. Because the verb "ooze" is commonly associated in Russian with the movement of blood, the "gutters" which are similar in linear form and liquid-carrying function to veins can be transposed into veins of the city which carry "cranberry"-red blood.[11] At the same time the unorthodox use of a "herring" to penetrate the persona implies a victimization of the persona, this posture can be superimposed upon the "wounds" of the city-scape, so that the identity of the persona and city overlap.[12] Meanwhile the galloping movement, an action associated more with horses than fish, adds further dynamic distortion to the picture.

The abandonment of traditional chiaroscuro was a feature of much of the pictorial experimentation in the early twentieth century. In Russia the painter M. Larionov formulated Rayonism (*Lučizm*), and a letter written by Larionov around January 1913 establishes Majakovskij's interest in the artist's ideas.[13] According to Larionov:

> Rayonism considers spatial forms, which can arise from the
> intersection of reflected rays of various objects, forms, iso-
> lated by the will of the artist. (See Xardžiev, 38.)

Similarly, Majakovskij's image of a letter on a "moon herring" that passes through the persona represents a visualization of the interaction between rays of light and objects in a scene. This interpretation is supported by the reference to "moon" (a source of naturally reflected light) and in particular the combination "moon herring" (*lunnyj sel'd*), which in Russian bears resemblance to the expressions for "moonlight" (*lunnyj svet*) and "crescent moon" (*lunnyj serp*). While the silvery color of herrings suggests the color of moonlight, the "galloping" action associated with it recalls the use of fish motifs in traditional still-life paintings because of the characteristic flickering effects achieved by the reflection of light from fish scales.[14] At the same time, if the "letter" is *located on* Majakovskij's "fish," the image viewed in the context of urban topography could describe the flow of light from an illuminated sign advertising fish and projected toward the persona. On the other hand, if the painted letter is *riding on* the "moon fish" (note the ambiguity in Russian between *na sel'de* as location and *na sel'de* as vehicle with a verb of motion) the image may designate the passage of light from the moon, through a painted sign, and into the vision of the persona. Whatever Majakovskij's moon herring represents, it functions in the visualized transmission of light between images in the poem; and like the translucent image planes in Cubist painting, the image of the "painted letter" appears to pass through the persona.

Spatial position and interrelationship of forms play a critical role in the formation of a mythic-religious framework in lines two through four of the poem. The presentation of the personified city as a penetrated image ("wounds") followed immediately by the penetrated image of a human persona ("through me") has been shown to allow an overlap between the two motifs. However, the suffering of the city, designated along the linear lines of "wounds of gutters," is then juxtaposed with a specifically cruciform pattern described by the linear passage of the "letter" through the persona. In this way a modern crucifixion is subtly indicated, but the traditional Biblical motif has been shifted to a contemporary context and translated by interaction between city and persona. In this regard, the image of the fish with the letter may be an odd variation of a traditional symbol of Christ.[15]

Whereas the persona in the first stanza of "Street-" is depicted as a passive element in the urbanscape, he takes an active role in the second section of the poem. As the "I" walks down the street, a spatial elaboration of the initial locational framework takes place. The forceful assertion of the persona is rendered in the prosaic terms of a construction worker: "I resonantly hammer-in the piles of (my) stride." (A "pile" [*svaja*] refers to a physical support, such as an abutment or pier, upon which a structure is erected.) The power and sense of construction counterpoints the idea of decay suggested earlier in the poem, and the hyperbolized concreteness associated with the persona's motion contrasts sharply with his former, permeable form ("through me"). While the word "resonantly" indicates an acoustic perception of the footsteps, the entire image is shifted onto the audial plane of the poem as a "drumroll" thrown "into tambourines of streets."

In addition to "drumroll," the word *drob'* is a hunter's term for "(small) shot," and its use in the description of the persona's encounter with the streets suggests a kind of confrontation. This "battle" motif is sustained by the heavy, marching stride of the persona and the drum-like roll of "tambourines." The battle lines are then shifted and realized through the crossed "spears" of the trams in the next lines of the lyric: "Trams tired from walking // have crossed (their) glistening spears." A variation on the Russian expression *skrestit' meči* ("to cross/measure swords"), the image describes the visual appearance of criss-crossed, overhead tram-poles in terms of the "battle" image framework.[16] While the walking motion of the persona is paralleled by the "walking" (*xod'ba*) of the trams, the persona's firm gait boldly contrasts with the machines' tiredness. The personification of the trams, based on a play with the Russian expression *ustalyj ot xod'by* ("tired from walking"), involves an ability to identify with the cityscape. The word "tired" may also be a temporal indicator in the poem, since "tiredness" may result from the end of a long day or the premature start to a new day. Regardless of the interpretation, the motif of crossed swords once again places the persona in the vicinity of a cruciform pattern formed in the urbanscape.

The movement established in the first two stanzas of the lyric is paralleled by the "stealing" motion of the square in the third. The designation "near," however, implies a point of reference. Rather than just a surrealistic projection of the urbanscape toward the persona, the image could concretely describe the apparent movement of a stationary square from the perspective of an approaching persona. Optical effects from moving frames of reference should also be considered further in the image. If *krivaja* is translated as "crooked," it may refer to the angular shape of a square. But *krivaja* also means "bent," and as such may describe the visual distortion of forms moving in a velocity framework different from that of the observer. At the same time, *krivaja* is "one-eyed" in Russian. The grotesque image of the square as an arm carrying an eye evokes a defined shape — a vertical line (the extended arm or hand) topped by a circular form (the "eye"). From the standpoint of the street image-framework, this shape could graphically describe the outline of a streetlamp, an urban image which appears frequently in Majakovskij's lyrics.[17] The raised arm also recalls a posture of religious offering.

"The sky was looking into the white gas // with the face of an eyeless basilisk." Since one of the figurative meanings of *šater* is "sky" (*nebo* or *nebosvod*), the progression from ground to celestial imagery involves extension of the initial framework *v šatrax*. The obscured, "rubbed-off faces" earlier in the poem are now replaced by the eyeless "face" of the basilisk. Distortions and fragmentation continue as the unexpected placement of an "eye" in a city square is followed by the removal of an eye from the mythological basilisk. The reference to this legendary dragon or king of serpents, who could kill by a mere glance at his victim, poses another paradox in the poem: how does a sky-basilisk who is "eyeless" actually "look" into white gas? The composition itself provides an answer, for the "eye" raised by the City appears in a position to serve both the square and the sky.[18] At the same time the no-eyed sky/basilisk represents a distorted counterpart to the earth-bound, one-eyed square, the juxtaposition of the images suggests a superimposition of the circular form of the street lamp over the circular form of the sky's "eye" — the moon or sun. Because of the overlap between urban and celestial frameworks, the "white gas" may refer to a variety of things — clouds, mist, the haze around the moon or sun, or the white aurora encircling a gas lamp. The "white gas" may also serve as an appropriately eerie setting for the basilisk which eclipses the more vibrant coloration earlier in the poem.

The "battle" framework described in the first two stanzas of the lyric comes to a climax in the third. As the square stealthily moves near, it is placed in confrontation with the gaze of the eyeless basilisk. This confrontation of man's world with that of Nature (the sky) includes a temporal shift from the contemporary urban world of trams and advertising signs to a remnant of ancient Greece. In addition, urban patterns suggestive of religious symbols are now displaced by a figure from the mythological past. Although potential for conflict arises in the appearance of a hostile basilisk, the poet defeats the monster by depriving it of the very source of its power — its "eye." Conventional logic or traditional beliefs are completely inverted, for it is the "one-eyed" city square that now has the power of sight.[19]

The picture-like quality of Majakovskij's "Street-" is perhaps most vividly summed-up by comparison with Malevič's *Englishman in Moscow* (1914). (See illustration.)[20] In broadest terms, both works have urban scenes which incorporate unusual combinations of images. The choice and juxtaposition of imagery, the use of overlapping planes and coloration discerned in Majakovskij's poem are paralleled in Malevič's painting, where green as well as red and white are major elements of the color scheme.[21] As the persona in "Street-" functions as a compositional element around which and through which other images appear, the figure of the Englishman in Malevič's work serves as a base for several encroaching image planes. Placed in the center of the picture, half the face of the Englishman is obscured by other images in the composition. The Englishman as an alien to Moscow provides a critical perspective which may explain the bizarre combination of images depicted. So too in Majakovskij's work, the unusual form and types of images are linked to the perspective of the persona. Much as Majakovskij advocated the use of striking images to

K. Malevič's *An Englishman in Moscow* (1913–1914)

revitalize poetry, so too Malevič based his art during 1913–1915 on strong image contrasts or "dissonance" of imagery (*Essays on Art,* I, 11).

One feature of Majakovskij's "Street-" is the manipulation of "eye" imagery. Similar to the "eye" of the square displacing the eye of the basilisk in Majakovskij's composition, Malevič superimposes the eye of a fish over one eye of the Englishman. The implied "eclipse" of the power of the heavens in "Street-" is paralleled in the painting by the words "partial eclipse" (*častičnoe zatmenie*), which also suggests a pun on the partial view of the Englishman's face. As Majakovskij disarms his basilisk ("eyeless"), Malevič literally undercuts the traditional use of eclipse as an apocalyptic image of foreboding by making the eclipse "partial." The fragmented placement of the words in Malevič's painting counterpoints the fractionation suggested by the word "partial." As Majakovskij's "Street-" presents a new view of concrete reality, so too Malevič prèsents the "common" in very uncommon combinations. John Bowlt describes Malevič's painting as follows: "Not in vain do the truncated words spread across the surface of 'Englishman in Moscow' denote 'partial eclipse' for here, as in other 'transrational' paintings, an unprecedented artistic reality of encroaching planes is, inexorably, concealing and sealing the bric-à-brac of the Victorian esthetic ("Journey into Non-Objectivity," 10). For Malevič, Cubism provides the new logic for the new reason.[22]

Many more parallels between the picture and the poem can be drawn. For example, the ladder in Malevič's painting is a kind of visual "abbreviation" for spatial shifts that occur in Majakovskij's lyric. The pinnacoidal churchtops (*v šatrax*) as markers on the urban skyline in "Street-" are countered by church cupolas in Malevič's work. Majakovskij's "painted letter" motif has correspondences in Malevič's colored letters, and the crossed "spears" of the poem are pictorially matched by the saw, sabre, bayonets, and crossed blades of scissors in Malevič's work. While depictions of cutting tools (such as a sword and scissors) serve as metaphors for the fragmented images in the composition, motifs of cutting devices may also represent the technique of sharp shifts and break-up of image planes apparent in the style of both Majakovskij and Malevič. (See Bowlt, *Russian Art,* 136.)[23] Majakovskij's "moon herring" is not only paralleled by Malevič's huge fish, but just as Majakovskij's herring is linked to a source of luminosity, so too Malevič's fish seems to be exuding light-like beams. A sense of line (streets, gutters, and tram "spears") and flow ("oozed out") in Majakovskij's poem is depicted in Malevič's work as well by means of emphasized curvature or angularity and a huge red arrow. Even Majakovskij's use of the verb *skakala* ("galloping") to describe movement unexpectedly attributed to a fish is paralleled by Malevič with the words *skakovoe obščestvo* ("racing society") provocatively placed above the right shoulder of the Englishman.

Like Majakovskij's verse-canvas, Malevič's pictorial use of displaced construction is associated with a sense of movement. The placement of objects askew (the ladder, for example), or in strange suspension (as the image of the candle) lend a feeling of dynamism to Malevič's painting. A highly specific "marker" of the artist's anti-aesthetic assertion in the picture is the large image of a spoon, for Malevič was known to have worn a wooden spoon in his lapel as part of his Cubo-Futurist guise. Originally a wooden spoon was glued onto the surface of the work, a physical encroachment of the prosaic world into the world of art. It was later replaced by the painted image (see Bowlt, "Journey into Non-Objectivity," 9).

Besides the mix of prosaic images employed by Majakovskij and Malevič, their two works demonstrate a likeness of compositional pattern.[24] More specifically, the cruciform structure described by the placement of images in Majakovskij's poem is paralleled by the cross-format evident in Malevič's painting. The cross was one of the compositional forms which intrigued Malevič, and it describes a major base for dispersal of motifs in his *Englishman in Moscow*. (Bowlt, *Russian Art*, 132). The vertical line established by the figure of the Englishman sharply contrasts with the sweeping horizontal line of the sword overlapping it. While repeated use of this compositional pattern may reflect Malevič's expressed interest in icon painting, the concomitant flattening and simplification of images (like the fish) in *Englishman in Moscow* as well as the incorporation of printed letters are features related to signboard art (Xardžiev, 117).[25]

Both Malevič and Majakovskij considered Cubo-Futurism a reaction against the art of the past. In 1915 Malevič wrote that "Cubism builds its pictures from the forms of lines and from a variety of painting textures, in which words and letters enter as a confrontation of various forms in the picture ..." (*Essays on Art*, I, 36). This concept echoes the effects rendered by Majakovskij's fragmentation of images and word-objects, implementation of image shift and distortion, and the battle-like confrontations among frameworks in his poem. Like a fish out of water, or an Englishman in Moscow, the persona of Majakovskij's work challenges the reader to look at the world anew.

Emory University

NOTES

1. K. S. Malevich, *Essays on Art 1915–1933*, tr. X. Glowacki-Prus and A. McMillin, ed. T. Andersen (2 Vols.; New York: George Wittenborn, 1971), II, 89.

2. See V. Markov, *Russian Futurism* (Berkeley: Univ. of California Press, 1968), 117-19.

3. E. J. Brown, *Mayakovsky, A Poet in the Revolution* (Princeton Univ. Press, 1973), 78.

4. J. E. Bowlt, "Journey into Non-Objectivity," *Journey into Non-Objectivity, The Graphic Work of Kazimir Malevich and Other Members of the Russian Avant-Garde* (Dallas Museum of Fine Arts catalogue, 1980), 9.

5. The poem was originally published without a title. The text used for analysis is taken from V. V. Majakovskij, *Polnoe sobranie sočinenij* (13 Vols.; Moscow: GIXL, 1955-61), I, 37.

6. The text of the Futurist manifesto *Poščečina po obščestvennomu vkusu* appears in V. Markov, *Manifesty i programmy russkix futuristov* (Munich: Wilhelm Fink, 1976), 50-51.

7. This is a feature of Cubism discussed by W. Judkins, *Fluctuant Representation in Synthetic Cubism: Picasso, Braque, Gris, 1910–1920* (New York: Garland, 1976), 22.

8. David Burljuk discusses the concept of shift or displacement (*sdvig*) as a major element of pictorial Cubism in his article "Kubizm" in the collection *Poščečina po obščestvennomu vkusu* (Moscow, 1912), 95-110.

9. The theme of decay within an urban context is a common motif in Majakovskij's poetry. This has aroused many questions about Majakovskij's true attitudes toward the city. Čukovskij, for example, amicably mocked Majakovskij's credibility as a "good urbanist." See K. Čukovskij, *Ègofuturisty i kubo-futuristy, obrazcy futuristićeskix proizvedenij* (1914; rpt. Letchworth, England: Prideaux, 1976), 32.

10. N. Xardžiev and V. Trenin, *Poètičeskaja kul'tura Majakovskogo* (Moscow: Iskusstvo, 1970), 44.

11. The use of "cranberries" in Majakovskij's lyric suggests an elaborate inversion of the cranberry-juice "blood" employed in the Symbolist play *Balagančik* (1906) by Aleksander Blok. See A. Blok, *Sočinenija* (2 Vols.; Moscow: GIXL, 1933), 548.

12. The concept of identifying with the pain of the city not only recurs throughout Majakovskij's early lyrics, but is also a theme shared by the Italian Futurists. See *Futurist Manifestos*, tr. R. Brain, R. Flint, J. Higgit, ed. U. Apollonio (London: Thames and Hudson, 1973), 29.

13. N. Xardžiev, "Poèzija i živopis'," *K istorii russkogo avangarda* (Stockholm: Hylaea Prints, Almqvist and Wiksell International, 1976), 39. Although Xardžiev does not provide the precise date of this letter, the reference by Larionov to the upcoming publication of *Sadok sudej II* would place the letter sometime between Larionov's invitation to speak on art (sent at the beginning of January 1913) and the appearance of *Sadok sudej II* in late February 1913.

14. Coincidentally, the first Rayonist painting exhibited by Larionov was a still life with a fish entitled *Rayonist Sausage and Mackerel* (exhibited December 1912 – January 1913). See M. Dabrowski, "The Formation and Development of Rayonism," *Art Journal*, 34/3 (Spring 1975), 203-4.

15. The fish was an early symbol for Christ since the word in Greek formed the initial letters of the expression "Jesus Christ, Son of God, Savior." See F. R. Webber, *Church Symbolism*, 2nd ed. rev. (Detroit: Gale Research, 1971), 59.

16. The phrase used in an earlier version of the poem (*skrestili sinij molnij kop'ja*) further supports an interpretation of "spears" as the tram poles which connect with overhead wires. For variant, see *PSS*, I, 376.

17. Support for this interpretation is found in an earlier version of the poem, where the phrase "in a fretted arm/hand" (*v reznoj ruke*) still more precisely describes the appearance of a lamp post. See *PSS*, I, 376.

18. While the multiple role of the eye suggests a variation on the visual pun or *trompe l'oeil*, eye imagery often appears in Majakovskij's work. His friend and mentor David Burljuk was actually blind in one eye.

19. Use of the basilisk in a context which involves the contrast of urban and sky imagery indicates the emergence of a new mythology, a mythology based on the contemporary city.

20. Permission to reproduce K. Malevič's *An Englishman in Moscow* (1913–1914) was graciously granted by the Stedelijk Museum, Amsterdam.

21.   J. E. Bowlt, *Russian Art 1875-1975: A Collection of Essays* (New York: MSS Information, 1976), 135, notes that green was rarely used in Malevič's paintings.

22.   In 1913 Malevič wrote, "art is that which not everyone can understand ... one cannot draw a single line without rational and thoughtful control ..."; he called this "new reason" "transrational" (*zaumnyj*) and contended that "this intelligence has found Cubism as its means of expression." See *Malevich: The Artist, Infinity, Suprematism; Unpublished Writings 1913-1933*, ed. T. Andersen (Vols.; Copenhagen: Borgens Forlag, 1978), IV, 203-4.

23.   It is Bowlt's contention that the scissors and sword "act as symbols of visual dismemberment."

24.   Bowlt (*Russian Art*, 135-36) notes that Malevič's images of a sword, ladder, fish, arrow and "partial eclipse" were probably drawn from Kručenyx's opera *Pobeda nad solncem*. Publication of Majakovskij's *Uličnoe*, however, predates the first performance of Kručenyx's opera in December 1913.

25.   Malevič himself said that it was from his study of icons that he turned to a period of "the urban sign." See Xardžiev, 118.

THE METRICAL TYPOLOGY OF ANNA AXMATOVA

Anthony J. Hartman

In recent years the metrical and rhythmical typology of Russian verse has been investigated in its overall characteristics and development by a number of scholars. In particular, Kiril Taranovsky and M. L. Gasparov have made major contributions in their investigations of Russian versification during the nineteenth and twentiety centuries.[1] However, for a more complete understanding of the history of Russian versification one needs not only an overview but detailed information concerning the practice of individual poets, whose usage may or may not conform to the general development. Such typologies have appeared for the poetry of Puškin, Blok, Brjusov, and others.[2] Until now, studies of Axmatova have not been primarily concerned with her versification, and only passing references are usually made to certain aspects of her practice.[3] Exceptions are Kolmogorov's and Proxorov's analysis of Axmatova's use of the four-stress *dol'nik* in "U samogo morja" and Thompson's discussion of her three-stress *dol'nik*.[4] A detailed investigation of Axmatova's metrical usage in all of her work is necessary to accurately place her practice within the context of Russian versification and to properly assess her contribution.

One of the major concerns of the literature on Axmatova's work is the question of the periodization of her long poetic career. A number of different schemes have been suggested; some are based on biographical information, some on historical events, and others on thematic considerations. According to Dobin, the appearance of *Anno Domini* in 1922 marked the end of Axmatova's early period (97). Verheul also accepts this date, at least provisionally, as the dividing line between Axmatova's early and late periods (3). Others have favored an earlier dividing line. In the 1920s, contemporary critics pointed to a change in Axmatova's poetry which seemed to develop between the collection *Četki* (1914) and *Belaja staja* (1917).[5] Žirmunskij, Mirsky, and Kornej Čukovskij all noted the more serious character of Axmatova's poetry beginning with *Belaja staja*. Among later scholars, Pavlovskij sees *Belaja staja* as ending the first period, and divides Axmatova's work into three periods: pre-revolutionary, post-revolutionary, and Soviet, i.e., post-1940 (69-70). However, as Verheul points out, such a division is based, perhaps, too much on external, historical events, rather than on the internal development of Axmatova's verse (2-3). In her biography of Axmatova, Haight distinguishes six biographical periods, and traces a parallel thematic development. The early verse is divided into two periods — pre-war and 1914 to 1924, and the later verse is divided into three periods: 1924 to 1941, 1941 to 1956, and 1956 to

1966. The periodization approximates that which Verheul reaches at the conclusion of his analysis of the emergence of the theme of time as the central preoccupation of Axmatova's poetry (222-23).

Axmatova's verse will be examined here from a diachronic as well as synchronic point of view in order to reveal whether her metrical usage provides support for any of the suggested periodizations. As a *modus operandi*, two main periods will be distinguished, 1909 to 1922, and 1923 to 1965. Axmatova's versification will be discussed in terms of its metrical typology, that is, the relative frequency with which the various meters appear in her work. According to B. I. Jarxo's principles, a typology ought to include: 1) the total number of meters, 2) the synchronic and diachronic frequency of each meter, 3) the division of meters into the broad categories of lyric, narrative, and dramatic verse, and 4) a comparison with the typology of other poets.[6]

In addition to the material in Fillipov and Struve's two-volume edition *Sočinenija*, more recent editions have also been included.[7] A total of 9603 lines of Axmatova's original verse were analyzed. Her translations in verse will not be discussed. The percentages referred to in the analysis are based on the number of lines rather than the number of poems in the various meters, since this approach gives a more accurate representation of the place a given meter occupies in the poet's work. If the number of poems in each meter had provided the basis for the calculations, a poem of four lines would have had the same weight as a poem of twenty or thirty lines.

The typology of twentieth-century verse is characterized by several parallel systems of versification (Gasparov, *SRS*, 39-75). In addition to the syllabotonic system of binary and ternary meters, used since the eighteenth century, various types of stress-meters and non-metrical verse have been developed in the twentieth century. The most common of these is the *dol'nik*, in which the number of syllables between ictuses, or metrical stresses, varies from one to two. Accentual verse, where the interval varies from zero to three in strict accentual verse (*taktovik*) and up to four or five syllables in loose accentual verse, is less frequent; non-metrical verse is relatively rare. In addition, polymetrical forms, in which a number of different meters constitute a structural element of a single work, have become more frequent in the twentieth century.

The metrical typology of Axmatova's verse taken as a whole manifests a clear predominance of binary and ternary meters over all others:

Table 1: Metrical Typology for All Lines

Meters	Lines	Percentage
Binary	5090	53.0
Ternary	1946	20.2

Dol'nik	2203	23.0
Strict Accentual	26	0.3
Folk	31	0.3
Polymetrical	307	3.2
Total	9603	100.0

Only the *dol'nik* is represented by a significant number of lines in meters other than binary and ternary. Accentual meters and folk meters are found only in isolated poems; there is no non-metrical verse; polymetrical verse is rare, comprising less than 5% of all the lines. (A more detailed typology and a summary of the abbreviations used are found in the Appendix.)

The percentage of binary meters shows a continuation of the tendency discernible at the end of the nineteenth and the beginning of the twentieth century away from binary meters and toward the increased use of ternary and stress-meters. Rudnev's data for Puškin, Fet, Brjusov, and Blok (*Blokovskij sbornik*, 236, 237) together with comparable figures for Axmatova, illustrate this development:

Table 2: Development of Russian Metrical Typology

Meters	Puškin	Fet	Brjusov	Blok	Axmatova
Binary	94.3	77.7	63.7	60.1	53.0
Ternary	1.4	14.9	13.9	16.9	20.2
Non-classical	3.8	6.3	11.7	11.7	23.6
Polymetrical	0.6	1.2	10.7	11.3	3.2

Rudnev's figures are based on all the verse of these poets, with no genre or chronological distinctions. The somewhat vague term "non-classical" includes all other meters other than binary, ternary, and polymetrical verse.

Axmatova's only deviation from the general tendencies is evinced in her use of polymetrical verse, which occurs less frequently in her verse than in either Blok's or Brjusov's. Otherwise, the directions are clearly continued; lines in binary meters occur 7-10% less frequently in Axmatova's verse than in that of Blok and Brjusov, while ternary meters occur 3-6% more frequently. Axmatova's "non-classical" meters — predominantly the *dol'nik* — are about 11% more frequent than in these poets.

If genres are distinguished, it is immediately apparent that Axmatova is primarily a lyric poet. Only four works, which have 90 or more lines, have been treated as long poems: "Prolog, ili son vo sne," "Putem vseja zemli," "Poèma bez geroja," and "U samogo morja." Poetic cycles have been broken down, and the constituent poems classified as lyric verse.

Table 3 shows that the relative proportion of lines in Axmatova's lyric and narrative verse approximates the levels found by Rudnev in the poetry of Blok and Brjusov (*Teorija stixa*, 118-19):

Table 3: Genres

	Blok	Brjusov	Axmatova
Lyric	81.2	82.5	87.0
Narrative	12.0	12.6	13.0
Dramatic	6.8	4.9	0.0

The slightly higher frequency of lines in lyric verse for Axmatova is a reflection of the absence of dramatic verse. The predominance of lyric verse places these poets in the tradition of Tjutčev and Fet (90-100% lyric), rather than that of Puškin, Lermontov, and Nekrasov, where only 30-50% of the lines appear in lyric verse.

When genres are distinguished, the typology of Axmatova's lyric verse closely resembles that for all lines, while the long works are dominated by the *dol'nik* (the number of lines are in parentheses):

Table 4: Typology of Genres

Meters	Lyrics		Long Poems	
Binary	60.6	(5071)	1.5	(19)
Ternary	21.0	(1758)	15.2	(188)
Dol'nik	15.1	(1267)	75.9	(936)
Accentual	0.3	(26)	0.0	(0)
Folk	0.4	(31)	0.0	(0)
Polymetrical	2.6	(216)	7.4	(91)

Axmatova's preference for the *dol'nik* in longer narrative forms is a distinctive element in her versification. As a point of comparison, one can again refer to the typology of Blok and Brjusov:[8]

Table 5: Typology of Lyric and Narrative Verse

	Classical	Non-classical	Polymetrical
Brjusov			
Lyric	83.6	12.4	4.0
Narrative	57.1	11.7	30.2
Blok			
Lyric	84.5	12.7	2.8
Narrative	70.0	11.7	18.3
Axmatova			
Lyric	81.6	15.8	2.6
Narrative	16.7	75.9	7.4

Although the percentage of classical meters is reduced in Brjusov's and Blok's narrative works, they nevertheless account for a majority of the lines. The non-classical meters remain about the same in both lyric and narrative verse, and polymetrical forms appear with greater frequency in the narrative verse. The *dol'nik* thus occupies the place in Axmatova's narrative works that the binary meters did in Blok's and Brjusov's. Kolmogorov and Proxorov (85) have noted that, with the exception of the Russian hexameter (employed since the eighteenth century in translations of classical epics), the first use of the *dol'nik* in a long poem in the history of Russian verse is represented by Axmatova's "U samogo morja" (Dk3 — 48 lines, Dk4 — 227 — lines).

A diachronic investigation of Axmatova's typology reveals a development which bears a relation both to the thematic evolution of her own verse and to the developments in twentieth-century versification as a whole (see Appendix for detailed typology of lyric verse):

Table 6: Diachronic Metrical Typology

	Lyrics		Long Poems	
	1909–1922	1923–1965	1909–1922	1923–1965
Binary	61.5 (2810)	59.5 (2261)	0.0 (0)	2.0 (19)
Ternary	19.3 (876)	23.2 (882)	0.0 (0)	19.6 (188)
Dol'nik	17.4 (796)	12.3 (471)	100.0 (275)	68.9 (661)
Accentual	0.3 (14)	0.3 (12)	0.0 (0)	0.0 (0)
Folk	0.0 (0)	0.8 (31)	0.0 (0)	0.0 (0)
Polymetrical	1.5 (68)	3.9 (148)	0.0 (0)	9.5 (91)
Total	100.0 (4564)	100.0 (3805)	100.0 (275)	100.0 (959)

A trend toward larger genres in Axmatova's later verse, which is apparent in the above table, has been noted by other scholars (Žirmunskij, *Tvorčestvo...*, 114-26). In the early period, the only long work is "U samogo morja" (275 lines of a total 4839, or 5.7%), while in the later period there are three works which account for 959 lines from a total of 4764 lines (20.1%). The long poems have a rather stable metrical typology; although there is more variety in metrical forms, the *dol'nik* continues to be the most important meter in the later period.

The typology of Axmatova's lyric verse, on the other hand, exhibits differences between the early and late periods, both in its general outline and in the most common individual meters. Although the binary verse remains at approximately the same level in both periods, the proportion of iambic to trochaic verse changes from 35.0% iambic and 25.3% trochaic in the early verse to 47.1% iambic and 12.4% trochaic in the late. There is also an increase in the proportion of ternary lines, a decline in the *dol'nik*, and a slight rise in the percentage of polymetrical verse in the late period.

Comparison with Gasparov's figures (51) shows that the typology of Axmatova's early verse corresponds closely to what is typical for the Russian lyric from 1925 to 1936:

Table 7:   Twentieth-century Russian Lyric Verse   Axmatova

	1890–24	1925–35	1936–45	1946–57	1958–68	1909–22	1923–65
Iambic	49.5	34.0	41.0	45.0	50.0	35.8	47.1
Trochaic	19.5	25.0	24.5	21.5	17.5	25.7	12.4
All Binary	69.0	59.0	65.5	66.5	67.5	61.5	59.5
Ternary	14.5	15.0	21.0	22.0	18.5	19.3	23.2
Other	16.5	26.0	13.5	11.5	14.0	19.2	17.3

The decade from 1925 to 1935 stands out from the preceding and following decades by virtue of the low percentage of iambic meters and the high percentage of meters other than binary and ternary. The typology of Axmatova's early verse exhibits a similarly low level of iambic meters, but the level of "other" meters (primarily the *dol'nik* — 17.4%) is lower and more closely approaches the proportion of "other" meters in Gasparov's figures from 1890 to 1924. While the proportion of trochaic meters in Axmatova's early verse reflects the levels found in the decade from 1925 to 1935, the ternary meters are slightly more frequent than typical for this decade, and thus anticipate the higher levels characteristic of later decades and of her own verse from 1923 to 1965. The developments in the typology of Axmatova's later verse tend to parallel those in Russian lyric verse after 1935. Both exhibit increases in iambic and ternary verse and a decline in trochaic and *dol'nik* verse.

If free and mixed meters (in which the number of ictuses per line varies randomly or according to a fixed pattern) and polymetrical verse are regarded as single meters, then one may say that Axmatova employed forty-two different metrical forms. Most of these are rare since they are found in less than 5% of the lines, and only a small number are minor (5-10% of the lines) or major (over 10% of the lines). If genres are not distinguished, Axmatova employed Dk3 in the largest number of lines (17.1%) and I5 only slightly less frequently (16.1%). The predominance of the *dol'nik* over all other meters emerges more clearly if, as in Gasparov's figures, all the *dol'nik* forms are combined (23.0%). It is necessary, however, to distinguish the lyric from the long poems, because their typologies differ so greatly. As has already been pointed out, the most distinctive feature of the long poems is the predominance of the *dol'nik* (Dk3 — 57.7%, Dk4 — 18.4%). Am2 and polymetrical verse are minor (10.7% and 7.4%, respectively). These four metrical forms account for 94% of the lines in the long poems.

When the individual meters in the lyric verse are considered, Axmatova's typology reveals a shift from the relative equality of four major meters from 1909 to 1922 (I5 — 13.9%, Dk3 — 13.2%, T4 — 13.0%, I4 — 11.9%) to a single major meter from 1923 to 1965 (I5 — 23.8%). (See Appendix.) While there are two minor meters in the early verse (An3 — 9.2% and T5 — 6.0%), there are four in the later (I4 — 9.8%, An3 — 9.3%, Dk3 — 8.5%, and T5 — 6.5%). Although Gasparov's study shows that an increase in the frequency of I5 is a development which is typical for twentieth-century Russian lyric verse, I5 does not exceed all other meters by so wide a margin as in the typology of Axmatova's late verse. According to Gasparov (48-49), I4 tends to appear from 1936 to 1957 with nearly the same frequency as I5 (I4 — 13.5 to 16.6%, I5 — 16.2% to 17.4%), and from 1957 to 1968, I4 regains first place by a narrow margin (I4 — 21.2% and I5 — 20.2%). The reduced level of the *dol'nik* and T4 in Axmatova's late verse is more typical of the evolution in the typology of the Russian lyric. However, the presence of An3 among the minor meters is not expected since ternary meters are usually only encountered among the rare meters. As is typical for Russian verse, the rare meters in Axmatova's typology are predominantly ternary, free meters, and mixed meters.

The shift away from the *dol'nik* to I5, which is characteristic of Axmatova's typology in the late period, took place in the middle of her early period, after 1915. The development of the *dol'nik* and I5 during Axmatova's early period can be followed in Table 8. Since many of Axmatova's late poems are difficult to date precisely, the later period has not been subdivided. The lines from poems in free and mixed meters have not been included in the total.

Table 8: Diachronic typology of I5 and Dk3

	Total lines	I5		Dk3	
1909–1911	(667)	11.4%	(76)	21.9%	(146)
1912–1913	(783)	17.5%	(137)	19.4%	(152)
1914–1915	(847)	11.9%	(101)	27.1%	(230)
1916–1917	(617)	29.8%	(184)	1.9%	(24)
1918–1922	(669)	20.5%	(137)	6.3%	(42)
1923–1965	(2849)	31.8%	(906)	11.4%	(324)

There is a clear break after 1915, when the occurence of Dk3 falls from over one-fourth of the lines in the 1914 to 1915 interval to about 2% in the 1916 to 1917 interval, and I5 rises from about 12% to almost 30% in the same periods. The relative position of Dk3 and I5 from 1916 to 1922 is the same as from 1923 to 1965.

Several scholars and critics have noted a change in Axmatova's verse beginning with the book *Belaja staja* (1917). Èjxenbaum observed that Axmatova turned from the *dol'nik* to syllabo-tonic meters, in particular I5, beginning with this book.[9] Changes in theme and style have also been pointed out. Žirmunskij stated that in Axmatova's late verse there is a significant number of poems "which do not belong to the genre of the intimate lyric in the strict sense of the word, but which are lyric reflections on moral-didactic and civic themes in the broad sense" (*Tvorčestvo ...*, 114). Such poems appear as early as *Belaja staja* and increase in number, particularly after 1940. Examples of these reflective works are the cycles "Èpičeskie motivy" (1913–1916) and "Severnye èlegii" (1941–1965), which were composed in I5.

Detailed investigation of Axmatova's metrical typology to a large extent confirms the commonly held view that compared to Blok or Majakovskij, Axmatova was not an innovator in her versification. Her use of Dk4 in "U samogo morja" is the only exception to this generalization. Although Axmatova's frequent use of the *dol'nik* in her lyric verse prior to 1915 was one of the features which impressed contemporaries as being new, in fact, the use of the *dol'nik* represents a continuation of one of the principle developments associated with the Symbolists, rather than a new direction.[10] Stress-meters other than the *dol'nik* do not occupy a significant place in her metrical typology, as they do in that of the more innovative Futurists and Constructivists (Gasparov, 72).

Axmatova's lyric verse from 1923 to 1965 exhibits several of the conservative tendencies which appeared in the typology of Russian verse after 1935. It has been shown here, however, that this metrical conservatism in Axmatova's later verse is not necessarily the result of the influence of Russian practice after 1935, but that it represents a continuation of trends toward more traditional meters which were manifested in her verse as early as 1915. The metrical changes in Axmatova's verse after 1915 accompany the thematic and stylistic changes which Žirmunskij and others noted in *Belaja staja*.

The chronological development of the typology of Axmatova's verse suggests a periodization of her work in which the early period lasted from 1909 to 1915. The two main features of Axmatova's late lyric, a reduction in Dk3 and a corresponding increase in I5, are found in the early verse of 1916 to 1922. Although uncertainty in dating makes the division of the period 1923 to 1965 difficult, the larger role of long poems between 1940 and 1950 and of translations after 1950 make it possible to distinguish four periods: 1909 to 1915, 1916 to 1939, 1940 to 1950, and 1950 to 1965. Such a periodization offers some support for Verheul's divisions in the development of the theme of time in Axmatova's poetry. The typology indicates, however, that the second period does not begin with the appearance of *Anno Domini* (1921–1922), but as early as 1916 in *Belaja staja*. While Verheul distinguishes additional periods between 1916 and 1939 (1921–1923, the 1920's and the 1930's), there are insufficient data to make similar subdivisions on the basis of the metrical typology.

The analysis of Axmatova's metrical typology shows that although it is not innovative in its overall characteristics, it formed a dynamic aspect of her poetry, an aspect which changed and developed along with other elements of her poetic practice.

Appendix: Axmatova's Metrical Typology

The following abbreviations have been used: I — iambic, T — trochaic, An — anapestic, Am — amphibrachic, Da — dactylic, Dk — *dol'nik*, A — accentual, and PM — polymetrical. The number which appears after the abbreviation indicates the number of ictuses per line. Free meters (*vol'nye razmery*) and mixed meters (*raznostopnye razmery*) are indicated by the letters F and M. Transitional-to-free meters, in which variation in the number of ictuses is found in only 12% to 20% of the lines, appear as Trans-F. Iambic and trochaic meters with a strong caesura have been listed separately.[11]

	All lines		Long poems		Lyrics		1909–1922		1923–1965	
	Lines	%	Lines	%	Lines	%	Lines	%	Lines	%
I. Binary	5090	53.0	19	1.5	5071	60.6	2810	61.5	2261	59.5
1. Iambic										
I3	148	1.5	0	0.0	148	1.8	116	2.5	32	0.8
I4	914	9.5	0	0.0	914	10.9	542	11.9	372	9.8
I5	1550	16.1	11	0.9	1539	18.4	633	13.9	906	23.8
I6	132	1.4	0	0.0	132	1.6	61	1.3	71	1.9
Trans-F	116	1.2	0	0.0	116	1.4	36	0.8	80	2.1
IF	256	2.7	0	0.0	256	3.1	84	1.8	172	4.5
IM	284	3.0	0	0.0	284	3.4	126	2.8	158	4.2
Total	3400	35.4	11	0.9	3389	40.5	1598	35.0	1791	47.1
2. Trochaic										
T3	58	0.6	0	0.0	58	0.7	16	0.3	42	1.1
T4	693	7.2	0	0.0	693	8.3	591	13.0	102	2.7
T5	522	5.4	0	0.0	522	6.2	275	6.0	247	6.5
Trans-F	55	0.6	0	0.0	55	0.7	48	1.0	7	0.2
TF	56	0.6	0	0.0	56	0.7	56	1.2	0	0.0
TM	254	2.6	8	0.6	246	2.9	174	3.8	72	1.9
Total	1638	17.0	8	0.6	1630	19.5	1160	25.3	470	12.4

	All lines		Long poems		Lyrics		1909–1922		1923–1965	
3. Strong Caesura										
I4	35	0.4	0	0.0	35	0.4	35	0.8	0	0.0
T6	17	0.2	0	0.0	17	0.2	17	0.4	0	0.0
II. Ternary	1946	20.2	188	15.2	1758	21.0	876	19.3	882	23.2
1. Amphibrach										
Am2	132	1.4	132	10.7	0	0.0	0	0.0	0	0.0
Am3	321	3.3	0	0.0	321	3.8	169	3.7	152	4.0
Am4	99	1.0	0	0.0	99	1.2	3	0.1	96	2.5
Am5	24	0.2	0	0.0	24	0.3	12	0.3	12	0.3
AmF	40	0.4	0	0.0	40	0.5	0	0.0	40	1.1
AmM	144	1.5	0	0.0	144	1.7	58	1.3	86	2.3
Total	760	7.8	132	10.7	628	7.5	242	5.4	386	10.2
2. Anapest										
An2	44	0.5	0	0.0	44	0.5	0	0.0	44	1.2
An3	828	8.6	56	4.5	772	9.2	418	9.2	354	9.3
An4	10	0.1	0	0.0	10	0.1	10	0.2	0	0.0
An5	19	0.2	0	0.0	19	0.2	11	0.2	8	0.2
AnF	6	0.1	0	0.0	6	0.1	6	0.1	0	0.0
AnM	72	0.7	0	0.0	72	0.9	72	1.6	0	0.0
Total	979	10.2	56	4.5	923	11.0	517	11.3	406	10.7
3. Dactylic										
Da3	40	0.4	0	0.0	40	0.5	32	0.7	8	0.2
Da4	53	0.5	0	0.0	53	0.6	42	0.9	11	0.3
Da5	2	0.1	0	0.0	2	0.1	0	0.0	2	0.1
Trans-F	5	0.1	0	0.0	5	0.1	0	0.0	5	0.1
DaF	9	0.1	0	0.0	9	0.1	0	0.0	9	0.2
DaM	67	0.7	0	0.0	67	0.8	35	0.8	32	0.8
Total	176	1.9	0	0.0	176	2.1	109	2.4	67	1.7
4. Variable Anacrusis	31	0.3	0	0.0	31	0.4	8	0.2	23	0.6
III. *Dol'nik*										
Dk3	1637	17.1	709	57.5	928	11.1	604	13.2	324	8.5
0-anac.	20	0.2	0	0.0	20	0.2	20	0.4	0	0.0
1-syll. anac.	133	1.4	12	1.0	121	1.5	96	2.1	25	0.6
2-syll. anac.	1148	12.0	649	52.6	499	6.0	264	5.8	235	6.2
variable anac.	336	3.5	48	3.9	288	3.4	224	4.9	64	1.7
Dk4	321	3.3	227	18.4	94	1.1	37	0.8	57	1.5
Dk6	9	0.1	0	0.0	9	0.1	0	0.0	9	0.2
DkF	49	0.5	0	0.0	49	0.6	23	0.5	26	0.7
DkM	187	2.0	0	0.0	187	2.2	132	2.9	55	1.4
Total	2203	23.0	936	75.9	1267	15.1	796	17.4	471	12.3

METRICAL TYPOLOGY

	All lines		Long poems		Lyrics		1909–1922		1923–1965	
IV. Accentual Strict	26	0.3	0	0.0	26	0.3	14	0.3	12	0.3
V. Folk	31	0.3	0	0.0	31	0.4	0	0.0	31	0.8
VI. PM	307	3.2	91	7.4	216	2.6	68	1.5	148	3.9
TOTAL	9603	100.0	1234	100.0	8369	100.0	4564	100.0	3805	100.0

Russian Research Center, Harvard University

NOTES

1. Kiril Taranovsky, *Ruski dvodelni ritmovi*, I-II, Posebna izdanja, knjiga CCXVII, Odeljene Literature i Jezika, Knjiga 5, ed. Petar Kolendić (Belgrade: izdavačko Preduzeće Narodne Republike Srbije, 1953); M. L. Gasparov, *Sovremennyj russkij stix* (Moscow: Nauka, 1974).
2. *Russkoe stixosloženie XIX v.: materialy po metrike i strofike russkix poètov*, ed. M. L. Gasparov, M. M. Giršman, L. I. Timofeev (Moscow: Nauka, 1979); James Bailey, "The Metrical and Rhythmical Typology of K. K. Slučevskij's Poetry," *International Journal of Slavic Linguistics and Poetics*, 18 (1975), 93-117; L. I. Timofeev, "Na puti k istorii russkogo stixosloženija," *Izvestija AN SSSR, serija literatury i jazyka*, 29, No. 5 (1970), 442-46; P. A. Rudnev, "Metričeskij repertuar A. Bloka," in *Blokovskij sbornik*, II, ed. Z. G. Minc et al. (Tartu: Tartu Univ., 1972), 218-67; P. A. Rudnev, "Iz metričeskogo repertuara russkix poètov XIX-načala XX v. (Puškin, Lermontov, Nekrasov, Tjutčev, Fet, Brjusov, Blok)," in *Teorija stixa*, ed. V. E. Xolševnikov (Leningrad: Nauka, 1968), 107-44. See also the following bibliographies: G. S. Smith, "A Bibliography of Soviet Publications on Russian Versification since 1958," *Russian Literature Triquarterly*, No. 6 (1973), 679-94; Ian K. Lilly and Barry P. Scherr, "Russian Verse Theory since 1960; A Commentary and Bibliography," *International Journal of Slavic Linguistics and Poetics*, 22 (1976), 75-116; V. S. Baevskij and S. I. Gindin, "Dopolnitel'naja bibliografia publikacij sovetskix učenyx po obščemu i russkomu stixovedeniju za 1958–1972 gg.," in *Problemy stixovedenija*, ed. M. L. Gasparov et al. (Erevan: Erevan Univ., 1976), 241-76.
3. E. S. Dobin, *Poèzija Anny Axmatovoj* (Leningrad: Sov. pisatel', 1968); A. I. Pavlovskij, *Anna Axmatova' Očerk tvorčestva* (Leningrad: Lenizdat, 1966); V. M. Žirmunskij, *Tvorčestvo Anny Axmatovoj* (Leningrad: Nauka, 1973); Kees Verheul, *The Theme of Time in the Poetry of Anna Akhmatova* (The Hague: Mouton, 1971); Sam Driver, *Anna Akhmatova* (New York: Twayne, 1972); Amanda Haight, *Anna Akhmatova: A Poetic Pilgrimage* (New York: Oxford Univ. Press, 1976).
4. A. N. Kolmogorov and A. V. Proxorov, "O dol'nike sovremennoj russkoj poèzii," *Voprosy jazykoznanija*, 1963, No. 6, 84-95, 1964, No. 1, 75-94; R. D. B. Thompson, "The Anapaestic Dol'nik in the Poetry of Axmatova and Gumilev," in *Toward a Definition of Acmeism*, ed. Denis Mickiewicz, *Russian Language Journal, Supplementary Issue* (Spring, 1975), 42-58.
5. V. M. Žirmunskij, *Voprosy teorii literatury: Stat'i 1916–1925*, Slavistic Printings and Reprintings, No. 34 ('S-Gravenhage: Mouton, 1962), 322-26; D. S. Mirsky, *Contemporary Russian Literature 1881–1925* (London: George Routledge, 1926), 259; Kornej Čukovskij, "Axmatova i Majakovskij," *Dom iskusstv*, 1 (1920), 23-24.
6. B. I. Jarxo, I. K. Romanovič, N. V. Lapšina, *Metričeskij spravočnik k stixotvorenijam A. S. Puškina* (Moscow-Leningrad, 1934); "Iz materialov 'Metričeskogo spravočnika k stixotvorenijam M. Ju. Lermontova,'" ed. M. L. Gasparov, *Voprosy jazykoznanija*, 1966, No. 2, 124-37. See also Bailey, "Slučevskij's Poetry," 93-94; *Russkoe stixosloženie XIX v.: materialy*, 3-11.

7.   Anna Axmatova, *Sočinenija*, ed. G. P. Struve and B. A. Filippov, 2nd ed. rev. and enl. (2 vols.; Munich: Interlanguage Literary Associates, 1967–1968); *Stixotvorenija i poèmy*, comp., text prep., and notes V. M. Žirmunskij, (Biblioteka poèta; Leningrad: Sov. pisatel', 1976); *Pamjati A. Axmatovoj: Stixi, pis'ma, vospominanija* (Paris: YMCA Press, 1974); Jeanne Van Der Eng-Liedmeier and Kees Verheul, *Tale Without a Hero and Twenty-two Poems by Anna Axmatova*, (Dutch Studies in Russian Literature, 3; The Hague: Mouton, 1973).

8.   Since Rudnev (*Teorija stixa*, 118-19) provides percentages based on the total number of lines, rather than on the total number of lines of narrative and lyric verse, it was necessary to re-calculate percentages for classical, non-classical, and polymetrical verse within the genres by dividing the total percentage of narrative or lyric lines by the percentages in each of the verse systems.

9.   B. V. Èjxenbaum, "Anna Axmatova: Opyt analiza," *O poèzii* (Leningrad: Sov. pisatel', 1969), 86, 109.

10.   See N. V. Nedobrovo, "Anna Axmatova," *Russkaja Mysl'*, 1915, No. 7, 51-53; see also Žirmunskij, 106-08, and Gasparov, 71.

11.   James Bailey, "Russian Binary Meters with Strong Caesura from 1890 to 1920," *International Journal of Slavic Linguistics and Poetics*, 14 (1971), 111-33.

IN SEARCH OF CONTINUITY: RUSSIAN AND SOVIET SILENT FILMS

Hari S. Rorlich

Until recently, Soviet and foreign cinema historians seemed to be unaware of the continuity between films produced in Russia before 1917 and after the October Revolution. In his filmography of pre-revolutionary fiction films, Višnevskij remarks: "For many years the history of pre-revolutionary Russian films was treated superficially and onesidedly. All artistic value was denied to films of this period, and hence, the pseudoscientific theory that Soviet film production started from scratch. This idea was entirely wrong. By October 1917, Russian film producers had created a definite style and artistic school which were reflected in the best pictures of that period."[1] Soviet film historians such as Iezuitov, Lixačev, Rosolovskaja, Ždan, to name only a few, in presenting the full sequence of the development of Russian and Soviet cinema have also underlined the positive qualities of pre-revolutionary films.

In May 1896, the most energetic entrepreneurs of an intriguing and new form of art, the cinema, converged on an unexplored market: Russia. The coronation of Nicholas II presented foreign film-makers with a golden opportunity to capture on film a most spectacular event in a Russia which was still a mystery to Western Europeans. The Lumiere brothers of France were given exclusive rights to film the entire coronation ceremony. From a specially built platform erected in the Kremlin courtyard, the strange-looking machines clicked off the first Russian film. Although the film was shown only in the West, the Lumiere brothers laid claim to Russia's first film audience.

On 4 May 1908 the Aquarium theater in Petersburg was the setting for the first public demonstration of the Cinematographe. The first three short movies, *The Arrival of the Train at a Country Station, The Fight,* and *The Card-game,* were well received; this encouraged the Lumiere Company to open the first Russian film house at 46, Nevsky Prospect.[2]

The Lumiere brothers were soon followed by the Englishman Robert Paul with his *Animatograph* and by Edison's *Kinetophone,* which was demonstrated to large audiences in a Moscow summer garden, the Hermitage.

Their "moving photographs" were so successful that they became one of the major popular attractions at the annual Fair at Nizhni-Novgorod. The short film *The Arrival of the Train at a Country Station,* shown at that Fair had the following action: a train arrived, passing the camera as it slowed to a stop, and deposited on a platform somewhere in France a number of passengers carrying bundles and baggage. The passengers dispersed, leaving the screen empty; that was the end of the film, which lasted only about fifteen minutes. The spectators were overwhelmed; they refused to leave until they had another chance to be scared by the giant locomotive steaming towards them. Among them was a young man by the name of A. Peškov — Maksim Gor'kij — who was reporting on the Fair for the papers of Nizhni-Novgorod and Odessa. Deeply impressed by the film, he wrote in one of his columns in *Nižnegorod-skij Kiosk*:

> A railway train appears on the screen. It darts like an arrow straight towards you — look out! It seems as if it is about to rush into the darkness in which you are sitting and reduce you to a mangled sack of skin, full of crumpled flesh and shattered bones, and reduce this hall and this building, so packed with people, and transform it into fragments and into dust.[3]

Cheap entertainment was a pressing demand in Russia. Poor people in both town and village usually had at their disposal only the pleasure of group singing and dancing. It is not surprising, then, that when the so-called "moving shadows" (*dvižuščiesja teni*) came within their reach, they flocked to them. The short films attracted large audiences willing to wait hours in front of improvised fair ground theaters to see what Gor'kij called "the miracle." The rapidly growing interest for this new and relatively inexpensive form of entertainment resulted in the opening of the first permanent movie theaters. In 1903, there were already ten permanent movie houses in Moscow. With names such as "Iljuzija," "Miraž," or "Fantazija," they reflected the desire of the Russian spectator to be amused, and most of all to be surprised.[4]

The French film companies Pathé and Gaumont penetrated and monopolized the Russian market in the last decade of the nineteenth century. This, however, did not represent a hindrance for the Russian film makers. Among them, there were enterprising people such as Aleksandr Drankov and Aleksandr Xanzonkov, who were later to assume a leading role among Russian producers.

The political and social turmoil of the years 1904–05, the domestic impact of the Russo-Japanese War and the Revolution of 1905, created an ideal climate for the "birth" of the newsreel. There was on the part of the Russian audience an augmented thirst for news, and foreign film-makers seized upon this unexpected opportunity. In order to keep up with public demand for news they began producing short films depicting mostly current events. News from the Siberian-Manchurian fronts and the bloody January Massacre in Petersburg were captured on film by Felix Mesguič, the only foreign cameraman known to have witnessed both these events. The growth of anti-government feelings at the end of the Russo-Japanese War forced the government to take drastic steps to stifle this new and potentially dangerous disseminator of information. The government recognized the need to increase its surveillance of the cinema — the footage taken by Mesguič during the February events was confiscated. The official press launched a strong campaign to discredit the incipient documentary. Phrases such as "victims of cinematography," and "the dangers of living photography" began to appear frequently in government magazines and newspapers. Yet the same press that revealed the dangers of the newsreel as a means of agitating the masses simultaneously emphasized the need to produce domestic films depicting scenes from Russian life. This was, indeed, paradoxically an ominous development for the native producers of Russia. In the fall of 1907 A. Drankov established the first Russian studio, proclaiming war on the French film monopoly. His views were sustained by advertisements in newspapers and magazines which notified the public that "until now the Russian public, sitting in Russian theaters, paying Russian money, has not seen subjects from Russian life."[5]

Between February and October 1908 Drankov produced a series of seventeen films. One of his major successes as a film maker was the filming of Tolstoj. The writer's hatred of photographers was well known. On Tolstoj's eightieth birthday, however, with the help of Tolstoj's wife Sof'ja Andreevna, Drankov and his crew of two filmed Tolstoj sitting on the porch of his house at Jasnaja poljana. His next notable success was a dramatic movie depicting the legendary Stenka Razin. The ten-minute film was released on 15 October 1908 and became an instant box-office success. Drankov's success prompted a strong reaction from theater owners who were afraid of losing their spectators to the new medium, the so-called electric theaters *električeskie teatry*). They used their political influence to enact legislation which would limit the number of cinemas to be opened, their location, and even their operating hours (Lixačev, 26). These restrictions, however, did not prevent the theaters, concert halls and circuses from losing an appreciable number of their regulars. This was well illustrated by A. Serafimovič, who commented on the rise of this new form of entertainment:

> If you walk in the evening along the streets of the capital, of large provincial towns, local towns, large settlements and villages, on every street you will see the same phenomenon with the solitary flickering kerosene lights at an entrance illuminated by lamps, and by the entrance a crowd waiting in a line — the cinema. If you look in the auditorium the composition of the audience will amaze you. Everyone is there — students and gendarmes, writers and prostitutes, officers and cadets, all kinds of intellectuals, bearded and with pince-nez, and workers, shop assistants, tradesmen, society ladies, fashionable women, officials — in a word, everyone.[6]

By the beginning of World War I the Russian cinema had established itself as an independent and most popular form of entertainment, primarily among the urban population.

The War itself was an unexpected blessing for the Russian film industry. Already freed from foreign competition, the industry intensified its production and began improving the quality of its films. In March 1916, a government decree established the Skovelev Committee which was given sole responsibility for the filming and distribution of a special war newsreel called *The Mirror of War (Zerkalo vojny)*.

The main purpose of the official war documentaries was to nurture Russian patriotic feelings and to arouse anti-German fervor. Movies such as *Under the Bullets of the German Barbarians (Pod puljami germanskix varvarov), For the Honor and Glory of the Slavic Race (Za čest' i slavu slavjan), Secrets of the German Embassy (Tajny germanskogo posol'stva), Glory to Us (Nam Slava)* and *Death to the Enemy (Vragu Smert')* were meant to keep alive what Leonid Andreev called the "heroic aspirations and noble sentiments" of the Russian people. During the last years of the War, Russian film production boomed in quantity; it declined, however, in quality. The war movies produced during this period were crude and tasteless, thus defeating their very purpose. They added to the anti-government feelings of the spectators rather than arousing their fighting spirit. The strikes and demonstrations of the fall of 1916 alarmed the government. Protopopov, the Minister of the Interior of the Provisional Government, proposed to set up an official film committee under his direct control. The sole task of this committee was to use the cinema as a means of official propaganda among the masses. In his view, the film had to be used to instill "healthy political and social opinions among the populace. It could lessen the sharpened conflict between classes and bring patriotic and monarchist ideas to the people." (Taylor, 40.)

The stormy events of the October Revolution swept this proposal into oblivion, and it was left to the newly established Soviet regime to implement what had been suggested by Protopopov. As early as September 1917, when the General Conference of Workers' Educational Organizations addressed the issue of proletarian and Socialist culture, one of the resolutions adopted concerned the cinema. It stated the goals of the proletarian cinema. The participants adhered to Lunačarskij's position regarding the use of the cinema as a powerful weapon for the enlightenment of the working class and broad masses of people. The new regime fully understood the importance of the cinema as a medium that was primarily visual, thus capable of overcoming problems of language, culture, and literacy. Consequently the new regime wasted no time in establishing full control over the film industry.

But the Russian film industry had been disrupted by war and revolution. The production of films and their distribution had almost completely halted. The existing network of movie houses was in a deplorable state. Some of the people directly involved in the movie industry — film producers, directors, cameramen, technicians, and even actors had fled the country for fear of nationalization and repression. Under these circumstances, Lunačarskij, the People's Commissar for Enlightenment, and Lenin favored a gradual nationalization of the film industry, since bringing it under the total control of the Party too quickly would have provoked strong opposition and been counterproductive. Nonetheless, two years after the Revolution, on 27 August 1919, Lenin signed the decree of nationalization of all cinema enterprises. The decree placed the entire film industry under the total control of the People's Commissariat for Enlightenment — *NARKOMPROS*. The nationalized cinema was included in the All-Russian Photographic and Cinematographic Section of *NARKOMPROS, VFKO (Vserosijskij fotokinematografičeskij otdel)*.

At this time, no new feature films were being made. The few still functioning movie houses were showing pre-revolutionary movies which under the new circumstances had little appeal to the audiences of workers and peasants. The need to find a new type of cinema, with a more immediate propagandistic impact on the revolutionary masses, led to the development of *agitfilm* or *agitka*. The term implies positive stimulation: thought-provoking as well as inciting to action. The *agit* concept had been used to define other new developments in arts and society: *agitcomedy, agitposter,* and *agittrain*, before being applied to the new film form in 1919. As a new film form, *agitka* had a short and explicit subject with a direct and convincing message.

Lev Kulešov, Dziga Vertov, and Vladimir Majakovskij are prominent among those who became directly involved in writing and producing the new short films. The success with which the *agitki* met the political tasks of the Soviet regime should not be underestimated. *Agitki* such as *The October Revolution (Oktjabr'skaja revoljutsja)* and *Listen, Brothers (Slušajte brat'ja)* played a crucial role in the recruiting campaign for the Red Army.

The *agitka* had a decisive influence on the stylistic development of the Soviet film. Its simplicity and directness shaped the editing of the Soviet silents and led to what Eisenstein called "dynamic montage." The impact of *agitka* is felt in the theoretical teachings of Kulešov, in the documentaries and film manifests of Dziga Vertov's group Kino-Glaz, and in some of the first films of Eisenstein, Dovženko, and Pudovkin.

Dziga Vertov, one of the pioneers of the Soviet silent films, followed Lenin's advice and began to record "life at random" for newsreels and documentaries. In 1919, Vertov wrote his first artistic manifesto, condemning the play-film as an empty form of entertainment. Under the strong influence of Majakovskij's aesthetic views, Vertov proclaimed the mighty power of the camera as a direct participant to the action. "I am the film eye," wrote Vertov, "I am in perpetual motion. I approach and depart from objects. I climb under them. I move alongside the face of a running horse. I barge into a crowd. I run before running soldiers ...." (Taylor, 75.)

Life in front of the camera was permitted to run its natural course; the only creative control the film maker had was through what and how he chose to shoot and the way in which he placed one shot in relation to another by editing.

To illustrate his theories, Vertov produced a series of short films known as the *Kino-Glaz*. They were made on the streets, in market places, in prisons, at accident sites, and so forth. Vertov intended to cover contrasting kinds of material — the new and the old, children and adults, the cooperative and the open market, city and country, and bread and meat.

Vertov and his only cameraman, Kaufman, used concealed cameras in order not to interfere with life or their subjects, and to record life as it developed under the camera eye. Vertov never finished his series. The few finished documentaries such as *March On (Vpered)*, *The Man with the Camera (Čelovek s kinoapparatom)* and *Symphony of the Donbas (Entuziasm)*, however, summarized his artistic credo: "I, the machine, show you the world as only I can see it" (Taylor, 75).

The early silent Soviet films were socially purposeful. As Eisenstein wrote in 1930: "In the Soviet Union art is responsive to social aims and demands" (Leyda, 89). The film had to teach the workers and the peasants how to live, fight, and shape Socialist character. The newly formed Soviet film industry had to do more than record "life at random." Film content had to be controlled, to present "the image of Soviet Russia that the authorities wanted to project, both to their own citizens and to the world" (Taylor, 70-71). Consequently, in some of the early silent Soviet movies produced by masters such as Eisenstein, Pudovkin, and Dovženko, the main goal was to establish in the minds of the audience a clear delimitation between the opposing forces of "good" and "evil," or "past" and "present." This simplistic approach, which led to the creation of stereotyped heroes, was dictated in part by the technical limitations of the silent cinema, and above all, by the particular propagandistic and agitational needs of the Civil War and early Soviet period.

The revolutionary worker became the most important hero figure in the Soviet society and his depersonalized and universalized image dominated the screen. In Eisenstein's *Strike (Stačka*, 1924), *Battleship Potemkin (Bronenosec Potemkin*, 1925) or *The Old and the New (Staroe i novoe*, 1928) the worker is portrayed in the traditional, almost classical heroic mold: calm and courageous, compassionate and self-sacrificing, strong and yet romantic.

Eisenstein's early films show a certain documentary-like looseness of structure, which served the purpose of epic scale in the action of the film. The message was broadly socio-political, and there was little delineation of characters except as types.

Pudovkin's first feature film, *Mother* (*Mat'*, 1926) represents his answer to Eisenstein's *Battleship Potemkin*. The film was loosely based on Gor'kij's novel of the same name, and it was intended as an artistic justification of the October Revolution. The oppressed Russian masses rebel, rise up, and only the Soviet state can guarantee their liberty, security, and dignity. Pudovkin, unlike Eisenstein, was more interested in his characters as people rather than as symbols or human metaphors. He replaced the non-actors of Eisenstein's films with professional actors. He noted: "I had a strong instinctive inclination for living people whom I wanted to photograph and whose soul I wanted to fathom, just as Eisenstein had fathomed the soul of his Battleship Potemkin" (Leyda, 209). Unlike Eisenstein's movie, Pudovkin's *Mother* showed an unusually unified cinematic style. Although the characters in *Mother* are mostly archetypes, they are also individuals, with individual names, unlike Eisenstein's heroes with generic names such as "Worker," "Sailor," or "Soldier."

The chief distinction between Eisenstein's and Pudovkin's films lies in the fact that Pudovkin's characters are both human and universal, whereas in Eisenstein's movies they are symbols. Pudovkin successfully combined individual characters with the masses, thus making it easier for spectators to identify with his heroes.

With Dovženko, a totally different personality entered the Soviet silent film arena. A Ukrainian by birth, Dovženko brought into the film a strange combination of deep emotionality and lyricism, high epic sense, an almost folkloric naturalness, and rhetorical passion. After an unsuccessful 1938 attempt with *Zvenigora* — an anthology of legends linked by the symbol of hidden treasure — Dovženko made *Earth (Zemlja)* a year later. The story of this almost plotless silent film is simple. The setting is a Ukrainian village. A group of young peasants wants to buy a tractor in order to bring the future to their village a little faster. They encounter the opposition of the Kulaks, who, fearing that this tractor will strengthen unity among the peasants, kill the young village chairman. The simplicity of the plot can hardly speak for the overall qualities of the movie. The film is a lyrical poem, sustained by Dovženko's own philosophical approach to deep love for "the earth." Death, which plays an important part in this movie, is seen by Dovženko not as an end, a finish, but only as a necessary sacrifice, and an intrinsic part of the unending process of the reviving life. *Earth* was not understood, and Dovženko was accused of not being in tune with Soviet reality.

One of the most powerful attacks came from Demjan Bednyj, who was so outraged by *Earth* that he devoted a three-column article in *Izvestia* to denouncing it as "defeatist." His and other attacks contributed to the shortening of the distribution life of the film. Dovženko's *Earth*, however, survived its critics. His movie is both shocking and beautiful, poetic and yet highly dramatic. Dovženko's closeness to the people and the soil made him an outcast among the advocates of *agitka*. The unique visual lyricism of his silent films Earth and *Arsenal* was never again achieved after the hard line of Socialist Realism was imposed.

The young Soviet film industry in many respects continued to develop in the path established by the Russian pre-revolutionary cinema. As well as the Tsarist regime, the Soviet leadership fully understood the powers of film as a propaganda tool capable of influencing the attitudes of large numbers of people. The gradual establishment of movie houses in villages and working class suburbs resulted in the propagandizing of large audiences of peasants and workers.

The early silent films, despite all their technical errors, were used successfully to disseminate the government's social and political message, thus fulfilling the Party's line of political and ideological education. Some of these movies even had a certain degree of propagandistic ingenuity and imagination, a fact which often influenced the audience's behavior. Through "social participation" the early silent historical and artistic films involved the population in the fight against counterrevolutionary forces, and later in the fight against a backward economy and the "vestiges of capitalism."

Soviet films of the silent period had an explicit socio-political purpose and their ideological persuasiveness sowed the seeds of the future doctrine of Socialist Realism. Nevertheless, Soviet silent film pioneers such as Kulešov, Vertov, Eisenstein, Pudovkin, Dovženko, and many others brought new methods and dimensions of cinematographic thought to the art of movie making.

University of Southern California

NOTES

1.   Venjamin Višnevskij, *Film Chronicle* (Moscow: Goskinoizdat, 1945), 67-68.
2.   Jay Leyda, *Kino: A History of the Russian and Soviet Film* (London: Croom Helm; New York: Barnes & Noble, 1960), 17.
3.   "Beglye Zametki" — Nižnegorodskij listok — 4 Ijulja 1896," in Richard Taylor, *Film Propaganda in Soviet Russia and Nazi Germany* (New York: Hillary House, 1979), 35.
4.   B. S. Lixačev, *Kino v Rossii. materialy k istorii russkogo kino* (Leningrad: [s. n.], 1927) 25.
5.   *Cine — Phono*, 1907-08, No. 7, 12.
6.   A. Serafimovič, "Mašinnoe nadvigaetsja," *Cine — Phono*, 1911-12, No. 8, 14.

WITKACY AND SZAJNA:
PRELUDE TO AND REQUIEM FOR THE HOLOCAUST

E. J. Czerwinski

Perhaps the best way to approach Stanisław Ignacy Witkiewicz (1885–1939), better known as Witkacy, and his work is to compare him with Józef Szajna (born 1922), Poland's foremost scene designer and director, who has during the past ten years created a theater which will in all probability not survive Szajna. The fact is that it is almost impossible to "recreate" a Szajna production: he is his own art. The same may be true of Witkacy. Witkacy, unlike Szajna, rarely had the opportunity to direct his own works. Of the eighteen premieres of his plays (according to Janusz Degler[1] twelve of his plays were produced) none really satisfied the author, although he had mild praise for at least three productions. Szajna the predominantly visual artist always has, not surprisingly, the highest praise for his own plays, simply because he cannot in any way be separated from his productions and because he now directs all his plays. If he uses another author's text, he, like his countryman Jerzy Grotowski, manages to inject his own ideas, words, and philosophy into the structure and visual fabric of the play. Even during his collaboration with Skuszanka and Krasowski in Nowa Huta (1956–62), Szajna left his stamp on every work, from Shakespeare's *The Tempest* to John Steinbeck's *Of Mice and Men.*

Unfortunately, Witkacy the writer and visual artist never succeeded in amalgamating all his concepts into any single production. Directors, actors, and producers in Poland's theaters are still searching for the key to Witkacy. Before proceeding with our discussion of Szajna's development, let us examine Witkacy's reception in Poland's theaters during his lifetime.

The history of Witkacy's vicissitudes in Polish theaters is still incomplete. During his lifetime his plays were variously received: either praised, damned, or ignored. *Tumor Mózgowicz (Tumor Brainhard)* was the first Witkacy work produced in Poland, at the Słowacki Theater in Cracow, on 30 June 1921. Only three Polish critics (Boy, Orlicz, and Skoczylas) approached the play seriously, analyzing the text and evaluating the acting and overall production. The others merely excoriated the author of "Pure Form," repeating their own kind of heresy, that one cannot make sense of nonsense. *Tumor* has yet to be given a satisfactory unprejudiced reading in Poland or elsewhere.

It is indeed ironic that Anatol Stern, the Polish critic, as early as 1922 branded Witkacy an "Absurdist." Witkacy accepted Stern's epithet and carried on a debate after the premiere of *Pragmatyści (The Pragmatists)* on 29 December 1921, in the Elsinore (Elsynor) Theater, founded by the Skamander

Group. Witkacy himself directed the play, which received harsh reviews. He became known as an apologist for senselessness. Alone among writers of the Absurd in the twenties, Witkacy approached his art with dedication, attempting in every way to propagate his theory of Pure Form, which in essence sought to make sense of what seemed senseless or nonsense. Later, in the 1950s, Beckett, Ionesco, Albee, Mrożek, Różewicz, and Pinter rarely replied to critics' attacks. Witkacy had faith and artistic belief in his theory: the debate with his detractors was always logical and carried on coolly.[2]

The third premiere of Witkacy's works, *Kurka wodna (Water Chick)*, precipitated little excitement, even though the young Maria Modzelewska's portrayal of the Water Chick was the crowning event of the theatrical season. Directed by Teofil Trczinski, who concentrated on the problems inherent in the play, *Water Chick* develops a theme which is central to an understanding of Witkacy's theory of Pure Form, that the past is inexorably linked to man's fate and that nothing can absolve him of that bitter reality.

This theme is inextricably linked with Witkacy's father, a noted educator who *demanded* that his son become the great artist he later was to become. The elder Witkiewicz's educational views are an effective argument against heredity: environment makes of a man what he is and what he is capable of becoming. The exchange of letters between father and son chiefly concern matters of art and, as Degler points out, problems relating to the psychology of creativity. Witkacy always referred to his father's influence on him regarding questions of art.[3] He even touches upon this particular matter in the text of *Water Chick* (Degler, 57). Nevertheless, the critics again (particularly the influential Karol Irzykowski) attacked Witkacy, calling him a "swindler and a fake." Witkacy, in a voice subdued and almost patronizing, chided his critics: "You can dislike me as an artist; but to insist that I am not an artist at all, I consider a bit of an exaggeration. I am afraid that the judgement of future generations will not be too favorable toward some of my critics."[4]

The following two years — 1923–24 — were perhaps the happiest ones for Witkacy. Two of his plays, *W małym dworku (In a Little Mansion)* and *Wariat i zakonnica (The Madman and the Nun)*, were produced in Toruń. Although *In a Small Mansion* received only one review (favorable), interest in the production nonetheless was quite strong. However, only one performance was scheduled after the premiere on 8 July 1923. The theater director, Mieczysław Szpakiewicz, decided to produce *The Madman and the Nun* (the title of which was changed to *The Madman and the Nurse* due to censorship problems). The premiere took place on 26 April 1924. This time two reviews were printed, devoted more to Witkacy's Theory of Pure Form than to the play itself. Nonetheless *Madman* was a success and the provincial theater of Toruń, under

Szpakiewicz's direction, paved the way for Witkacy's reception in Warsaw nine months later.

What bewildered most critics (and still does today) is Witkacy's penchant for destroying (or straining) logic by first killing off some of his characters, only to have them blissfully resurrected in the second or third acts of the plays. Oftentimes, these same characters are destroyed again and again only to participate in their own comic requiem in the final moments of the last act. This artistic device of making death and life seem less important than other matters in the play is directly linked with Witkacy's Theory of Pure Form: one death (or Grand Gesture) is something of a wish-fulfillment that each of us harbors within ourselves to a lesser or greater degree; the second death (or sometimes a Grand Gesture) is a result of that wish-fulfillment. Witkacy presents each as if it were actually happening. He does not resort to psychological tricks or Pirandellian dreams where everything seems/is. The death occurs, life goes on. The Grand Gesture is not an actual development of the life-experience. Life is a theater-game and man must become theatrically involved. How else can man make sense of life? Man must create his own scenario and it must be composed of Pure Form, unburdened of content. *Mansion* and *Madman* best exemplified his theory.

Like Szajna in the 1970s, Witkacy was ready for Warsaw but Warsaw was prepared for the worst. Always a difficult city for the newcomer, Warsaw expected a disaster. They did not get it: *Jan Maciej Karol Wścieklica (Jan Maciej Karol Brainfever)* was a success, due largely to Jan Pawłowski, who played the leading role. The ensemble became marionettes who surrounded the living Jan Maciej: the individual's tragic plight in a world of puppets was underscored. As a result, *Brainfever* had a run of thirty-four performances in Warsaw and a month's tour throughout Poland. Pawłowski's Fredro Theater presented the first successful premiere of a Witkacy work (although the scene design did not altogether please Witkacy); the critic Boy deserves a great deal of credit for this success, since it was he that initially suggested to Pawłowski that the play be produced.

Even with the propitious results of this production, theaters hesitated to stage Witkacy's works. The Union of Christian Workers (which owned the Fredro Theater) objected to further performances of Witkacy's plays. Professional theaters were afraid to confront the opposition, even though, as a result of the success of *Brainfever*, interest in Witkacy was awakened. Witkacy had no alternative: in 1925 a new theater group was set up in Zakopane, the Formistic Theater Section of the Society of Podhalański Art. *Madman* and *Nowe Wyzwolenie (The New Deliverance)* were produced during this period.

In all fairness to Warsaw intellectuals, one must remember that then as now theater matters involved financial as well as politico-religious considerations. People associated with the theater in Warsaw hoped that the new theater in Zakopane would thrive. Boy as usual praised the venture and gave it his blessing. However, the critics and the public in Zakopane found Witkacy's exoticism unsuitable and argued for a more traditional repertory. Witkacy remained undaunted, insisting that such a theater was necessary and possible to maintain. He championed an artistic approach, "neither amateurish nor experimental." His theater was not meant to be a proving ground.

Unfortunately his proclamation fell on deaf ears. Witkacy learned the art of acting in this Formistic Theater, which influenced him later when he directed *W małym dworku (In a Small Mansion)* in Lwów and when he was to compose his final work, *Szewcy (Shoemakers,* 1934), a few years before his death.

Of the adventures of *Tumor Mózgowicz (Tumor Brainhard)* in Warsaw's Little Theater much has already been written. The actors' strike, led by Bogusław Samborski, an actor who had earlier played in *The Pragmatists*, almost destroyed Witkacy's chance to break into the repertory of Warsaw's theaters. Samborski in good conscience insisted that Witkacy had made "no progress" as a dramatist and that his plays were meant for "puppet theaters," not for the professional theater.

Witkacy summarized his own ideas concerning the actors' strike: "The naturalistic theater spoiled the actor in a certain sense ... My play, like my theater in general, does not allow him a place to realize his ambition [of showing off his ego] .... He is only a part of the whole company [in my theater]."[5]

Finally, on 26 May 1926, two of Witkacy's plays were premiered by the Little Theater: *The Madman and the Nun* and *The New Deliverance.* Even Witkacy's former detractor, Adolf Nowaczyński, came to praise the two plays, insisting however that Witkacy finally had accepted a naturalistic (realistic) approach to his themes and abandoned his Theory of Pure Form. Like other critics, Nowaczyński heaped encomiums on the head of the surprised Pole: "There are few innovators like Witkacy in Europe .... If only this man were to breathe regularly the miasma of large cities, he would today be one of the Polish writers of European fame and fashion and would be performed on every stage, first experimentally and ultimately professionally."[6]

Unfortunately, Nowaczyński's prognosis never materialized. After the premiere of *Mister Price, czyli bzik tropikalny (Mister Price, or Tropical Madness)* on 2 July 1926 in Warsaw's Independent Theater, Witkacy's career as a dramatist literally came to an end. Karol Irzykowski this time completely destroyed him with an unfavorable review.

The play indeed was badly produced and Witkacy did not even bother to answer his detractors, as he was always prone to do after a premiere. The fact that he collaborated on the script with Eugenia Dunin-Borkowska may have been responsible for the poor reception. Even Boy, who felt somehow obliged to protect Witkacy, found it lacking in inventiveness and felt that the work was a poor repetition of past Witkacy.[7] There was nothing left for Witkacy to do but establish his own theater and direct his own plays.

Since he had no capital to set up his own theater, Witkacy accepted the invitation of Ludwik Czarnowski to direct *In a Small Mansion* in the Little Theater in Lwów. His directorial debut in a professional theater was greatly enhanced by the presence of two great actresses — Stanisława Wysocka, who played the role of the Mother, and Irene Solska, who took on the small part of the cook. Little is known about the history of the production, nor can we assess Witkacy's success in realizing his theories, but the production appealed to the public.

During the next two years, 1927–28, only two premieres of Witkacy's works took place: *Persy Zwierżontkowskaja* (perhaps best translated as *Boobs Animalovskaja*) on 31 May 1927 in Lódz, and *Metafizyka dwugłowego cielecia* (*The Metaphysics of a Two-Headed Calf*) on 14 April 1928 in Poznán's New Theater. According to Degler, *Boobs Animalovskaja* (the text of which has yet to be found), marks the end of one phase of Witkiewicz's work on the theater. Judging from the partial resurrection of the text (through comments of the four critics who attended the premiere), the play is probably the quintessence of Witkacy. Andrzej Nullus summarized the themes found in the play: philosophically operating on a symbolic-realistic level, Witkacy explored the problem of the individual versus the collective. Witkacy felt that there was no place for the individual's beautiful story in this world, that in the twentieth century man was confronted by the mass-collective. However, Witkacy had hopes early in his career of saving art from the oncoming Great Fall of Culture — the Great Catastrophe — as he was wont to refer to it. Art in this New World would be a narcotic that would take man to a different land and would so condense his feelings that he would come to see the wonder of life. Witkacy honestly felt that art and theater had gone as far as they could go. The end had come and a new beginning was necessary. He was, in a way, anticipating the Holocaust that not only destroyed the foundations of art but almost annihilated mankind itself.

If *Boobs* was a success, *Metaphysics* was a fiasco: Edmund Wierciński, the director, attempted to parody Witkacy's theory of Pure Form and failed miserably. The end for Witkacy came in 1928 with this production. During the next ten years his plays were produced in various experimental theaters (the most successful being the *Cricot*, which Tadeusz Kantor in 1956 would revive as *Cricot II*).

Witkacy's poor reception during his lifetime should not blind us to the fact that he was years before his time. It is fashionable to say of him today that he reads better than he plays. So does Shakespeare, if we are to carry this absurd statement to its illogical conclusion. The fact is that one should read *and* see his plays: Witkacy painted his plays; words were merely a pretext for subconscious thoughts realized only on a stage, when a director and his cast follow every one of Witkacy's comments regarding acting, staging, and scene design. The artist-painter lived within the artist-writer.

Witkacy admitted that perhaps it was impossible to realize his Theory of Pure Form. But *striving* for Pure Form was almost as important as *realizing* Pure Form. He gave instructions to future directors concerning the production of his plays: allow the actors to recite the text mechanically (characters are not delineated by dialogue); keep the tempo fast; follow faithfully the author's comments and scene design; do not go beyond the text — it is "mad" enough in itself; and do not cut a word.

Witkacy pondered the question of creating a theater, like the one that once existed, where an audience could relive myths and experience religious feelings. In recent years Grotowski has tried to form such a theater. Witkacy failed in his attempt to establish a theater of catharsis. He dreamed of "a theater which in actuality [would be] a sacred place to relive metaphysical feelings." Witkacy created the Word; Grotowski tried to give it flesh. As for Szajna, agreeing with Witkacy that the end of the world has already taken place, he stubbornly repeats a requiem in each of his productions.

There is more than a superficial similarity between Witkacy and Szajna. Both artists came to the theater through the graphic arts; Szajna has composed and written several of his productions (*Dante* and *Cervantes*), although he does not claim to be a dramatist by profession. Witkacy wrote extensively about his theory of "Pure Form," Szajna about his concept of "Open Theater" (not to be confused with Joe Chaikin's Open Theater). Yet the tie that binds these two geniuses is their sense of destiny: they consider themselves larger than life, beyond life, more than life. They are their own art — original, impossible to produce or reproduce, verging on yet barely avoiding the "incomprehensible." They are sensuous (Witkacy verbally more sensual); they are boldly, casually, knowingly alogical (Witkacy in his writing, Szajna in his graphic concepts); they are madmen, more sane than the rest of mortals; and they are sublime artists. To know Witkacy is to understand Szajna. Szajna, post-Absurdist, is Witkacy's own Tumor Brainhard.

Both artists are preoccupied with the Holocaust in their works. Witkacy predicted the end of art and committed suicide in 1939 when, supposedly, he saw the extermination of the world in the very act of Hitler's aggression;

Szajna, on the other hand, lived the Holocaust: he spent five years (from seventeen to twenty-two years of age) in several death camps. If Witkacy's works signal a prelude to the Holocaust, Szajna's works utter its Eternal Requiem.

Jósef Szajna is dedicated to his role as the Hound of Heaven and the modern equivalent of the Greek Eumenides. Having spent his youth in a death camp, the Polish stage designer, writer and director believes that God added twenty years to his life as a result of his experiences in Oświęcim (Auschwitz) and Buchenwald during World War II. Szajna's insistence that he has been accorded this "life-gift" is difficult to contradict. "I am here but I come from Underground," Szajna simply states, almost in imitation of Dostoevsky's meta-hero.[8] And although the Great War separates Szjana from Witkacy, the former seems a conscious extension of the latter.

Besides similar vocations both artists developed an artistic credo: Witkacy — the Theory of Pure Form; Szajna — the Open Theater. The term "Open Theater" is not a satisfactory one and hardly does justice to Szajna's revolutionary innovations. Critics insist that Witkacy's Theory of Pure Form is equally inadequate to describe the ideas of the genius from Zakopane. Often confused with Joe Chaikin's Open Theater, Szajna's concept of Open Theater is a highly personal one and cannot be duplicated, simply because there is only one Szajna. Like Witkacy's ideas, Szajna's theories will never be realized: the genius of these two artists is such that when death has its way, nothing but the ghost of their ideas will survive them. Witkacy and Szajna are their own art.

Szajna, however, persists in his desire to be understood: "After all, I am creating my theater for people — not for posterity. I use the term 'Open Theater' because I see theater as a place where perpetual motion takes place. People enter and exit; new plays are produced; life seems always renewed in the theater."

Perhaps a more appropriate but still an ineffective term is "Omnitheater," if for no other reason than that Szajna attempts to encompass everything, even the seats upon which the audience sits captive. It is safe to say that were Witkacy alive today, Szajna would have undoubtedly influenced him to extend his theater to envelop the auditorium.

These two Polish artists have much in common: both were misunderstood and berated early in their careers; both experimented with all aspects of theater — the literary, the visual, and the directorial; both were haunted by man's penchant to destroy his environment, his culture, and ultimately himself; and both died before their time — Witkacy by suicide, Szajna by a process of mass-murder, memorialized by the number on his left forearm – 13729. It is a tribute to man's resiliency that Szajna was able to step into a normal life after his incarceration, attending the Academy of Fine Arts in Craców and receiving his diplomas in 1952 and 1953.

His early work as a scene designer at the *Teatr Ludowy* (The People's Theater) in Nowa Huta (1956–62) led him to his successful collaboration with Krystyna Skuszanka and Jerzy Krasowski. During these years he was instrumental in introducing a new type of scene design to Polish theaters. His most successful projects were for Franz Werfel's *Jacobowski and the Colonel* (1958), John Steinbeck's *Of Mice and Men* (which Steinbeck himself applauded in 1963), and Shakespeare's *The Tempest* (1961).

During his tenure with Poland's husband-wife team, Szajna felt that credit was being misdirected. "These were my projects, my designs, my visions, but I was always given second-billing," he insisted. In 1963, however, Szajna was given an opportunity to head his own theater, when Skuszanka and Krasowski accepted new positions at the Polski Theater in Warsaw. A year before, in 1962, Szajna had collaborated with Jerzy Grotowski in the now famous Laboratory production of Wyspiański's *Akropolis (Acropolis)* and created a great stir by substituting a death camp locale for that of Wawel Castle, the play's customary setting. The critics were unanimous in their praise for Szajna's contributions. It was only natural, then, that Szajna was offered the position of Artistic Director of the People's Theater when Skuszanka and Krasowski left for Warsaw.

As director and scene designer, Szajna received damning reviews. Gogol''s *Inspector General* (1963) was a complete failure. Critics were baffled and the audience was mystified. Szajna managed to create a distance between actor and audience that was to remain until his production of Goethe's *Faust* at the Polski Theater in Warsaw in 1971.

In a way, all of his productions during this period (1963–71) seemed to be a search for a way to produce Szajna. Kantor, too, had the same problem until he created his finest production, *Umarła Klasa* (*The Dead Class*). Tadeusz Hołuj's *Puste pole* (*Empty Fields*) in 1965 seemed to come closest to Szajna's vision — of showing the public that a great horror had taken place, that things were still awry in the universe, that attention had to be given to the greatest misdeed that mankind had perpetrated since the crucifixion: "If Christ was the Son of God, then, we are His children; and His children have been mutilated. It did not happen almost two thousand years ago. It happened yesterday."

But the public refused to listen. They were baffled by the grotesque art that Szajna created. Prostheses belonged in hospitals; the paraphernalia of the gas chambers belonged in the museums of Oświęcim. Szajna disagreed. He chose Kafka's *The Castle* and Majakovskij's *Mysterium Buffo* in 1966 to illustrate that there were inlets of the mind that had been trampled on, even before the

Holocaust, and that these dramatists had apocalyptic visions of the future. It is significant that the following year, 1967, Szajna decided to produce the works of his countryman with whom he (and Tadeusz Kantor) had most empathy, Witkacy. *Oni* (*They*) and *Nowe Wyzwolenie* (*The New Liberation*) were designed and directed by Szajna at the *Teatr Stary* (The Old Theater) in Craców in 1967 and paved the way for Szajna's subsequent work at his Teatr Studio in Warsaw in 1972.

Szajna's production of *Witkacy* stunned Warsaw critics and audiences. It was obvious that Szajna and Witkacy had finally made it to Warsaw, a city that was less than kind to both artists prior to 1972. Certainly Kantor's early productions of Witkacy's works did much to revitalize the latter's reputation. In 1962, Konstanty Puzyna collated and edited two volumes of Witkacy's extant works and a number of theaters were swept up in the Witkacy revival.[9] But Szajna produced the definitive Witkacy. It marked the beginning of Szajna's collaboration with the great masters of literature. Selecting certain texts from various plays, Szajna fashioned a literary collage that underscored his visual collage. His actors were merely brushes and tools of the master-painter. In the giant sculpture of a human being that occupies the center of the production, Szajna seemed to hail his conquering hero — Witkacy — who had created plays that voiced Szajna's own concern with the human condition. In producing *Witkacy*, Szajna had created his own theater.

Since 1972, Szajna has become Poland's leading innovator, surpassing even the reputation of Tadeusz Kantor, whose production of *The Dead Class* won the coveted Obie Award in 1979 as the best foreign production in New York's Off-Broadway theaters. Unfortunately, the honor was never bestowed on Szajna, whose productions of *Dante* and *Replika* at the Brooklyn Academy of Music in 1976 certainly deserved the same honor.

Undaunted, Szajna continues his quest of Open Theater. By his own admission, Szajna set out to compose his autobiography, "not an *apologia pro vita mia*, but a hymn to man, a divine or undivine comedy. We have been formulating our moral patterns for centuries, but attitudes based on these patterns broke down when people began building crematoria for other living people ... The creative act alone defies the nothingness of man." Judging by his three most strongly autobiographical productions — *Replika, Dante,* and *Cervantes* — it would seem that Szajna has, if not vanquished, at least come to grips with death, as Witkacy never did.

In 1973, at the World Festival of Theaters in Nancy, Szajna unveiled *Replika* (a third version) to a stunned audience. The main idea of the work is contained in the title, *Replika*. In Polish, the word means an answer, an answer by the artist who himself experienced the inferno of the concentration camps. But

Replika also means a reproduction, a recreation of the world of annihilation. In short, Szajna had finally composed his long-awaited Requiem. From a refuse heap a new generation emerges: "The offal of civilization — mannequins, wheels and shoes, bits of piping, newspapers and sacks, ropes, jute and plastic, all sprinkled with soil, comprising something of a vast rubbish heap."[10] All these he scattered amidst the audience. Man emerges, but it is the puppets he plays with that are the symbols of life. A superman appears and becomes the leader of the group. He brandishes a fire extinguisher, attempting to destroy the "new mankind." In the process, he destroys himself.

"What is it all about?" Szajna asks, and then proceeds to answer his own question: "About the agony of our world and about our great optimism. Because death is our time and time is our death. That is why art is at once an epitaph and an apotheosis."

Witkacy would have agreed. This phoenix that encompasses both death and resurrection is grandly presented in *Dante* (1974). Ironically, Dante's text is almost unimportant; words often merely repeat ideas, and at other times they only accompany Krzysztof Penderecki's haunting music. Here, more than in any other of his productions, Szajna has attempted to make the entire theater a stage. A ladder leads from the balcony to the stage, forming a cross on which the dregs of humanity sit. These form the real world. On the stage-proper, Szajna projects his vision of hell and heaven. Visual compositions change before the spectators' eyes, and Dante is resurrected.

Following *Dante*, Szajna created a magnificent pictorial vision in *Cervantes* (1976). In this production a platform also projects into the auditorium. Suspended from the balcony at the end of the platform is a huge puppet with a death's head, lamps shining in its eye sockets, its arms made of chains, and its ladder-torso with a television set lodged in its belly. It is Szajna's vision of God, Devil, and Power. Before this surrealistic tribunal, Cervantes conducts a cruel examination of conscience in which he is both judge and executioner. Cervantes' epitaph is also Szajna's: "Woe, woe to him whom human depravity has never stirred to revolt, who has never felt the urge to tilt at windmills." (*Cervantes*, unpublished text).

Cervantes is present in the play, but first and foremost there is Szajna — Szajna who alone understands the convoluted metaphors and images that he spins around the heads of his audience. Unlike Witkacy, Szajna eschews the written word: "This is not a time for words. Witkacy created great prose-poems, but modern man claims he cannot understand them. I have created a mini-world, Witkacy's catastrophic vision of future-culture. But my mini-world has become a *teatrum mundi* because my setting is the Nazi camps." The survivors who emerge from the rubbish heap in *Replika* are rising from the dead: "We are all Christs," Szajna simply states. "One can blame the Nazis for being a bit too human: some of us survived — just like all those characters in Witkacy's plays who are reborn in the last act of his plays. Unfortunately, this is our last act."

Szajna, however, despite his pessimism, continues to create. He is currently working on a production of *Moby Dick*. "But it is very difficult," he explains. "Captain Ahab never realizes that he himself has swallowed the white whale. How am I to project that idea on my small stage?"

The problem, as pointed out by Bożena Wojnowska in her article on Witkacy's philosophy of Catastrophism, was also a central one for Witkiewicz.[11] Both artists were convinced that God's gigantic toy — the universe (in the form of a spinning top in Szajna's *Replika*) — was fast running down. Witkacy found it unbearable to witness and committed suicide; Szajna took part in his own death and continues to compose his own and his fellow-man's Requiem.

The State University of New York at Stony Brook

NOTES

1. Janusz Degler, *Witkacy: W teatrze międzywojennym* (Warsaw, 1973).

2. Even after 1956, Witkacy was rarely produced on his own terms: experiments by Tadeusz Kantor (*Cricot II*), Krzysztof Pankiewicz or even by Szajna were impressive but far from Witkacy's dream of Witkacy. The problem, probably, is that artists who have attempted Witkacy have had egos and personalities almost as Herculean as Witkacy's own.

3. See Stanisław Witkiewicz, *Listy do syna*, ed. Danek-Wojnowska and Miciński (Warsaw, 1969), and J. Witkiewicz, "Życiorys Stanisława Ignacego Witkiewicza," in *Stanisław Ignacy Witkiewicz: Człowiek i twórca*, ed. T. Kotarbiński and J. E. Płomieński (Warsaw, 1957). For Witkacy's own views concerning his father's influence, see "Bilans formizmu," *Głos Plastyków*, 1938, No. 8-12.

4. *Teatr,* 1922, No. 221, 222.

5. I. D. (Deutscher), "U autora *Tumora Mózgowicza*. Wywiad *Naszego Przeglądu* ze St. I. Witkiewiczem," *Nasz Przegląd*, 13 April 1926.

6. "Teatr Mały," *Gazeta Warszawska Poranna*, 29 May 1926.

7. Several recent productions of this play in Poland tend to disprove Boy's claim, especially the production at the *Współczesny* (*Contemporary*) Theater in 1974.

8. Interview conducted with Szajna 9 June 1975. Subsequent quotations were recorded in interviews conducted during the past six years.

9. *Dramaty*, ed., comp. and introd. Konstanty Puzyna (2 vols.; Warsaw, 1962; 2nd ed. rev. Warsaw, 1972).

10. Program, *Teatr Studio*, for *Replika* (1973), 5.

11. "Uwagi o Karastrofizmie Stanisława Ignacego Witkiewicza," *Studia o Stanisławie Ignacym Witkiewiczu* (Wrocław, 1972), 287-300.

PART IV

THE SOVIET PERIOD

THE ROLE OF THE "ONE"
IN GOR'KIJ'S "TWENTY-SIX AND ONE"

George Gutsche

Gor'kij's famous and frequently anthologized story of 1899, "Dvadcat' šesť i odna" ("Twenty-six and One"), has received surprisingly little critical and scholarly attention. Studies of the work have tended to emphasize the author's vivid descriptions of the plight of the twenty-six pretzel-makers and have given very little prominence to the heroine of the story, a sixteen-year old maid named Tanja, who works for embroiderers in the same building, but under much better conditions and with a higher status than that of the pretzel-makers.[1] There is a need for a reassessment of her role which explores the implications of the moral and psychological relationship between her and the twenty-six. Tanja — the "One" — is *central* to the meaning of the story and recognizing the importance of her role enhances our understanding of wider implications of the work and its place in the author's creative development.[2]

The story "Twenty-Six and One" focuses on the development of a relationship between the twenty-six workers and Tanja; she makes daily visits to the basement factory, where the men give her freshly baked pretzels and become infatuated with her. An ex-soldier comes to work as a roll-baker in another section of the building. The new roll-baker, like Tanja and unlike the other roll-bakers and embroiderers who will not speak to the pretzel-makers, is friendly to the twenty-six: he visits them, jokes with them, and brags about his prowess with women. His bravado, however, in time begins to exasperate the men and provokes them into offering their idol Tanja as a sexual challenge. The soldier agrees to the test and in several weeks proves successful. The twenty-six berate Tanja, but she maintains her composure and responds to their curses with invective of her own. Strong and seemingly unflappable, she proudly walks out of their life.

The narrator of the story is one of the workers. There is little that distinguishes him from the author; in his autobiography Gor'kij identified the bakery of the story as one he had worked in in Kazan'. Although the bakery and working conditions may reflect reality, there is no evidence that the events and characters of the story have real-life counterparts.[3]

Conservative critics of the time saw the story as, if not pornographic, at least amoral in its apparent refusal to condemn Tanja and the ex-soldier.[4] On the other hand, Marxist critics of the time and later have rightly pointed to the power of Gor'kij's description of the basement factory, with frequent references to the filthy conditions and oppressive routine. More questionable is their suggestion (Kalašnikov, 171; Divil'kovskij, 512-13; Filippov, 510) that working conditions and the demoralized spiritual condition of the workers are primary in the story. In their view, the workers desperately reach out for any hope, even an illusion. Tanja serves only to highlight the negative aspects of their situation. Since the workers do not respect themselves, they do not allow her the right to be wrong and to make mistakes on her own. This view does not do justice to Tanja's role in the story.

Furthermore, although the psychological clash of weak and strong wills in the story has been noted before, it has not been pursued in any detail; nor has the significance of other psychological and moral issues, such as the consequences of belief in transcendent deities, been explored.

Questions remain about the character of Tanja, who has been understood as a personification of rebellion against conventions and, less sympathetically, as a girl with a "proclivity to evil."[5] A similar range of contradictory judgments surrounds the interpretation of the men and their actions. In particular, the question of what they saw in Tanja and what losing the wager meant to them has not been satisfactorily resolved.

The story obviously goes far beyond conventional moral judgments relating to the propriety of Tanja's involvement with the soldier. The real issue here, as in most of Gor'kij's early stories, is struggling against the routine and conventional, exerting one's will, and expressing emotions that are truly human. His depiction of Tanja here, just as his previous depictions of tramps (*bosjaki*), reflects his ideas about and attraction to the "uncommon," those who would not accept the status quo.

Although the heroine of this story is not a tramp, there is no question that she falls within the category of Gor'kij's types who challenge conventional morality, who assert their will, and who derive strength from confrontation with adversity. She dominates the story and in no sense represents a secondary personage, serving only to exemplify the men's desperation.

The range and development of emotions hold the key to the story's meaning. From the outset we are provided with a psychological spectrum — what we can expect from the bakery workers and from Tanja. Her appearance on the scene is prepared by an introduction of the men and the conditions under which they work. Some notion of their potential for authentic human feeling is given early, by their spontaneous turn to song in order to break the routine of their labor: in the words of the narrator, "singing stirred our hearts with a gentle tickling pain, making old wounds smart, and awakening our longing" (9). The men's wishing and desiring something better provide a transition to Tanja's appearance.

She brings them pleasure merely by appearing: she greets them, takes the pretzels they offer her, and leaves them in "pleasant" discussion. From the outset their affection is tinged with solicitude — an element which bodes ill for future developments, for giving advice, even if unheeded, implies a desire to impose their will on hers. There can be no question that the men want someone or something to idolize. Tempers quickly flare if someone questions their deity: they insist that everyone love her without qualification and they regard anyone who goes against them as an "enemy" (12).

Their intolerance of heresy, with respect to their idol, is paralleled by their dislike — which the narrator admits derives from envy for better working conditions and social status — toward the four roll-bakers. One of the four, a new baker, the ex-soldier, is an exception because he, like Tanja, treats them as human beings. Their good feelings toward him are tempered, however, by apprehensions about his womanizing. They take pride in Tanja's indifference to him and and even feel "elevated" by it, loving her all the more for scorning him (15).

The situation to this point has been artfully constructed — all that remains is to make what was unstated explicit. The turning point occurs when the ex-soldier, drunk, visits the men and begins his customary boasting. The chief baker of the twenty-six, whom the narrator later characterizes as more intelligent than the rest, angrily belittles the soldier's sexual victories. He expresses his fury with an image — the soldier has been dealing with "saplings" (*eločki*), and Tanja is a "full-grown pine" (*sosna*) (15).

The other workers are fascinated with the challenge, and grow animated and noisy. After the wager has been made, with a two-week limit, their solicitude for Tanja is replaced by curiosity (both "burning and pleasing") about her fate. They are eager and confident, and for a while they fear that they have not wounded the soldier deeply enough, and that the match will be called off.

Their initial curiosity undergoes changes; they begin to work nervously, to argue with each other, and also "to become more intelligent, to talk better and at greater length" (17). They realize they are playing a game of cosmic dimensions with the Devil, and with Tanja representing their stake in the outcome. The soldier's attempts to win over Tanja give them a feeling of "elation" (*vozbuždenie*), so that they live more intensely and unwittingly do extra work.

Although they continue to be affectionate toward Tanja, their curiosity, "cold and sharp, like a steel knife" (18), complicates this emotion. And as the two-week deadline approaches, they examine Tanja for evidence of weakness. When the day of truth comes, they meet her silently instead of amicably. The head baker, now sullen, does not hurry to give her pretzels — the customary offering — and she, surprised by her reception, becomes "pale and nervous" and then suddenly leaves (19). The failure to provide their idol with the daily sacrifice presages their misfortune since, as the narrator admitted earlier, she existed for them only because of the pretzels. What is curious here is that all act as if the wager has been lost already, when in fact (though perhaps not in intention) nothing has happened yet.

The men have obviously realized, even before proof has been offered, the uncomfortable truth that Tanja is not a goddess, but a normal human being. Deprived of their comforting illusion they lose their spirit ("Nam bylo grustno i bespokojno," 19) and dejectedly watch through the window as the soldier follows Tanja into a cellar into the yard. Her troubled face (*ozabočennoe*) upon entering is clearly contrasted with her shining eyes and smiling lips ("... glaza u nee sijali radost'ju i sčastiem, a guby — ulybalis'," 20) as she leaves. The soldier is not visibly different when he emerges, and he quickly disappears from the story. Tanja, however, is met with verbal abuse and whistling. When the twenty-six go out into the yard, surround her, and begin to taunt her she remains silent, taken aback. Their feelings are authentic: anger over their loss, perhaps jealousy, and a desire to make her feel their pain. The narrator asks himself why they do not beat her (20). One of them grabs at her sleeve — a violation of the unwritten code concerning what is permitted; her eyes flash (*sverknuli*), she straightens her hair, and then she calls them "unhappy convicts" (*arestanty nesčastnye*), no longer using the affectionate diminutive (*arestantiki*) with which she used to greet them on her daily visits. Walking upright, beautiful, and proud ("prjamaja, krasivaja, i gordaja") through the circle as if the men did not exist, she calls them rabble and vipers ("svo-oloč' ... ga-ady ..." 21). They are stunned into silence and left alone in the dirt and rain.

The emotions Gor'kij offers in these scenes exemplify authentic living. Curiosity, rage, elation, suspense, and all the elements associated with the confrontation drive home the truth that living human beings are alive because they feel strongly. We know that what Gor'kij himself viewed as positive in the character of his fellow workers at the Kazan' bakery was the "gleam of sadness in their bloated faces," and the "spark of wrath and indignation flush in their eyes." Their worst quality — what he tried to eliminate in his efforts to educate them — was their "patient endurance" and "hopeless resignation" (*The Autobiography of Maxim Gorky*, 537). Several generalizations in the story and a series of images effectively emphasize the point.

For example, the narrator states early that human beings respect every form of beauty (10) and cannot live without something to worship. Gor'kij's conviction that people need something to worship ultimately led to his philosophy of "God-building" (*bogostroitel'stvo*) which he expressed artistically in his later "Ispoved'" ("The Confession," 1908).[6] Working people, in Gor'-kij's view, were natural "God-builders," with their enormous vital and creative energy, their spiritual kinship, and their cohesion as a group. But directing "God-building" energy into conventional patterns of religious belief involv-ing transcendent deities was not, to him, the answer. From the story we can conclude that idealizing individuals can lead to disillusionment, but there is no obvious implication concerning an appropriate object of worship (for exam-ple, a form of social organization or the social whole, as he would suggest in later years). What he offers is simply an artistic illustration of the human need for ideals.

Another generalization of the narrator refers to the desire people have to impose their love without respect for their beloved (11). This generalization runs to the heart of the story, for the men offer Tanja a burdensome love that does not allow her the freedom to make her own decisions (see Divil'kovskij, 512).

The narrator's comments about cursing are also relevant. First he says that there is always a reason for cursing a comrade, but the men in the bakery rarely cursed because they were "half-dead," like "statues," with their feelings stifled by the burden of their work. What is crucial is that Tanja, first by inspiring in them love, and then by provoking their hatred, has elevated them and made them human enough to curse. Even their cursing represents an assertion of their humanity.

A final generalization, though made with particular reference to the soldier, carries implications for the twenty-six workers as well. The narrator discusses how some people derive vitality from a cherished disease of their mind or body (16). Even though they do not enjoy it, and may even complain about it, they attract attention and compassion with it. Boredom, or a poor life, can lead to the acquisition of a vice that could function in this way. The soldier derives self-esteem from his powers of seduction. That is why he is so offended by the workers' doubts that he could succeed with Tanja. But the workers, too, in idolizing Tanja, set themselves up to lose their vitality and reason for living, for idealization — with the wrong ideals — can also become a "cherished disease."

The imagery gives yet another dimension to the story. In addition to the dominant images of the twenty-six men as convicts and the bakery as their prison, there are also depersonalizing images of the workers as machines, stone statues, sheep, oxen, and more positively and ironically (in view of their social status), the foundation of the building. In contrast, a number of inanimate objects are brought to life, perhaps emphasizing the ominous nature of exploitive labor: boiling water "purrs" in a melancholy way (*zadumčivo i grustno*), a shovel "scuffles and throws," "darts in and out," and, in a most striking fashion, the oven of the bakery is seen as the head of a monster (*skazačnoe čudovišče*) with a mouth and jaws, vent-eyes (*bezžalostnye i besstrastnye*) that stare at the workers, and scorching breath; we are told it is capable of hating the workers ("prezirali ix xolodnym prezreniem mudrosti," 3).[7]

Into this world of dehumanized and alienated workers and animated equipment, Tanja enters as an idol (*božok*). A set of images emphasizes her elevated and superhuman status: she is viewed as a substitute for the sun (9), and a falling star (10). When she comes for pretzels — a ritual (*svjaščennyj obrjad*) in which the pretzels are offerings or sacrificies (*žertvy*), she always appears four steps above the workers (11). Her identity as a personal object of worship to them, as an idol (*idol*), as a holy being (*svjatynja*), and as a vessel containing "their best," is explicitly noted by the narrator time and again. Only during the confrontation between Tanja and the men are all on the same level — a sign of her lost divinity and transcendence.

There is also significant imagery associated with the men when they sing (9). Their singing can move the walls of their prison and evoke thoughts of freedom and space ("a road stretching into the distance" and a "bonfire in the steppe"). The author is not only expressing his belief in the power of art to improve reality, but also suggesting the potential of the men for authentic human feeling, evoked in this case in spontaneous artistic expression.

The religious dimension of the story — associated with much of the imagery — attracts our attention at several different levels. The slaves (*raby*) and their furnace idol at the beginning of the story are replaced by worshipers and a new deity, described in biblical terms (light and darkness); moreover, there is a new ritual (a daily visit and an offering), and a new code of behavior concerning appropriate requests (what she will and will not do) and physical contact (the men cannot touch her). The plot, too, has religious overtones: the Messiah undergoes a test arranged with the help of a disciple (the head baker), disappoints her disciples in the test by showing human qualities, but nonetheless ultimately rises above them, though not in any supernatural sense. Gor'kij is clearly paying his disrespects to conventional Christianity by suggesting that though it may have considerable power to evoke strong human emotions, it may ultimately break the human spirit because it is founded on transcendence.[8]

Gor'kij may also have been referring subtextually to Sophiology, which as a doctrine became known to the public through the poetry of Vladimir Solov'ev in the 1880s and 1890s. Holy Wisdom as the "Maiden of the Resplendent Gates," a feminine deity who "tarrieth at the Entrances," suggests Tanja in her relationship to the pretzel-makers and her customary appearance at the basement door.[9] Gor'kij shows in the story that lowly factory workers, just like Symbolist poets, not only can appreciate the purist of artistic forms — music — but also create feminine deities.

The story cannot be read as a condemnation of sexuality, notwithstanding the author's well-known preference for maternal types.[10] Tanja's age, inquisitive and lively nature, and most of all her openness to new experience at the expense of restrictive social conventions, predispose her to amatory experimentation with the ex-soldier. Moreover, she emerges from the experience not as Anna Karenina, spiritually and physically sullied, but radiant and happy. The very same traits that allowed her to break conventions and associate with the twenty-six workers — most notably that independence of spirit which allows people to see others as people regardless of social status — ironically would lead to the conflict of the men with her. After all, it was their adherence to and imposition of a rigidly defined behavioral code that determined their reaction to her actions.

Gor'kij, in a manner that suggests some awareness of Nietzsche's *Beyond Good and Evil*, has placed Tanja beyond conventional moral categories, has promoted her "free spirit" and the strong emotions she arouses, and through her has advanced the view that people must learn to live without comforting illusions, whether about moral absolutes or transcendent deities.[11]

If we read the work as a defense of the independent spirit and strong emotions, then the test itself is positive. Challenging the soldier was a spontaneous gesture on the part of the oldest and most intelligent baker; the challenge was made in a moment of anger, but nonetheless can be understood as deriving from an underlying concern of all of them about the reality of their idol.[12] They admit they wanted to test her. Their doubts are implicitly reflected in their overreactions to suggestions that Tanja was not worthy of the special treatment they gave her. Their deep-seated desire to test their idol combines with resentment over the bravado of the soldier, envy of his success, and perhaps an element of masochism. All of this sets the stage for the waiting period, during which the workers feel truly alive, and the dramatic conclusion.

The story is existential insofar as it presents human beings in situations where their actions lead to feelings of being authentically alive. In much the same way that Dostoevskij's Underground Man purposely brings about his own suffering in order to savor the experience of that suffering, Gor'kij's bakery workers participate in a test which allows them to suffer and thus feel alive. Indeed, the focus is on the experiences themselves (whether positive or negative by conventional standards); we know that Gor'kij at this time was most concerned with the psychological implications of confrontations between strong wills and convention. The generic subtitle of the work, "Poèma" calls attention not only to the lyrical aspects of the story, but also to its epic qualities; strong wills and emotions are truly heroic in a situation where oppression, routine, and suffocating restrictions are the norm.[13]

It is clearly Tanja who embodies the epic spirit of the work, since her vitality and strength stand out in relief against the workers' dejected acceptance of their sunless world.[14] She predominates despite the fact that the story represents their point of view, their milieu, their predisposition to idealize, and their ideal destroyed by reality. In Tanja, Gor'kij presents a model of "authentic" behavior, and of the kind of courage that is necessary if, for example, social conditions are to be changed. Tanja gives no indication of social or political consciousness, but she nonetheless shows the psychological attributes without which action is impossible.

The author does not provide in the work an explicit program of social action. Instead he presents, through the characters in the work, a view of human psychology, and promotes by suggestion, and primarily through the character of Tanja, the values of remaining open to experience, receptive to all emotions, and fearless in the struggle with conventions. As the bearer of these positive moral and psychological attributes she can hardly be denied a claim to significance in the story. Indeed, understanding her role in this light enhances our appreciation of important issues the story raises.

Northern Illinois University

NOTES

1. The following sources were used in this study: Jeffrey Bartkovich, "Maxim Gorky's 'Twenty-Six Men and a Girl': The Destruction of an Illusion," *Studies in Short Fiction,* 10 (1973), 287–88; N. Gekker, "Dvadcať šesť i odna': Poèma M. Gor'kogo," in *Kritičeskie staťi o proizvedenijax Maksima Gor'kogo* (St. Petersburg, 1901), 210–15; L. E. Obolenskij, "'Dvadcať šesť i odna.' Poèma M. Gor'kogo," *Kritičeskie staťi,* 233–35; A. I. Ovčarenko, "Obrazy rabočix v rannem tvorčestve M. Gor'kogo," *O položiteľnom geroe v tvorčestve M. Gor'kogo 1892–1907: Staťi* (Moscow, Sov. pisateľ, 1956), 129–33; V. A. Kalašnikov, *Pisateľ i ego geroi: O polemičeskoj napravlennosti i nekotoryx drugix osobennostjax rannix rasskazov M. Gor'kogo* (Minsk: Nauka i texnika, 1969), 170–71; F. M. Borras, *Maxim Gorky: The Writer* (Oxford: Oxford Univ. Press, 1967), 86–88; Helen Muchnic, *From Gorky to Pasternak* (New York: Vintage, 1961), 70–72; and B. V. Mixajlovskij, *Tvorčestvo M. Gor'kogo i mirovaja literatura 1892–1916* (Moscow: Nauka, 1965), 185–86. Mixajlovskij, Gekker, Ovčarenko, and Kalašnikov focus on the workers and the significance of their disillusionment. Several early interpretations (cited in notes to the edition of the story used in this study: M. Gor'kij, *Polnoe sobranie sočinenij,* [25 Vols.; Moscow: AN SSSR 1970], 7–21, 509–513) by A. A. Diviľkovskij (in 1905) and M. M. Filippov (1901) also give principal attention to the men.

2. The date of composition (1889) suggests the story's transitional status. It was written after the major "tramp" stories ("Čelkaš" and "Makar Čudra") yet before Gor'kij's powerful drama

treatment of the theme of "inspiring lies," *Na dne* (1902). The human longing for ideals, for something to worship, was a literary theme used by Gor'kij in a variety of forms throughout his literary and journalistic career.

3. Gor'kij talks of the Kazan' bakery and his experiences there in his autobiography, *Moi universitety*; see *The Autobiography of Maxim Gorky* (New York: Collier Books, 1962), 537 ff.; F. M. Borras, 87-88, suggests a biographical dimension: the story represented a way for Gor'kij to express his disappointment over the ways humans (in particular, a woman he had idealized) fell short of his expectations. This interpretation again diminishes the significance of Tanja's role as a positive character. The artistic function of the narrator is discussed by Ovčarenko, 182.

4. See remarks on "reactionary criticism," especially the comments of F. Dobronravov (1902) and M. O. Menšikov (1900), in the 1970 edition, 511. V. A. Kalašnikov, 171, similarly speaks of the workers' superiority to Tanja, who turns out to be *pošlaja*, "vulgar," and insignificant in comparison with their image of her.

5. Filia Holtzman, *The Young Maxim Gorky: 1868-1902* (New York: Columbia Univ. Press, 1948), 136, includes Tanja among Gor'kij's early "heroes of protest and unrest"; she, like Lojko Zobar, Rada (from "Čelkaš"), Čelkaš, Konovalov, Foma Gordeev, and others, are "symbolic personifications of rebellion against all the restrictions and prohibitions in Russian life." Bartkovich, 287, however, applies moral criteria ("proclivity to evil"), as does Muchnic, 72, who refers to the pathos of Tanja's "fall," her loss of "innocence and the respect of men."

6. For a discussion of this period in Gor'kij's life, see George L. Kline, *Religious and Anti-Religious Thought in Russia* (Chicago: Univ. of Chicago, 1968), 112-16.

7. A similar image was used in "Suprugi Orlovy" (1897), where a tavern is pictured as a beast's mouth, swallowing the Russian people.

8. The apocryphal Russian story of the Virgin's visit to Hell (*Xoždenie bogorodicy po mukam*) is also a possible subtext.

9. Although there is no direct evidence of Gor'kij's familiarity with the poetry or philosophy of Vladimir Solov'ev, there is much to indicate that Gor'kij was well aware of literary and cultural movements of his day. See A. Ninov, *M. Gor'kij i Iv. Bunin: Istorija otnošenij — problemy tvorčestva* (Leningrad: Sov. pisatel', 1973), 74-130; S. Elizarov, "Bor'ba M. Gor'kogo protiv reakcionnyx tendencij v literature," in *Stat'i o Gor'kom: Sbornik* (Moscow: GIXL, 1957), 269-347; and A. A. Volkov, *M. Gor'kij i literaturnoe dviženie konca XIX i načalo XX vekov* (Moscow: Sov. pisatel', 1954). A discussion of Solov'ev's views, and in particular the concept of Sophia, may be found in Samuel D. Cioran, *Vladimir Solov'ev and the Knighthood of the Divine Sophia* (Waterloo, Ontario: Wilfrid Laurier Univ. Press, 1977), especially 42-63; the reference to Sophia at the "Entrances," which comes from Proverbs viii and ix, is given on p. 18 in note 13. Just as Gor'kij seems to have given Sophia a concrete exemplification, so he would later give, as Ninov, 83-84, notes, the modernist motif of poet as smithy an expanded, more mundane ("social-revolutionary") meaning in his play *Meščane* (1901).

10. Tolstoj, as Gor'kij later reported, viewed Tanja as a rebel, obeying not "social laws," but an "inner" law; see Maxim Gorky, *Reminiscences* (New York: Dover, 1946), 47-48.

11. Betty Forman, "Nietzsche and Gorky in the 1890's: The Case for an Early Influence," in *Western Philosophical Systems in Russian Literature*, ed. Anthony M. Mlikotin (Los Angeles: Univ. of Southern California Press, 1980), 163, notes that Nietzsche's "On the Prejudice of Philosophers" (a section of *Beyond Good and Evil*) appeared in Russian translation shortly before "Dvadcat' šest' i odna" was published. She also suggests (161) parallels between Gor'kij and Nietzsche in their glorification of strength, pride, and beauty in the exceptional individual, and their preoccupation with inspiring and ennobling illusions (or "lies").

12. Muchnic, 72, sees this element of the story as an expression of "man's tragic inclination to destroy himself unwittingly, setting traps for what he lives and loves by."

13. Although *Poèma* designates a narrative poem, the term was also applied to prose works (by Gogol' and later writers). A. A. Volkov, *Put' xudožnika: M. Gor'kij do Oktjabrja* (Moscow: GIXL, 1969), 55, associates the genre subtitle with the work's "poetic feeling" as well as its

moral-heroic dimension; his focus, however, is on the workers, not Tanja. Ovčarenko, 132-33, refers to the harmony of tone and genre, the story's "exalted essence" and musical qualities (which are analyzed in terms of syntactic parallelism, anaphora, contrasts, and rhetorical questions). The *Kratkaja literaturnaja ènciklopedija*, T. V. (1968), 934-35, indicates that the *poèma* in the late nineteenth and early twentieth centuries had a mixture of lyrical and epic sources.

14. There is a wide range of often divergent and contradictory interpretations of the ending of the story. One of the early critics, Gekker (214-15), saw hope for the twenty-six, suggesting that they would keep looking for a better, more reliable ideal. He also suggested that Tanja would also find disillusionment in the future. Ovčarenko, 131, sees in the ending an affirmation of the workers' bright future in the destruction of their illusions about Tanja; the removal of an idol "pleases" (!) the narrator because it improves the workers' chances for "renewing" life. What is important, according to Ovčarenko, is that they have shown the ability to find unanimity, to defend mutual ideas, and to live better through their common love of the *good*. Next time they will love what is *truly* good. Kalašnikov, 171, similarly states that they retain their faith in the beauty of people. Muchnic, 72, on the other hand, sees nothing positive in the workers' lot. Even with her lost innocence, Tanja is in love, free, and healthy, while they are sick and imprisoned. Bartkovich, 288, also emphasizes the worker's ultimate hopelessness and the author's nihilism. Although the text clearly supports the view that the workers' future will remain bleak, the position I argue is that Tanja's positive role rescues the story from "nihilism."

FROM SOCIALIST REALISM TO SOLŽENICYNISM

John Schillinger

Years before the official advent of Socialist Realism, Evgenij Zamjatin anticipated it in his visionary work, *We*. Zamjatin achieved this through the character of D-503, an indoctrinated intellectual whose daily journal entries praise
the benefits of sacrificing personal freedom to a totalitarian state and revere
the wisdom of the Benefactor, the omnipotent leader who unerringly guides
the destiny of the One State. D-503's observations are, however, heavily laden
with self irony and become increasingly tinged with self doubt.

More recently, the character of Lev Rubin in Solženicyn's *The First Circle*
plays a similar role in ironizing a social system and its proponents. Clearly,
Rubin parallels D-503 with his unshakable belief in Stalin and the "progressive forces of history," coupled with his conviction that the means are justified
by the ends; and Solženicyn ironizes Lev Rubin's misperception of the essence
of his society just as he ironizes literature created to support it.

But unlike Zamjatin, Solženicyn is not entirely free of the Socialist Realist
tradition. As Geoffrey Hosking observes in *Beyond Socialist Realism*, Soviet
literature, including the works of Solženicyn, may be shown to exhibit a
cyclical quality.[1] Early Soviet literary heroes in fact owe much to the courageous protagonists of the Russian *bylina*, while Socialist Realism of the Stalin
era turned to eighteenth-century Russian literature for its emphasis on the
stability of society. The resulting "Socialist Classicism" of that later stage
represented a profound change in the message of Soviet literature, a transition
from revolution to conservatism.

In effect, Solženicyn's works reject this trend and return to the spirit of early
Soviet literature with characters reminiscent of the visionaries created by
Gor'kij and Černyševskij. In these works, courageous individuals challenge
current authority, more faithfully recalling *bylina* heroes than do their new
Socialist Realist counterparts. Though Solženicyn retains an early feature of
the Socialist Realist tradition, he has turned it to his own purpose.

In his refusal to sympathize with Party policy or to depict reality in its
revolutionary development, Solženicyn's departure from Socialist Realism is
unmistakable. Solženicyn neither glorifies the Purpose of Soviet society nor
educates the readership in the spirit of Socialism. Repeatedly stripping away
the varnish from Socialist Realist reality and tearing down facades which
obscure the truth from his characters, Solženicyn challenges Socialist Realism
with Solženicynism, a literary response based upon a different set of goals
which treats Socialist Realism as a topic itself.[2]

From his earliest published works, Solženicyn's protagonists may be easily recognized by their antipathy to Socialist Realist facades.[3] Published because of its value for Xruščev's anti-Stalin campaign, *One Day in the Life of Ivan Denisovič* violated Soviet literary canon by going behind the facade of Socialist Realist reality to a Stalinist labor camp. X-123, a prison-wise old timeserver in this first work whose very name uncannily evokes Zamjatin's *We*, reflects this spirit of challenge in a conversation with Cesar', a former movie cameraman. X-123 rejects Cesar''s contention that Sergej Èjzenštejn was a genius for his work in *Ivan the Terrible* and, for its implied justification of Stalin, calls it vile politics instead. As for artistic achievement, he feels that too much art is no art at all, particularly when it masks such an ulterior motive.[4] When Cesar' attempts to defend Èjzenštejn by asking what other treatment of the subject would have been permitted, X-123 becomes indignant. "Ah! What would they let through? Then don't say that he is a genius! Say he's a toady, that he carried out orders like a dog. Geniuses don't hurry to adapt their treatment to the taste of tyrants!"[5] X-123 counters Cesar''s objections that it isn't *what* but *how* that matters in art, by declaring: "Your *how* can go to hell if it doesn't raise the right feelings in me!" (I, 64.)

It is this attempt to mask reality, to turn literature into a Potemkin facade camouflaging true conditions, which particularly galls X-123 and others in Solženicyn's works. Elizaveta Anatol'evna, the hospital janitress in *Cancer Ward*, emphasizes this point when she explains that she reads only French novels because they "don't hurt you so much." Because of the agony she has endured as a victim of state persecution, she cannot bear to read the inevitably optimistic Soviet books by authors who seem blissfully ignorant of the negative side of life. Though the French authors may also be less than realistic, Elizaveta Anatol'evna maintains that she can read in peace because she knows nothing about France:

> "I don't know any books closer to our life that wouldn't irritate me. In some of them they take the reader for a fool. In others there aren't any lies, and the authors are therefore very proud of themselves. They conduct extensive research into what country lane a great poet went down in the year 1800 .... Yes, perhaps it wasn't easy for them to work all that out, but how safe it was! They took the easy way out! But they had nothing to do with those who are alive and suffering today." (II, 529.)

Solženicyn's departure from Socialist Realism is also evident in *For the Good of the Cause*, published in *Novyj Mir* shortly after *One Day*.[6] At first this short work appears to be another Socialist Realist story about the initiative and energy of idealistic Soviet youth. Unbounded in their enthusiasm, groups of young technical institute students compose songs about their radio equipment and sing them as they walk between buildings. They themselves are completing the construction of new facilities for their institute to the utter amazement and admiration of the regular building crew, who frankly admit the work is superior to their own. Cries of disappointment fill the air when it is announced that it is too late to put in a month of voluntary labor on the collective farm before the fall school term, and their idealistic and selfless faculty advisor is ever watchful that their spirit not be dampened by indifference.

This sterotyped course of events is abruptly ended with a transition from Socialist Realism to Solženicynism. Just as the students finalize plans to move into their new quarters, a highly placed bureaucrat takes over the building for his own electrical appliance works. The students are left disheartened and disillusioned; and when they are not given the truth of the matter, their faculty advisor reacts bitterly with idealistic fervor customary in early Soviet literature:

> "... whenever anything good happens to us we announce it, cover the walls with posters, broadcast it over the loudspeaker system, right? But if it's something bad or something difficult must they find out wherever they want and whisper what they wish? No! .... Lenin taught us: don't be afraid to speak up. Free speech is a healing sword!" (I, 277.)

Not only has Solženicyn transformed the initial action of this short story into a parody of the hackneyed Socialist Realist success story by twisting the expected outcome, he has returned to earlier ideals by enlisting no less an authority than Lenin himself to attack the very essence of Soviet literature so repugnant to X-123 and Elizaveta Anatol'evna. The truth, says Solženicyn, is best, no matter how uncomfortable. Just as Kostoglotov in *Cancer Ward* seeks medical books to learn the truth about his treatment, so he advises Elizaveta Anatol'evna to "burden" her son with the facts about the world he lives in rather than allow him to be deceived by a facade.

There are naturally those in Solženicyn's works who are inextricably bound to a defense of Socialist Realism. Their statements are generally self ironizing and guide the reader to the opposite point of view. The very omission of world literature from the frame of reference of these characters serves only to make the great authors more enticing.[7] Of all characters in this category, it is Stalin who is both the chief beneficiary and most ardent advocate of the Socialist Realist perspective.

Not surprisingly, the Greatest of all the Great finds a small book in brown binding entitled *Iosif Vissarionovič Stalin: A Short Biography* immensely appealing. The narrator even contends that the Greatest Genius of Geniuses has nearly memorized its entire two hundred fifty pages. Though superficially this work would not properly belong to the genre of Socialist Realist literature, it illustrates the conventions associated with successful Soviet fiction of the period. In the text, Stalin is characterized as the model Comrade, ever striving toward the Purpose, selflessly displaying his powerful will, wise foresight, and indomitable courage for the benefit of his countrymen.[8] Stalin's portrait is further enhanced by statements which cast him as Lenin's right-hand man, the strategic genius of the Revolution, and the wise and experienced leader who brought his country through the Great War of the Fatherland by dint of the crushing might of his logic. Stalin's own acceptance of these patent exaggerations and fabrications ("Yes, the people had been fortunate .... Without false modesty — it was all true," III, 128) reinforces the idea that works which present the proper attitude for the edification of the Soviet citizen are certain to receive official blessing.

Socialist Realism is not always synonymous with idealization. *Tito, the Traitor's Marshal* is another biography particularly pleasing to Stalin. The equally distorted picture of reality in this work, however, is intended to vilify rather than praise its subject.

Stalin's high opinion of other works, such as movies depicting his role in Soviet history, is similarly self-serving. After viewing Virta's *The Battle of Stalingrad* and Višnevskij's *Unforgettable 1919*, he muses that his role in the Civil War and the Great War of the Fatherland is finally being depicted more accurately. Everyone could now see what a big man he had been, and he himself remembered how he had intervened to correct the rash and too trustful Lenin. Like those exposed to the films and literature that portray him, Stalin is susceptible to the convincingly rewritten scenarios associated with the Socialist Realist depiction of history.

Since Stalin appears unable to distinguish between truth and embellishment in a film based upon his own life, it is hardly surprising that he can easily accept the presentation of other similarly corrected subjects. The narrator ironizes this point by eavesdropping on Stalin's thoughts:

> In general, things were going very well on the collective farms. Stalin had become certain of this while seeing the film *Cossacks of the Kuban'* and reading the novel *Cavalier of the Golden Star*. The authors had visited collective farms, had seen and depicted everything, and what they had shown was obviously good. (III, 134.)[9]

This represents the achievement of the goal set for Socialist Realism, the acceptance of "varnished reality" as fact.

But even when the departure is so great that Stalin himself notices it, the effect remains and is appreciated for capturing the "spirit of Socialism." Virta's scenario for *The Battle of Stalingrad* depicts a nighttime dialogue between Stalin and an unnamed Friend, though Stalin acknowledges that there never had been such a Friend because of the constant insincerity and perfidy of people. Still, tears come to Stalin's eyes as he views the scene, and he thinks to himself, "Now that was an artist for you!" Obviously, Stalin favors the *how* in art that sidesteps the truth to serve the proper ideology.

Many of the works which make such a favorable impression upon Stalin are mentioned by other characters as well, and a comparison of attitudes is instructive. Predictably, Colonel Mamurin, the former Chief of Special Communications (thrown into prison when Stalin encountered some static on a telephone connection), seeks solace in books like Babaevskij's *Cavalier of the Golden Star*. But the *zek*, Xorobrov, will have nothing to do with another of Stalin's favorites when he voices his opinion as to what movie might be brought in for screening ("... don't bother bringing in shit like *Cossacks of the Kuban'*!"). The Serb, Dušan Radovič, is equally unappreciative of *Tito, the Traitor's Marshal*, which he comes upon in Major General Makarygin's study. Of the "dishonest" literature that passed through his hands in the past twelve years, observes the narrator, none of the infamous, sycophantic, and totally false books had been as vile and foul as this one. Briefly flipping through it, Radovič could see who needed it and why, as well as "what kind of bastard" the author was. Used as a common denominator, literature clearly identifies adversaries on either side of Stalin's regime.

A more extended discussion of *Unforgettable 1919* reveals more cautiously expressed disparities in attitude. Dinèra, one of Major General Makarygin's three daughters, is the wife of a well known author, Nikolaj Galaxov. Less restrained in her remarks because of Galaxov's prominence, Dinèra's attacks on the shortcomings of Soviet literature are just within bounds, and at times are even directed at her husband's works. Her judgments are fresh in an otherwise stultifying atmosphere of literary criticism formulated not by critics, but by the positions they occupy. In a discussion of the stage version of *Unforgettable 1919* with the critic, Aleksej Lanskij, Dinèra characterizes Višnevskij's version of how Stalin saved the entire Revolution and all of Russia as "a realistic piece, of course, a sensitive image of the Leader, historically accurate, but ... that's all ..." (IV, 490). Having made her obligatory *pro forma* concessions to the Best Friend of Mankind, Dinèra criticizes other elements of the play with far less restraint. Astonished that her evaluation could be so indifferent, a young man next to her describes how the people in the audience wept at the touching portrayal of Stalin. But Dinèra ignores the easily achieved emotional impact and presses the point that excluding Stalin, the other characters lack names and personalities. Some stock figures, she insists, have even been taken straight out of other, already too familiar plays. Worse yet, it is a simple matter to determine at the outset who is good, who is bad, and how it will end. "And why don't you like that?" Lanskij asks. "Why do you have to have false and superficial entertainment? ... Do you think that in real life our fathers doubted how the Civil War would turn out?" (IV, 491.) Obviously, Lanskij is thoroughly imbued with the spirit of Socialist Realism.

Dinèra is also skeptical of a system that relieves playwrights from opening night worries so common in the West by generating plays that never flop. Lanskij's pat explanation, like his reverence for the father of Socialist Realism, Maksim Gor'kij, again demonstrates his internalization of the Party line. Plays do not fail in the Soviet Union, he assures her, simply because the people and the playwrights share the same artistic and general view of the world. This supposed unanimity of opinion associated with the one-party system and the classless society yet to come is pointedly ironized by Solženicyn. Dinèra's biting reply is exemplary of this treatment: "You can save that for an article. I know that thesis: that the people are not interested in your personal opinion; that as a critic you must express the truth, and there is only one truth ...." (IV, 491.)

Of all the characters placed in a defensive position *vis-à-vis* Socialist Realism in *The First Circle*, Dinèra's husband, Nikolaj Galaxov, who embodies the plight of a less visible set of Soviet authors, is examined the most extensively. Though only thirty-seven, Galaxov enjoys nationwide recognition as a poet, playwright, and novelist. A complete edition of his collected poetry is being set to print, hundreds of theaters (following the lead of the capital) are staging his plays, and the appearance of his novel was followed by the award of the Stalin Prize.

Like most of his readers, Nadja Neržina's Hungarian roommate, Eržika, enjoys Galaxov's works because he evokes a beautiful picture of a world in which all suffering is easily conquered. Never are his characters shaken by doubt, for their devotion to the Purpose gives them singleminded assurance. It is this vapidity upon which Galaxov has raised the edifice of his fleeting fame. Never will Galaxov attain immortality. When the *zek* Xorobrov attempts to read Galaxov's *Selected Works*, he feels he is being mocked. If the war had not come along, he hypothesizes, writers like Galaxov would simply have become professional eulogists.

Unlike Lanskij, Galaxov understands his position. Most of his colleagues also sacrificed immortality to write books that "served the people." Their works were published in large editions, mass distributed, and energetically promoted. Like Dinèra's playwrights, these authors were assured of success because their message was correct. Galaxov's brother-in-law Innokentij Volodin presses the point in their conversaiton at Makarygin's party. Echoing Xorobrov's ironic comment on the theme of war in Galaxov's works, Volodin congratulates Galaxov on his good fortune in having a war to use as a background for his works. "The conflicts, the tragedies — from where else could you have taken them?" (IV, 502.) Both men are quite aware of the answer to this question.

Volodin also asks if literature really has to repeat military statutes, newspapers, or slogans; if so, is it still literature? The problem, Volodin observes bluntly, is that a great writer is in a sense a "second government," which is why a regime only loves its minor writers. In fact, he adds "we have the remarkable example of a literature created not for readers but for writers" (IV, 503).

Under the influence of wine, Volodin continues this train of thought and asks Galaxov what ideas he has brought to his "tortured era." "Beyond, of course, those unquestioned ideas that Socialist Realism provides for you" (IV, 504). Surprisingly, Galaxov confesses that there is much he cannot say in literary cirlces, and indicates his disappointment at his failure to achieve the stature of a Puškin. An interruption by Volodin's wife saves Galaxov from actually voicing his innermost feelings, but the author allows us to eavesdrop on his thoughts. Like many of his fellow authors, Galaxov believed that times would change, and anticipated the day when he would be able to truthfully record present events and could revise his old books as well. "Right now," he feels, "it was better to write about that quarter, eighth, sixteenth — oh, what the hell, that thirty-second part of the truth that was possible. It's better to have a little something than nothing at all." (IV, 506.)

In truth, Galaxov is actually depressed by the compromises he must make. Each time he begins a new work, Galaxov swears he will make no concessions, but inevitably he capitulates to the ominous presence of the fearsome critic, Žabov (a thinly disguised deprecatory reference [žaba: toad] to Ždanov), whom he imagines to be standing over him as he writes. Galaxov vividly pictures the devastating attacks that this all-powerful critic could launch against any of his literary indiscretions, and soon the familiar, dull paragraphs begin to fall obediently into place in his manuscript. Solženicyn himself stands as a living model of the course of action Galaxov fears.[10]

Convinced that it woud be safer to describe moon people than to risk treating real life, Galaxov decides to write a play describing the Soviet diplomats' struggle for peace against the plotting Imperialists. Ironically, he turns to his diplomat brother-in-law for background information, unaware that Volodin's hours in freedom are numbered — precisely because he had humanely attempted to serve the cause of world peace.[11] The contrasting ethics of the two men become apparent early in their conversation when Volodin remarks that writers always remind him of investigators. Galaxov replies:

"You mean they remind us of our conscience?"
"Reading your magazines, I'd say, not always."
"But we're not peering inside man for his crimes,
but for his merits, his good qualities."
"It's just because of this that your work negates
the work of the conscience." (IV, 501.)

Volodin has moved from the philosophy of "you only have one life" to that of "you only have one conscience." His decision to risk his sheltered life and career by acting according to his convictions contrasts sharply with Galaxov's capitulation to Žabov and Socialist Realism.

In *Cancer Ward*, two characters, Pavel Rusanov and his daughter Avieta, are advocates of the Party's approach to literature. An opportunist to the core, Panel Rusanov supports everything that is personally beneficial. Though his favorite reading material is *Pravda*, which keeps him abreast of changes by which he may be affected, Rusanov is aware of the "optimistic and patriotic" works of A. N. Tolstoj (sarcastically dubbed Aleksej Non-Tolstoj by the *zeks* in *The First Circle*) and is particularly repelled by what he knows of the pacifist ideas of L. N. Tolstoj. Ruthless and unprincipled on his own part, Rusanov easily dispatches the giant of Russian literature with the irrefutable words of the authorities: "The moral perfection of Lev Tolstoj and company," he says didactically, "was described once and for all by Lenin. And by Stalin. And by Gor'kij." (II, 157.)[12] Still, though he has read a number of Socialist Realist works, Rusanov is not really a true believer who can find relief or pleasure in them. When his daughter mentions that she has brought a number of such books ("Even the titles lift one's spirit") for him to read during his convalescence, Rusanov unexpectedly asks, "But didn't you bring anything with a bit of sentiment?" And though he has not read them, he adds, "I know everything that's in these myself" (II, 320-21). Once the message inevitably conveyed by such books is grasped, there is little benefit in reading endless variations on the same theme.

Unlike her father and Galaxov, Avieta displays genuine enthusiasm for Soviet literature. Calculating and level-headed, Avieta knows she will be rewarded for conveying the proper message and is confident of a successful literary career. She easily allays her father's fears:

"How can it fail to work out? You're being naive! Gor'kij said: anyone can become a writer! With work, you can achieve anything. But if the worst comes to the worst, I'll become a children's writer." (II, 319.)

Aggressive and outwardly dedicated to Party principles, Avieta combines innate business sense with what at times could be mistaken for guilelessness. Avieta is a blend of a rosy-cheeked and determined young Komsomol member and a world-wise member of the priviligentsia who has mastered her father's technique of turning the Party's avowed commitment to the Purpose to her own advantage.

As certain of the outcome as Dinèra Galaxova's playwrights, Avieta tells her father that she will ignore the individual and go straight to the collective for her material. It will be impossible to criticize her she says, because there will be no ideological mistakes. And if they attack her for artistic flaws, "... well, good heavens, who don't they attack for that?" (II, 320). The most vital point, she insists, is to have tact and to be responsive to the times in order to avoid trouble with the critics. One could hardly imagine a more damning indictment of the status of art in any society.[13]

Avieta's concept of creating a novel is equally simplistic. The Stalin-prize authors, she says, have delightfully simple relationships with each other and enjoy a merry life. "But when the time approaches to write a novel, they lock themselves up in a dacha for two or three months, and there's your novel! ... Yes, I'm going to make every effort to get into the Writers' Union." (II, 319.)

Those on the opposite side, whose comments probe the meaning of literature rather than its potential for self-aggrandizement or propaganda, manifest contempt, disappointment, or pain at the thought of Socialist Realist literature. Their irreverence for sacred cows is captured in the aphoristic brevity of an exchange between two *zeks* in their sleeping quarters in *The First Circle*:

> "Who here's reading Gor'kij?" ...
> "I am."
> "What for?" (IV, 440.)

Unlike those who personally benefit from Party-sanctioned literature, the *zeks* enjoy the freedom of ignoring the sycophantic in favor of the more stimulating artistic works of world literature. Be it Hemingway, Hugo, Dumas, or Goethe, the mention of any author or title is sure to prompt a discussion among men who actively enjoy debate and analysis. As a respite from their daily drudgery, such conversations allow their inquisitive minds to assert a form of individuality otherwise absent from their lives. Opinions tend to be strongly held and defended, and discussions of the most inconsequential topics can easily become heated arguments. None fear remaining "outside the community" for failing to accept the idols of the theatre so detested by Šulubin in *Cancer Ward*.

According to the narrator, when Hobbes said blood would be shed over the theorum that the sum of the angles of a triangle is equal to one hundred eighty degrees only if it injured someone's interests, he knew nothing about prisoners. Given their intellectual freedom and the pressing need to escape the ennui and physical constraints of their existence, the *zeks* are eager for diversion. In *The First Circle* this is particularly reflected in creative verbalization such as

Sologdin's consciously unique manner of speaking, and in self-expression in some form of literature.[14] Neržin's carefully guarded writings and Rubin's painstakingly worded proposals to aid Soviet society exemplify this form of creativity.

Prison conditions are especially suited to the oral tradition of literature represented in Potapov's ironic rendition of "Buddha's Smile," a tale which provides release for the inmates by satirizing the system which imprisons them and functions as a response to Socialist Realism by excessively stripping, rather than varnishing reality. Similarly, Rubin's mock trial of Prince Igor' of the twelfth-century *Tale of the Campaign of Igor'* also offers sanity-saving relief in the black humor which emerges from his archly ironic utilization of lines from Russian literature's oldest monument to emphasize the injustice of the trial proceedings each of the men had experienced.

The intensity with which the *zeks* live by the word is evident in the significance they attach to speech itself. It is even symbolic in the philologist Lev Rubin's total absorption in the assiduous study of individual words and his tragic inability to grasp their true meaning once distorted by Stalin. The integrity of the word is central to the relationships and structure of *The First Circle*, centered as it is in an institute established to destroy the inviolability of the spoken word, to manipulate the word in such a way that it deceives and traps unsuspecting citizens.

It is precisely this milieu which, in keeping with the tenor of Stalin's brash decision to contradict Marx himself by reclassifying language as a "tool of production," epitomizes the plight of the people. As Stalin well knows, whoever controls the tools of production determines the basis of all relationships in any society. Rubin's role in prison is thus closely related to Galaxov's portrayal as a Socialist Realist author, since both manipulate words in a way that directly influences their society for the benefit of the state.

In a literary atmosphere established by its very title, *The First Circle* prominently features the plight of the "wise men" who have risen to the best and highest level of prison camp hell. But though Rubin ponders the Faustian impossibility of ever making mankind happy, and Adamson reads *The Count of Monte Cristo* rather than books which burn with the truth, one senses in most the determination to assert self-will and combat the regime on its own or on more ethical grounds. Neržin's insistence on his right to read Esenin's poems and his refusal to bother with Hemingway's "poor mixed-up bulls," as well as Ruska's interest in Mommsen's *History of Rome* serve as literary indications of independence, resistance, and social judgment.

The acceptance or rejection of the regime itself can even be seen in the comments of *zeks* discussing the nature of art. While Belinskij separated the question of art from his discussions of social problems reflected in literature, Solženicyn turns a discussion of artistic theory into an attack on social conditions. Solženicyn's *zek* painter Kondrašev-Ivanov approaches Pasternak's Živago as a theorist of pure art. Indifferent about nothing, Kondrašev-Ivanov has a reputation for extreme opinions. His entire existence lies in his devotion to art. In a conversation with Rubin and Neržin, Kondrašev-Ivanov declares that a painter does not simply copy from nature but tries to represent as much as possible the totality of his perceptions and impressions, and perceives incongruities in nature which ought to be there and should be depicted. Unexpectedly placing himself in an ironic position, Rubin objects that this "ought to be" (the essence of Socialist Realism) represents a potential danger. But Kondrašev-Ivanov insists that he must go beyond the external features of a subject and try to capture other elements, such as nobility, if such traits are or could be there. "Why shouldn't I help someone find himself and raise himself up?" (IV, 454.)

Neržin calls Kondrašev-Ivanov a one-hundred percent Socialist Realist for this stand, but Rubin presses further by asking if it constitutes a denial of objectivity in art, a question which is both an unwitting attack on Socialist Realism and a revealing look at Rubin's attitude toward the truth of such works. This initiates the transition to Solženicyn's point, for Kondrašev-Ivanov not only maintains that he is proud of his own non-objectivity, but insists that Rubin himself is also not objective, in spite of his cherished belief that he is supremely objective:

> "The truth, which is supposed to be the final result of long investigation — is it possible we don't see before us a sort of twilight truth prior to any investigations? ... You have been absorbed in the comparison of a hundred of the world's languages, you have buried yourself in dictionaries ... but you are already convinced that you will prove that all words derive from the word 'hand.' Is that objectivity?" (IV, 455.)

Kondrašev-Ivanov, of course, is no Socialist Realist. His cherished portraits contain a subjectively rendered message of strength, courage, and idealism which emerge as individual challenges to the repressive force of the regime. Rubin, however, through his devotion to the Party's avowed mission, sees objectivity in a very subjective representation of reality. For Rubin, objectivity in art is the Socialist Realist portrayal of reality in its "revolutionary development" as an affirmation of Party and Purpose.[15] Kondrašev-Ivanov's position is highly individualistic and allies art with an appeal for the spirit and strength necessary to both withstand and rise above the levelling process of Societ actuality.

Neržin is quick to express his aversion for Rubin's brand of art which must embody teleological movement toward the Purpose: "Why the hell do I need progress? I like art because there can't be any 'progress' in it." (IV, 456.) Just try to improve on Rembrandt, he challenges.

Potapov cuts off the discussion by observing that, according to Rubin, no work of art can be understood without knowing how it came to be created and "the social justification for it." He then captures the essence of this "social justification" in "Buddha's Smile," a devastating illustration of how impossibly blatant deception might be perpetrated in the name of the Purpose. This image of reality, the equivalent of Socialist Realism, is quite different from Kondrašev-Ivanov's ethical aspirations for subjectivity in art.

Klara Makarygina, the State Prosecutor's youngest daughter, serves as a bridge between the enclosed world of the Mavrino prison research institute and the outside world of the priviligentsia. Having vainly attempted a career in literature at her sister Dinèra's urging, Klara was unimpressed by Gor'kij and Majakovskij, the paragons of Soviet prose and poetry. Neither could she understand why so much time was wasted on the positions and social ideas of Soviet writers and the writers of the "brother peoples" of the Soviet Union. She was expected to "tremble over every comma" in works she heartily detested, and she longed instead to study authors who had something important to say about life. This was the more difficult because her teacher rejected Tolstoj's novels as too long and ponderous, and likely to confuse the clear critical essays written about him; and writers like Dostoevskij were simply dismissed as being among a group of authors totally unknown to anyone. At the university, they did not mention the real world she had already encountered. Instead, they studied a variety of literature which, just as Elizaveta Anatol'evna had observed, "treated everything on earth except what one could see with one's own eyes" (III, 332).

Klara's own glimpses of the real world cause her to abandon the study of literature and enter an institute for communications engineers. In her first job as supervisor of inmates at Mavrino she is confronted with another facade reminiscent of her experiences with literature. What she encounters conflicts radically with what she has been told by the prison authorities. After frightening warnings that the *zeks* are vicious, desperate men with wolves' fangs, Klara finds them to be normal, sensitive human beings. They even appear to be innocent. Her brother-in-law Volodin temporarily reinforces her with praise for beginning to "figure things out," but even he is soon to plunge into the lower circles of GULag hell; and Klara herself seems destined to fall like a ripe apple into the arms of Lanskij, the literary critic and ardent proponent of the regime. The system is implacable, and the truth always in jeopardy. Insight can always be suppressed forcibly, if not voluntarily from a sense of vulnerability.

Nadja Neržina's roommate Muza is not so prone to capitulation. A graduate student of literature, she measures the values she has found in literary masterpieces against what she encounters in her own life. When another roommate announces that she plans to fool her lover by shamming virginity, Muza is repelled. She is only too conscious of the response of the literary heroines she understands and respects, and the disparity in ethics is overwhelming. When two men approach her to become an informer, she refuses at the expense of her career, and probably her life, knowing that she could not spy on her roommates and later discuss the human qualities of Hamlet and Don Quixote with her students. Muza's idealism is firmly established. The heroes of Russian literature, she says, are after "justice and good." She, like Neržin and Volodin, will emulate them.

In *Cancer Ward*, the characters who reveal Solženicyn's quest for the truth are similarly drawn away from Socialist Realist literature. Efrem Podduev, who has had little concern for others during the course of his boisterous life, is greatly affected by Tolstoj's *What Men Live By*. He is, in fact, so moved by the possibility that men are meant to live by love, that he goes from patient to patient to see if any of them share the same opinion. Many of the answers (food, air, water, homeland) are superficial, and Rusanov typically avoids the issue by alluding to the interests of society and ideological principles. When Podduev gives him Tolstoj's answer, Rusanov ponders briefly, "L-o-v-e! ... N-n-o-o, that 's not our morality" (II, 123).[16]

But Rusanov's own morality has little in common with the idealistic message of the many Socialist Realist books he can no longer bear to read. Other citizens seem to share his opinion. As a student in *For the Good of the Cause* describes them:

> "There are so many of those novels turning yellow in the bookstore windows, and all the shelves are packed with them. You come in a year later and they're still in the same place .... Later they pile them up and take them back. The driver says they're going to be turned back into pulp and then paper again. So why were they printed?" (I, 245.)

Young Demka, who has decided to study literature at the university, functions as a spiritual offshoot of Kostoglotov, and innocently provides an ironic view of Soviet literature. In the last century, he finds, there were ten authors and all were great. Now there are so many Soviet authors you have only to change one letter in their last name and you have a new one. No one could have time to read all of their books, and you were better off if you did not. Completely unknown writers win Stalin prizes and disappear forever. Even the titles of the works are easily confused, such as *The Big Life* and *The Big Family*. The critics had called one healthy and the other harmful, but Demka cannot remember which was which. Even Pavel Rusanov has difficulty keeping such titles straight. When he rejects one of the books his daughter brings him on the grounds that he has already read it, she tells him, "You read *The Earth in Bloom*; this is *Mountains in Bloom*" (II, 320).

Demka also has trouble grasping terminology. Having just learned that to see things objectively means to see them as they are in life, Demka is dismayed to find an article attacking Vera Panova for "treading the marshy ground of objectivism." By following Kostoglotov's admonitions to trust his eyes but not his ears, Demka's well meaning inquisitiveness soon begins to reveal negative elements in Soviet literature, and he turns to the "real-live poetess" Avieta Rusanova for answers.

Overcoming his shyness only with great difficulty, Demka asks the dazzling Avieta her opinion of the need for sincerity in literature. This is not an idle question, for he has just finished Vladimir Pomerancev's article on sincerity in literature, which had recently appeared in *Novyj Mir*.[17] Anticipating the coming "thaw" in Soviet literature, the liberal attitude of the article is quite unlike that of Avieta's reply. As if she had been called upon to make a speech, Avieta rejects sincerity as a major criterion for judging a book on the assertion that sincerely expressed incorrect or alien ideas can be harmful to society. Subjective sincerity, as she terms it, can conflict with the truthful dialectical presentation of life.

When Demka fails to comprehend her answer, she turns to a metaphor through which Solženicyn effectively ironizes her position. Facts can be too depressing, she explains. One should plow deep to reveal the seeds of the future which otherwise cannot be seen. When Demka asks if such plowing would not destroy the seedlings, she says brusquely that she is not talking about agriculture. But Demka's objection has not been lost upon the reader. You need not dwell on the bad things to tell the truth, she continues, "One may speak fearlessly about what is good so that it might become even better" (II, 322). The truth, Avieta insists, can be radiant, uplifting, festive, and optimistic, because people want life to be embellished. But like Solženicyn's other positive characters, Demka sees a higher function for literature. "Literature," he mutters awkwardly, "is the teacher of life" (II, 322). And neither Demka nor the others are speaking of educating Soviet society in accordance with the critic Žabov's message.

Avieta, however, is relentless. She emphasizes the difficulty of describing what will some day exist compared with the ease of describing what can be seen today but is "not necessarily" true. The truth is what *must* be, she tells Demka:

"Our wonderful tomorrow is what has to be described."

"But what will they describe tomorrow, then?"
the slow-witted lad's forehead wrinkled.
"Tomorrow? ... Well, tomorrow they'll describe
the day after tomorrow." (II, 323-24.)

Convinced that Pomerancev's article has unjustifiably accused Soviet writers
of insincerity, adamant that her father had done nothing reprehensible when
he denounced his neighbor years earlier only to annex his apartment space,
and certain that Rusanov would overcome his tumor, Avieta is repeatedly
erroneous in her judgment. Demka's role as the somewhat naive bearer of
irony exposes her ill-founded reasoning, and he becomes increasingly more
certain of himself. Though Kostoglotov later warns Demka that he will simply
ruin himself trying to study literature and soberly advises him to work on
radio sets instead, Demka is intractable: "Oh, screw the radio sets! ... I love
the truth." (II, 434.)

Šulubin, one of the more tragic figures in *Cancer Ward*, has lived to suffer
for his decision to place survival over the truth. A broken man, disowned by
the family for whom he sacrificed himself, Šulubin had become a librarian, a
man of books. Regretfully, he had always done what he had been told, and
reflecting upon his past, one event in particular comes to mind. To preserve
the illusion of happiness at the moment, he had taken "books full of truth"
and burned them in the stove. Now his life seems senseless. He failed to meet
the ethical challenge overcome by Solženicyn's strongest protagonists and
voiced by Kostoglotov: "There is nothing in the world for which I'd agree to
pay any price!" (II, 90).

It is because those like Nikolaj Galaxov and Avieta Rusanova *have* a price
that Stalin's regime persists and is celebrated in its literature. Solženicynism,
the challenge of Neržin, Muza, Demka, Elizaveta Anatol'evna, and the others
who value literature as they do life, calls for the regime to tear down the facade
of Socialist Realism so that in confrontation with the real truth, the nation
might move without deceit toward its Purpose.

Oklahoma State University

NOTES

1. Vladislav Krasnov, *Beyond Socialist Realism* (New York: Holmes and Meier, 1980), 1-28.
2. Deming Brown emphasizes the strength of Solženicyn's attack upon this "Stalinist
literary whoredom" in "*Cancer Ward* and *The First Circle*," *Slavic Review*, 15, No. 2 (June 1969),
312. For a definition and analysis of Socialist Realism, see Andrej Sinjavskij (pseud. Abram
Tertz), *The Trial Begins* and *On Socialist Realism* (New York: Vintage Books, 1960), 147-59.
Except for Sinjavskij's higher opinion of Majakovskij, this treatise could easily have been written

by Solženicyn. Not only are Sinjavskij's basic opinions strongly echoed in *The First Circle* and *Cancer Ward*, but comments by characters about specific works like Višnevskij's *Optimistic Tragedy* also indicate distinct resonance.

3. For a cogent analysis of the ethical implications of action and attitude manifest in Solženicyn's characters, see Herbert Eagle, "Existentialism and Ideology in *The First Circle*," *Modern Fiction Studies*, 23, No. 1 (Spring 1977), 47-61.

4. The function of Cesar' and other characters with artistic frames of reference in *Cancer Ward* and *The First Circle* is analyzed by J. V. Clardy, "Alexander Solzhenitsyn's Concept of the Artist's Relationship to Society," *Slavonic and East European Review,* 52, No. 1 (January 1974), 1-9.

5. Aleksandr Solženicyn, *Odin den' Ivana Denisoviča; Sobranie sočinenij* (6 vols.; Frankfurt: Possev, 1969-70) I, 64. All subsequent references will be made to this edition, and all translations are my own.

6. See Heinrich Böll, "Solzhenitsyn and New Realism," in *Aleksander Solzhenitsyn: Critical Essays and Documentary Materials*, ed. J. Dunlop, R. Haugh, and A. Klimoff (Belmont, MA: Nordland, 1973), 185-87.

7. Lev Rubin, the humane and consequently tortured *zek* apologist for the Stalin regime, is the sole character capable both of a genuine appreciation for world literature and unswerving loyalty to the Party. An intellectual dedicated to the study of language, Rubin is unable to comprehend that he has been deceived by Stalin's words — which adds particular emphasis to Solženicyn's depiction of the extent to which Stalin could succeed in duping Soviet citizens.

8. Note that this Socialist Realist portrayal of Stalin is equally true of Solženicyn's own hero, Gleb Neržin. The difference lies in the ironic intent in the depiction of Stalin.

9. Besides an extensive analysis of Stalin's depiction in *The First Circle*, Gary Kern, "Solzhenitsyn's Portrait of Stalin," *Slavic Review*, 33, No. 1 (March 1974), 4-7, offers useful insights into Solženicyn's methods of presenting the personal perspectives of his characters.

10. See Walter Kaufmann, "Solzhenitsyn and Autonomy," in *Solzhenitsyn*, ed. Kathryn Feuer (Englewood Cliffs, N. J.: Prentice-Hall, 1976), especially 158, for a discussion of this point.

11. For a more extensive analysis of Solženicyn's use of irony, see my article "Irony and the Influence of the Potemkin Facade in *V Kruge Pervom*," *Russian Language Journal*, 32, No. 112 (Spring 1978), 149-63.

12. Here Rusanov effectively illustrates Šulubin's theory (after Bacon) of the pernicious influence of "idols of the theatre": the acceptance of the opinion of others rather than judging by personal experience.

13. Even Belinskij, the ultimate authority and precursor of Soviet literary criticism, valued art and rejected the purely didactic and instructive in literature as late as in his "Vzgljad na russkuju literaturu 1847 goda," and affirmed that art must be first of all, "then it can be the expression of the spirit and direction of a society in a given epoch." V. G. Belinskij, *Polnoe sobranie sočinenij* (13 vols.; Moscow: AN SSSR, 1953-59), X, 303.

14. Bruno Bettelheim, *The Informed Heart* (New York: The Free Press, 1960), 111-15, describes the need for self expression in a prison camp situation as a defense mechanism against the disintegration of the personality. Though equally true of man's position in an impersonal society, the defense of individuality in extreme situations such as concentration and labor camps is necessarily more intense and the leveling forces are more clearly delineated. While Bettelheim avoided depersonalization by assuming a role independent of the prison authorities and rules as he observed his fellow prisoners and speculated about their behavior, the *zeks'* literary creativity is most often revealed in subjective expressions of their attitudes toward the regime, its policies, and their treatment. Self expression in this manner not only provides a sense of release or even a modicum of revenge, it contributes toward a feeling of self respect stemming from constructive activity that is personally controlled. Ivan Denisovič's labors over his brick wall are of identical value.

15. The subjective nature of Rubin's "objectivity" is painfully evident in his decision to assist

in the identification of Volodin's tape-recorded voice. "Objectively," Rubin had reasoned, the man whose voice he had heard warning a humanitarian of danger was attacking the "positive forces of history." See also Edward J. Brown, "Solženicyn's Cast of Characters," *Slavic and East European Journal*, 25, No. 2 (Summer 1971), 165-66.

16.   Solženicyn's many-faceted treatment of the theme of love is examined at length in my article, "The Function of Love in Solzhenitsyn's *The First Circle*," *Studies in Twentiety-Century Literature*, 1, No. 2 (Spring 1977), 183-98.

17.   Vladimir Pomerancev, "Ob iskrennosti v literature," *Novyj mir*, 1953, No. 12, 218-45.

RELIGIOUS SYMBOLISM IN
VALENTIN RASPUTIN'S TALE *LIVE AND REMEMBER*

Gerald E. Mikkelson

> Greater love has no man than
> this, that a man lay down his
> life for his friends. John 15:13

Most Western scholars agree that in the 1970s the overall quality of Russian literature declined in comparison to the 1960s. This is particularly true of works published officially in the Soviet Union. Narovčatov's *Novyj mir* was decidedly less bold and innovative than Tvardovskij's. Polevoj's *Junost'* had lost its youthful vigor and adventurousness. Only two literary journals, *Družba narodov* and *Naš sovremennik*, have sustained any artistic momentum. An astonishing number of talented writers has joined the emigration — Vasilij Aksenov, Lev Kopelev, and Vladimir Vojnovič are only the most recent. Some who remain — like Andrej Bitov, Fazil' Iskander, Bella Axmadulina, Andrej Voznesenskij, and even Vladimir Solouxin — see their most cherished and daring creations appear only in the West and in *samizdat*. Occasionally a novel of great significance like Vasilij Belov's *On the Eve* (*Kanuny*, 1975) is published at home, though extensively expurgated and without the usual first printing in serial form in a journal. More and more major works, once again, are being written for the drawer, and the formerly distinct literary voices of authors like Viktor Astafev, Boris Možaev, Fedor Abramov, Jurij Nagibin, and others, are becoming practically inaudible through censorship, compromise, and trivialization.

Against this rather dreary picture of Soviet Russian literature of the 1970s, two figures stand out in sharp relief. One is Jurij Trifonov, whose already substantial literary career reached a brilliant culmination in his last three novels — *Another Life* (*Drugaja žizn'*, 1975), *The House on the Quay* (*Dom na naberežnoj*, 1976), and *The Old Man* (*Starik*, 1978). These works, which combine an uncompromisingly honest depiction of modern Soviet urban philistinism with a relentless pursuit of historical truth about the Soviet experience, will assure their author of a hallowed place in the literary record of this period. His sudden death at the age of 55 is much to be regretted. The other most remarkable Russian writer of the 1970s in Valentin Rasputin.

Valentin Grigor'evič Rasputin was born in 1937 in Ust'-Uda, a Siberian village on the upper reaches of the Angara River about half way between Irkutsk and Bratsk. Rasputin began his literary career in the 1960s as a newspaper and television correspondent who wrote amusing but somewhat inconsequential sketches and short stories on the side. His first two longer fictional works, *Money for Maria* (*Den'gi dlja Marii*, 1966) and *The Last Deadline* (*Poslednij srok*, 1971) called attention to Rasputin as one of Russia's more promising younger writers. Since the publication of his most recent tales, called *Live and Remember* (*Živi i pomni*, 1974) and *Farewell to Matyora* (*Proščanie s Materoj*, 1976), many consider him Russia's greatest writer living in the Soviet Union today.[1] He resides to this date in Irkutsk.[2]

Because the setting of his major works is the Siberian village and his principal characters have their roots in the traditional Russian value system and the agricultural cycle of life, Rasputin is frequently discussed in connection with Fedor Abramov, Sergej Zalygin, Vasilij Belov, and the other writers of the so-called "rural prose" of the 1960s and 1970s. Ronald Hingley is correct in classifying Rasputin as one of the contemporary authors who "go out of their way to portray Russian rural life as a worthwhile cultural milieu wholly distinct from that of the towns."[3] And Deming Brown properly includes Rasputin among the "village writers" who engage in "an intensive examination, and usually a celebration, of folk traditions, values, and customs, and of Russian antiquity and cultural monuments."[4] The central theme of Rasputin's works is, as stated by Boris Pankin, "the theme of the bases, the foundations of folk life, of the connections of the present with the past and future."[5] These *derevenščiki* are a force in Soviet Russian literature today.

Despite certain similarities of style, theme, and authorial point of view within the rural prose school, Rasputin, as his writing matured during the first half of the 1970s, managed to establish his own literary place and to become a subject of critical debate. While enjoying immense popularity among readers and unanimous recognition of his talent among critics, Rasputin delved into ever more controversial themes and penetrated more deeply into issues of sociological and philosophical importance. As Deming Brown has asserted, "what makes Rasputin stand out among writers who use the village setting is his concern with questions of a universal nature."[6] And it is precisely this willingness to confront sensitive topics — life–death, tradition–technological progress, marital love–civic duty — that makes Rasputin's prose a source of anxiety and disagreement among certain Soviet critics and literary authorities. One such work is *Live and Remember*, a dramatic and moving wartime tale about a Soviet army deserter and his wife. Many readers and critics regard this tale as Rasputin's most successful work.[7]

The action in *Live and Remember* takes place in 1945, the last year of World War II, from mid-January through late May. The setting is the small Siberian village of Atamanovka, located northwest of Irkutsk on the right bank of the Angara River. The story begins when an old man Mixeič Gus'kov, horsekeeper for the kolkhoz notices that his carpenter's ax has vanished from its hiding

place under a floorboard in the bathhouse. Also gone are some homegrown
tobacco and a pair of hunter's skis. Mixeič's daughter-in-law, Nastena, while
lying awake in bed that evening, reaches the terrifying conclusion that her
husband, Andrej Gus'kov, who was reported missing one month before, after
having been away at war since the summer of 1941, is the only person who
could have known where the ax was hidden. To test her suspicion, she leaves a
loaf of bread in the bathhouse. Four days later it too has disappeared. And she
finds a cigarette butt in the cold ashes of the bathhouse stove. That Saturday
she lights a fire in the stove and waits in the darkness until the huge black form
who is her husband comes in from the cold.

Andrej, after recovering from his third serious wound in the war and
expecting a furlough, was released from a Novosibirsk army hospital with
orders to return to his unit at the front. He was dumbfounded. He was so
certain that he would be home in a few weeks that he even persuaded Nastena
not to visit him in Novosibirsk. Then, at the railroad station, tired of war and
bitter at being deprived of his much deserved leave, Andrej makes the fateful
decision to board a train bound for the East, in effect becoming a deserter.
Having disembarked in Irkutsk, he is given lodging for more than a month by
a cherubic deaf-mute named Tanja. Abandoning her without warning, Andrej
walks for three nights down the Angara, avoiding detection, finally arriving
exhausted at his family's bathhouse. Early the next morning, laden with the
ax, tobacco, and skis, he crosses the river on the ice and takes refuge in a long
abandoned river shack behind the hill, so that even the smoke from his
chimney can not be seen from Atamanovka. Thus Andrej's desperate ambition is realized — to get away from war, and to rejoin his wife.

Thus also begins his protracted, agonizing struggle to survive in the wilder-
ness, to remain in contact with Nastena, and to avoid being detected by anyone
else — even his parents, Semenovna and Mixeič. Through an ever-thickening
web of subterfuge and lies, and at great risk to herself, Nastena begins to cross
the river to visit Andrej, to supply him with provisions — including a shot gun,
powder, and ammunition — and to achieve the intimacy and depth of affection that eluded them during their four years of married life before the war.
Andrej is burdened by guilt for his act of treason. Nastena is weighed down by
pity for her husband and by the duplicity she must practice to avoid arousing
suspicion among her friends and Andrej's parents. Previously childless, she
soon becomes pregnant, which means there is no turning back for either of
them. Andrej's fate is sealed by deserting, Nastena's by remaining at his side.
Their rendezvous continue until mid-March when the river ice becomes
unsafe. Nearly two months pass without a meeting, during which Andrej, left
to himself in the bush, turns gaunt, sallow, and morose. In early May the war

ends, the Angara is open, the swallows return for the summer, and Nastena pretends that somehow they will wriggle free from their predicament, that somehow Andrej will be pardoned for his crime. All this is to no avail. Nastena's pregnancy is detected, rumors concerning Nastena and Andrej spread through the village, authorities arrive to resume their investigation, and, finally, rowing feverishly across the river in a desperate attempt to warn Andrej of their pursuit, Nastena stops, moves to the end of the boat, and allows herself to fall into the deep, surging waters of the Angara. A few days later, her body is washed up on the shore and returned to Atamanovka for burial. Andrej, who heard the voices and the commotion, escapes to a nearby island cave, and perhaps farther into the *taiga*, but for how long, we do not know, for the story ends at this point.

The principal themes of the tale are the wrenching effects of the war on the course of one's life, the motivations and consequences of Andrej's desertion, the harshness of the law, and of the community's judgment on someone who has broken their code, the role of fate in people's attitudes, the bonds of the characters with nature (the Angara River, the seasons, the terrain, the flora, the fauna), and the role of love in human destiny, especially its connections with suffering, with martyrdom.

None of these themes is treated in an abstract, schematic manner. They arise spontaneously as an organic concomitant of the action and of the relations among the characters. The novel has an authentically realistic foundation; its setting and circumstances are historically motivated, and its dramatic conflicts are vividly described in a straightforward, unembellished manner, with smoothly flowing alternations of dialogue and omniscient narrative, variations in tempo, and a blending of literary prose with colloquial speech. The characters are believable and distinctive.

Apart from Rasputin's keen perspicacity as an observer of nature and of human activity, and his unfailing skill as a storyteller, what is most interesting in *Live and Remember* is the novel's underlying symbolic structure. A glimpse into its double design reveals a recognizably Christian parable on predestination, the power of love, suffering, and martyrdom. The characters, even as they interact on a realistic plane in plausible social surroundings, are also players in a cosmic drama involving as antagonists the forces of good and evil, prayer and blasphemy, condemnation and forgiveness, life and death.

The evidence for this hypothesis can be found on many levels of the novel's structure and language. The author, or, more exactly, the third-person narrator of the tale, often identifies the time of year of certain episodes by reference not to the month or date, but to the church calendar, to the most recent or current Orthodox feast day, for example, Christmas (January 7, N.S.),

Epiphany,[8] St. Elijah's Day (August 2, N.S.), or The Intercession of the Most
Holy Theotokos (*Pokrov*, October 14, N.S.). This device serves as evidence of
the survival in Soviet times of these remnants of Russia's Christian culture in
the language if not in the ritual observances of the novel's characters and its
narrator. What is more important, certain other major feast days, while not
mentioned specifically, are called to mind because of their concurrence with
events. For instance, Nastena realizes she is pregnant and informs Andrej
during the last part of March, not long before the Annunciation (*Blagoveščenie
Presvjatyja Bogorodicy*, April 7, N.S.). During Andrej's emotionally
charged response to this news, he shouts (among other things), "*Nastena!
Bogorodica moja!*"[9]

The novel's main female character, Nastena, is apparently a believer and, at
least in times of emergency and need, resorts to prayer. After telling Andrej of
her pregnancy, and not quite believing it herself, she recalls the anguish of her
previous seven long years of childlessness:

> Lord, how can it be?! ... Can it be that God has taken pity on her and bestowed
> upon her this good fortune? Can it be that after so many years of married life,
> after so many futile desires, efforts, and prayers, now, when all hope seemed lost,
> she had by some miracle become fertile and was carrying a child? (81.)

A few moments later, when Andrej asks her if she remembers how long they
waited and hoped for this moment, she replies: "Wasn't I the one who prayed
for nights on end, who kept asking for a child by you?" (83).

To be sure, Nastena's faith, in the typical Russian manner, is mixed with
folk supersition. A prayer is, among other things, a means of driving off
dangerous supernatural creatures and evil spirits.[10] During her first fateful
meeting with the bearded Andrej, after making love with him on the bathhouse floor, she asks him where he will go now. "To my brother, the gray
wolf," he replies, and departs for the Angara. As yet understanding little of
what is happening, Nastena asks herself if it might not have been a werewolf, a
changeling (*oboroten'*), instead of her husband. In the darkness it was hard to
tell. Werewolves, they say, can disguise themselves so that even in broad
daylight they cannot be distinguished from a real person: "Not knowing how
to form a proper cross, she crossed herself any old way and whispered the
words of a long forgotten prayer, left over from childhood and just returned to
memory" (20). Andrej as well, though even less accustomed to prayer, resorts
to prayer in times of crisis. During their first full day together in the cabin,
where she has brought him gunpowder and other provisions, he says, "I'll
pray for you to come" (47). Two months later, while waiting in the distance for
Nastena to light a fire in the bathhouse stove as a signal confirming her
pregnancy, Andrej is afraid that something dreadful may have happened:

"Could it have all fallen through? For the first time, it seems, in his entire vagabond life Gus'kov prayed to God: "Lord, don't leave me. Lord, make it so the bathhouse is warmed up. You can, it's not too late. Do only this one thing and then do with me as You think best, I'll agree to anything." (123-24.) It is not surprising that Andrej's prayer is so hurried and pragmatic, rather resembling an attempt to bargain with fate. Andrej is, after all, in a state of desperation and almost completely dependent on his wife. It is striking, nevertheless, that in a work of Soviet literature both protagonists should resort so naturally, so spontaneously, to prayer rather than to Communist discipline, to socially useful labor, or to the spirit of the collective when they encounter apparently insurmountable obstacles.[11]

There is also Andrej's pervasive sense of guilt. By deserting he has cut himself off from society, placed himself outside the law, become a fugitive from justice. Moreover, he has drawn his wife into the dread and narrowing circle of his own inevitably tragic fate. He has doomed them both. At times his sense of guilt reaches such proportions that he imagines himself possessed by devils. When he shoots and mortally wounds a defenseless goat, Andrej sees his own reflection in the dying animal's bloody, terror-stricken eyes: "They dilated in response, and he saw in their floating depths two hairy and repulsive petty demons' mugs resembling his own" (54). Later, after scavenging through an empty flour mill, Andrej is seized by a nearly overpowering desire to set fire to the place, to commit a wanton act of destruction in defiance of those who live more tranquil, normal lives than he. After all, he has matches and dry birch bark for kindling, and the ancient structure would burn quickly: "He remembered himself, he understood, that he should not set it afire and that in the end he wouldn't dare do it, but the devilish temptation was so strong, he so much wanted to leave a hot memory behind, that, no longer relying on his own will, no longer trusting it, he got hold of himself, and hurried away from the mill, to get distance from his sin" (123). And then, on May Day, venturing to a distant, unfamiliar village and luring away and killing a helpless suckling calf while its mother watches in horror, Andrej "even now wasn't sure whether it was only for the meat he had finished off the calf, or whether to please something else, which lately had taken up residence in him firmly and imperiously" (146). While Andrej is not so naive as to entertain notions about a reprieve for his crime, he does struggle in a variety of ways, not only to survive, but expiate his guilt, to exorcise his demons. Nastena, on the other hand, while she is initially more sanguine, perhaps naive, about the ultimate verdict of society, knows from the start that Andrej will not be able to bear the burden of his guilt alone. During their first meeting in the hunter's cabin, having heard Andrej explain his predicament, Nastena ponders his fate and her own:

Man cannot be without sin, or else he's not a man. But such a sin? Andrej won't bear the guilt, it's clear ... It's beyond his powers. So how can she foresake him now? ... He bared himself before her. How can she reject him now? One would need to have no heart, in place of a heart to have a scales which weighs what is advantageous, and what is not. One can't wave off a stranger, be he thrice unclean. And Andrej is one's own, kin. If not God, then life itself had joined them, so they could stand together, whatever might happen, whatever misfortune might occur. (51.)

Two months later, during the late March snow storm, when Andrej is trying to convince her that he is finished, that she will suffer only harm and torment because of her ties with him, Nastena answers in the same spirit: "Once you are guilty there, then I am guilty too. We'll answer together." (95.)

Nastena tries to convince Andrej that even his horrendous sin is forgiveable. Giving "them," that is, the authorities, and her people, the benefit of the doubt, she says: "My mother long ago used to say: 'There is no guilt that cannot be forgiven.' Aren't they human, after all? Once the war ends, we'll see. Maybe we'll be allowed to go repent, or something." (105.) Even near the end, having heard Andrej tell how deserters are executed by firing squad without legal niceties, she remains unconvinced. On her last visit across the Angara to Andrej, Nastena is still hoping for "a saving exodus":

The truth — it will grow through the rocks, it will arise in the middle of the Angara in its fastest and deepest place like a talking tree. No power can hide it. Would it not be better for Andrej to come out and confess his guilt? It is believed that there is more joy in heaven over one repentent sinner, than over ten righteous men. People must understand that one who has fallen to such a sin is not likely to be good for sin again. (178.)

This is, to be sure, a praiseworthy Christian approach to wrongdoing. "They," meaning the authorities, are not Christians, of course, and perhaps are not even fully human in this sense. To err is human, to forgive is not government policy, especially in wartime, especially in a Stalinist society. Repentance is not likely to produce a softening effect.

Gradually Nastena realizes that not only for Andrej is there no salvation in this world, but also that for her too this ordeal is a road to Calvary. While trying her best on May 9 to celebrate with her fellow villagers the end of the war, "it somehow seemed to her that this day was the last one that she would be able to spend with people; tomorrow she would be left alone, completely alone, in a kind of mute, pitch-dark emptiness" (153-54). Later, fearing the day when someone would discover her pregnancy, she tries to imagine herself being rescued at the last moment from disaster. But, "she did not succeed in glimpsing into this new life, for her it was as dark, as hidden, as funereal repose" (159). Not having seen Andrej for two months, she wonders what he is thinking. Something must be done: "Judgment is at hand, at hand — whether people's or the Lord's, or one's own — but at hand. Nothing in this world is given without a price." (164.) And when Semenovna, the mother-in-law, realizes that Nastena is pregnant and asks, "Hey there, girl, you been knocked up?" we learn that "Nastena's heart tore loose, well, this is it — the threshold of her road to Golgotha" (182).

On the day before the story ends, having abandoned her first attempt to warn Andrej by rowing across the river, because she was being followed, Nastena, while cutting through a special cemetery for the drowned, accidentally stumbles and, grabbing onto a leaning wooden cross, barely avoids falling into a freshly dug grave.

> Lord, where have I landed? Where have I landed?! Among the drowned. She felt a chill of horror, her feet were soaked and wouldn't move. She clambered on all fours out of the sunken grave and rolled downhill, toward the boat. Lord, have mercy! What's going on here?! What's the point of this? Didn't she have enough fears of her own? Not realizing that she might be heard, she grabbed the pole and with all her might pushed the skiff upstream away from this vile, accursed place. (194.)

This incident, following earlier hints that Nastena does not swim and seldom works on or near the water for fear of drowning, serves both to foreshadow the means by which she will die and to underscore the extraordinary courage, though born of desperation, which was required for her to take her own life in this way. More important, it is a metaphor of her martyrdom. For in sacrificing herself, Nastena not only puts an end to her own suffering, and accepts the fate she has come to regard as inevitable, but she also saves Andrej, at least from imminent arrest. And concerning the matter of guilt, it is her friends, the Atamanovka women, who pronounce the final word. For in the brief epilogue we learn that Miška, the hired man who brought Nastena's body back from Karda, was prevented from burying her among the drowned: "The women would not allow it. And Nastena was committed to the earth among her own, only a little to the side, near the leaning fence.[12] After the burial the women gathered at Nad'ka's for a simple wake and cried — they were sorry for Nastena." (200.) In this quiet and simple, but eloquent farewell to the earthly remains of Nastena, the women of Atamanovka indicate they have understood the full horror of her position, the unbearable intensity of her suffering, and the stark grandeur of her sacrifice. In their decision to bury her not in disgrace but in a proper Christian grave, with dignity, among their own, they express their empathy for a neighbor and a friend whose cup of life was no less bitter than their own, and who had remained against all odds faithful to her husband to the end. As Nastena had forgiven Andrej, and had expected God to forgive them both, so do these peasant women forgive Nastena. And the funeral rite becomes a gesture even of defiance to those in the village and in the larger establishment who would be quick to condemn transgressors of the law. Even old Mixeič, though disgraced by Andrej's desertion and angered by Nastena's complicity and concealment of son from father, does not regard either of them as lost. He pleads with Nastena to arrange one last meeting between them: "In the name of Christ, Nastena, let me see him. You won't be forgiven if you hide him from me. ... In the name of Christ, bring us together. We've got to turn him around before he's completely defiled." (187.)

The word *ispoganit'sja*, "to become defiled," is both a colloquial and an ecclesiastical expression. It refers not to physical spoilage or dirtying, but to moral degradation. It is derived from the Latin *paganus* (pagan) and means to become desecrated, un-Christian, and, ultimately, damned. Mixeič, to be sure, fears for his son's life, but more than that, for his human dignity, for his soul. By the next day, knowing that the authorities will arrive soon from Karda, Mixeič is urging Nastena to help Andrej escape: "Listen, girl. If he is here, have him leave at once, or something, before they catch him. The men, it seems, have got some plan. Innokentij Ivanovič has taken charge of them. This morning Nestor drove to Karda. This is no laughing matter." (197.)

Andrej, therefore, was perhaps wrong in assuming that he could not disclose his presence and his crime to Mixeič. For despite the pain of his humiliation, Mixeič in the end is motivated by the same familial instinct which drove Nastena to help Andrej in his distress. Thus the chain of compassion which connects Andrej to Nastena, and Nastena to her women friends, extends also to Mixeič. They stand together as intuitive proponents of the spirit of Christian forgiveness as opposed to the harsh and vindictive letter of the law that is applied to the deserter and his accomplices.

The hypothesis that *Live and Remember* is a Christian parable receives further support from an examination of the names of its principal characters. In the Russian tradition, they are carefully selected and emblematic.[13] The name Andrej, derived from the Greek *andreios* — brave, manly — is associated most vividly in the Russian historical consciousness with St. Andrew, the "first-called" disciple of Christ, *protokletus (Andrej pervozvannyj)*, who, according to the Primary Chronicle legend: "... during his trip to the Greek colonies on the Black Sea, had visited the territories that were later to become Russia. This legend became very popular with the Russians and laid the foundation for the later-developed theory of Russia as the guardian of the Orthodox faith. Andrew crossed through Russia from the mouth of the Dnieper River, passed the hills on which Kiev was later founded, and went as far north as the ancient city of Novgorod."[14] One is reminded that St. Andrew was particularly impressed with the indigenous custom of the steam bath and tendency to self-flagellation: "I noticed their wooden bathhouses. They warm them to extreme heat, then undress, and after anointing themselves with tallow, they take young reeds and lash their bodies. They actually lash themselves so violently that they barely escape alive. They then drench themselves with cold water, and thus are revived. They think nothing of doing this every day, and actually inflict such voluntary torture upon themselves." (Zenkovsky, 47.) Thus the name Andrej calls forth a whole cluster of associations — bravery and manliness, primacy (or "firstness"), Christianity in Russia, the *banja* ritual, and suffering.[15]

The most significant name in *Live and Remember* is that of the heroine. It is an example of double obfuscation, like Russia — to borrow Churchill's phrase — "a riddle wrapped in a mystery inside of an enigma." In the middle of the tale, when the protagonists, husband and wife, are reminiscing about their married life together, Nastena recalls that she had been given this particular variant of her name by Mixeič when she was introduced to her father-in-law by Andrej: "We arrived at home. You said, 'Well, this is my wife.' Your father asked: 'What's her name?' 'Nastja,' I replied. He reshaped it into Nastena. And so it stuck from that day on — Nastena and only Nastena." (97.) Nastena is an accepted but somewhat rare diminutive of Nastja, which is itself from the once common name Anastasia, in the Russian colloquial form *Nastasija* or *Nastas'ja*, or in folk form *Anastaseja* or *Nastaseja*, all derived from *Anastasija*, based on the Greek *Anastasis* which means a raising up, a rising (from *ana*, up, and *histemi*, to cause to stand), and resurrection. Thus, in line with the notion of Nastena's suffering, her bitter cup, her falling into the grave, her martyrdom for the sins of another, there is inherent in her name the possibility of resurrection. And one is reminded how Christ's resurrection is depicted in Russian iconography. This event, which was actually observed by no living man or woman, is shown in the iconostasis Festival tier among the twelve special feast days not as the rising up of the Lord, but as His descent into Hell to rescue Adam and Eve and the other righteous ones of the Old Testament times from damnation. In other words, the Russian Anastasis is not so much a *voskresenie* as it is a *sošestvie v ad*. In *Live and Remember*, Nastena represents both the One who descended and those including Andrej for whom Christ's descent was made. At the very end of the story we are told that Nastena:

> ... stepped over to the stern (of the boat) and glanced into the water. Deep, deep inside there was a shimmer — like in a beautiful, frightening fairy tale, — the sky streamed and quivered in it. How many people had dared to go there and how many more would still decide! A broad shadow swept across the Angara: night

was on the move. Her ears were filled with splashing — pure, gentle, enticing; in it rang little bells — tens, hundreds, thousands of them ... and these bells were beckoning someone to a holiday. Nastena felt overcome by sleep. Leaning with her knees against the gunnel, she tipped it lower and lower, staring intently into the depths with all the vision with which she had been endowed for her many years so come, and she saw that a match flared up at the very bottom. (200.)

Thus occurs Nastena's "descent into hell," her predestined, inevitable, and yet voluntary martyrdom, the giving up of her life and that of her unborn child for the sake of Andrej.

There are many more instances in the novel that could be cited to support its interpretation as a Christian parable on the level of symbolic structure. Even the candles Nastena brings from Karda to Andrej for lighting his cabin in the winter darkness had been obtained, we are told, "from some unspecified church in the area" (37). These candles, which originated in a church and are delivered by his protectress Nastena to Andrej in the darkness of his isolation and despair, can be taken not only as a household necessity, but as a symbol of light and hope.

Several conclusions can be drawn from the foregoing analysis. *Live and Remember* is primarily a tale not of Andrej, the deserter, but of Nastena, his wife. Her drama is the deeper one, whether we discuss her precarious position in Atamanovka society and in the Gus'kov family, or her anguishing spiritual dilemma. Nastena belongs firmly within the hallowed Russian social and literary tradition of dedicated, self-sacrificing women — for example, the Decembrist Volkonskij's wife Marija Nikolaevna (née Raevskaja), and Dostoevskij's heroines Sonja Marmeladova (*Crime and Punishment*)[16] and Grušen'ka (*The Brothers Karamazov*), who are willing to follow their men into exile, if necessary, into Gehenna. Nastena's suicide is neither a mistake, "a crude and unforgiveable blunder,"[17] nor a condemnation of Andrej, a "higher judgment of him,"[18] as some critics have suggested, but rather a valiant, last-minute attempt to save him from arrest, and from his sins. Nastena's death, while it is a great misfortune for the village, and a family tragedy, is also a release from torment, a resolution, and a martyrdom in the traditional Christian sense.

One Soviet critic has drawn a sharp contrast between Dostoevskij's Sonja Marmeladova, whose acts of mercy are unquestionably motivated by her faith in God, and Nastena, who allegedly "answers for each of her actions not before God but before people."[19] This assertion is highly questionable on both counts. From the very beginning of the story, Nastena's love and sense of wifely responsibility for Andrej cause her to behave with almost total disregard for the harsh verdict likely to be rendered by the authorities whose laws they have broken. She is willing to violate the legal code in obedience to her own conscience. As another Soviet critic has said:

> With all the powers of her sensitive soul and all the juices of her young body, expecting love and happiness, she embodies with her very existence ... an elemental and organic knowledge of the meaning of life for a person who is predestined to take part in the natural and well-balanced order of life, to perform her obligatory "service" in the eternal movement of natural life, and who is able as a reward for this "service" to receive only the sense of her own communion with the overall movement, with the general laws of being. (Starikova, 241.)

In other words, in service to a higher ideal Nastena is willing to go against her own society and even perish.

The purposefulness of Nastena's sacrifice is also underestimated by an American scholar. Deming Brown sees her as "a loving, loyal woman whose purity of heart blinds her to her unworthy husband's crime .... Increasingly tormented by guilt, fear of apprehension, and mental torture sadistically inflicted upon her by Gus'kov, Nastena kills herself and their unborn child by drowning in the Angara." (Brown, "Valentin Rasputin," 11.) Nowhere in this tale has it been suggested by the main character Nastena, or by the narrator, that she is blinded or that Andrej is unworthy or sadistic. Closer to the mark is N. N. Shneidman, who writes that, "according to the letter of the law Nastena is guilty. Hiding a deserter is a grave crime, but the author is compassionate to his heroine and he asks that she be forgiven; such is the tone of the narrative."[20]

More difficult to establish, perhaps, but nevertheless implied, is the case for Andrej's being forgiven, or at least pardoned for his crimes. Most Soviet commentators do not even allow for such a possibility. For them, Andrej is, quite simply, a coward, an egotist, and, worst of all, a traitor. Since he has betrayed himself, his wife, and his country, he deserves the most severe punishment that society can mete out. Only one critic, stressing the similarity between the treatments of crime and punishment in Dostoevskij and in Rasputin, allows for the consideration of possible mitigating circumstances, and distinguishes between the crime itself and its perpetrator. In his words, "Gus'kov is not by nature a traitor (just as Raskol'nikov is not a murderer)."[21] No final judgment can be pronounced on Andrej without examining and evaluating his record of military heroism, his three increasingly severe battlefield wounds, and the denial of home leave that prompted him to make his crucial and irreversible decision. Another Siberian writer of rural prose, Sergej Zalygin, has referred to Live and Remember as "the statement of a humane writer to a humane reader and society." And in appealing for a sympathetic approach to Nastena's predicament and suffering, he asserts that "only a humane society is concerned with the individual personality, with her experiences, with her fate" (179). One suspects, however, that this humaneness does not extend to Andrej Gus'kov.

At one extreme of Soviet commentary, not only is Andrej guilty of unforgiveable crimes, but Nastena's love itself also becomes a crime when it
motivates her to harbor a criminal in time of war, during which "this feeling,"
according to one critic, "has no right to exist .... There are historical epochs
when any natural human feeling can and should to one degree or another yield
the right-of-way to civic duty, when love itself can turn out to be a crime"
(Kuznecov, 341). The problem is that readers of the novel are supposed to
observe reality and to evaluate the characters' behavior through the prism of
World War II when, it is suggested, all individual emotional life had to be
suspended, and all abstract moral judgments subordinated to the task of
achieving military victory. One needs to ask whether such requirements are
truly necessary even in wartime, and whether this particular historical epoch
(that is, when love can be a crime) has not lasted, in the opinion of the critic,
well beyond the end of World War II, in fact, even as long as Soviet power has
existed. Is the Soviet reader to remain forever blinded and gagged by the
alleged exigencies of a kind of epistomological and ethical martial law?

There is a more moderate strain of Soviet commentary on *Live and
Remember* that suggests that Nastena and perhaps even Andrej behave in a
way that is perfectly natural, understandable, and even justifiable, considering
the extreme historical circumstances in which they find themselves. Nastena,
in particular, is viewed as a character whose instincts and actions are consistent with her native origins and with her sense of personal mission and of the
meaning of life. One critic writes that Nastena is a "symbolic mother ... whose
image is created to a large extent in the spirit of the folk-poetic tradition"
(Seleznev, 60); and another that "we believe each sincere bodily movement by
Nastena in her attempts to perform to the end her woman's 'service,' we are
with her on the road to Calvary of a natural human being in an unnatural
situation" (Starikova, 243). In other words, what is out of kilter is not the
feelings, or the logic, or the value system of the principal character, but rather
her situation, her surroundings, her society. In these terms, *Live and
Remember*, if it does not provide an apologia, at least pleads for a hearing in
the case of Nastena (and Andrej) against the state. Were such a hearing
actually conducted in an impartial court of law, it would be proper for the
defense attorney to raise specific questions. What actual danger was presented
to the community by the meetings between Andrej and Nastena? Had not
Andrej already fought long enough? Bravely enough? Been wounded enough?
Should he not have been given a furlough? A discharge? Was not the war
nearly over when Andrej deserted? Was not victory in sight? Could not the
military and civil authorities have afforded to relax their regimen of extreme
deprivation and penalties?

In addition, the reader might also ask: should not the victory celebration have been accompanied by a spirit of amnesty, making the summary execution of Andrej if he is apprehended and the suicide of Nastena quite superfluous? Would not the indigenous Russian folk customs and practices, if still flourishing in this small Siberian village, have sanctioned a more broadly humane, perhaps Christian, resolution to this novel's central dilemma? Does not the epilogue, which shows the village women burying their friend and neighbor with dignity, provide a silent rebuke to the harshness of the existing regime, and an eloquent defense of a more tolerant and forgiving approach to human foibles?

Several commentators, both Western and Soviet, have suggested that Rasputin is something more than a novelist of manners, more than a consummate Realist. Seleznev calls him a "writer of philosophical cast" (55). Starikova refers to the "dual quality of ... (his) prose — the reliable account of the eye-witness concerning mundane matters and, simultaneously, the poetic parable of high moral meaning and artistic generalization" (238) that allows Rasputin's works to be examined on a variety of levels and scales. She adds that it is "Rasputin's mission to convert the elemental culture of the old Russian peasantry, which is passing from the historical arena, into an imperishable attribute of contemporary national culture" (246). Deming Brown has pointed out that, for Rasputin and certain other writers of village prose, the preoccupation with Russian folk traditions, values, customs, and antiquity "represents to a great extent a search for values to replace those of a Marxist-Leninist ideology that quite obviously does not satisfy many fundamental spiritual needs" (*Soviet Russian Literature,* 252). Geoffrey Hosking adds that, now that Russian rural communal life is largely destroyed, "the residual morality is Christian or even pre-Christian rather than communist" (81).

All these critical comments lend support to the hypothesis of this study that one of the ways of understanding the situation, events, and characters in *Live and Remember* is by viewing the tale's symbolic structure as a modern-day Christian parable, and Nastena as a suffering saint, as a martyr for the sake of Andrej, as a righteous woman in the Biblical sense (like Solženicyn's Matrena) without whom the village cannot stand, nor can the city, nor can the country as a whole.

University of Kansas

NOTES

1. This opinion was repeatedly expressed, for example, by Vladimir Solouxin during his visit to the United States in 1979.

2.   As an aside, it has always seemed fascinating that certain localities in Russia can produce at a particular moment in history a whole plethora of literary talent. In the Golden Age of the Russian Realist novel in the nineteenth century, it was the region south of Moscow — the manor houses, provincial towns, and rolling hills of Tula, Orel, and Voronež; in the early twentieth century, it was the imperial capital, Petersburg; in the 1920s — Odessa. But now, quite apart from the major urban centers, there have emerged distinctive schools of writing in at least two rather remote provincial towns: Vologda, the northern birthplace of contemporary Russian rural poets Jašin, Rubcov, and Vikulov, as well as the prose writers Tendrjakov, and Belov; and Irkutsk, the Siberian home of playwright Aleksandr Vampilov, short-story writer Evgenij Guščin, and novelist Valentin Rasputin. An explanation of these phenomena should probably be left to the cultural anthropologist or the literary historian with a strong sociological bent.

3.   Ronald Hingley, *Russian Writers and Soviet Society, 1917–1978* (London: Weidenfeld an Nicolson, 1979), 163.

4.   Deming Brown, *Soviet Russian Literature Since Stalin* (Cambridge: Cambridge University Press, 1978), 251.

5.   Boris Pankin, "Proščanija i vstreči s Materoj: zametki o proze Valentina Rasputina," *Družba narodov*, 1978, No. 2, 248.

6.   Deming Brown, "Valentin Rasputin: A General View," an unpublished paper delivered at the International Slavic Conference at Garmisch, Germany, in October 1980.

7.   For example, Pankin, 241, who suggests that *Živi i pomni* is the "only example in Valentin Rasputin's *oeuvres* in which the idea (*zamysl*) and the execution (*vploščenie*) turned out to be in complete harmony with each other."

8.   The first episodes in the bathhouse take place during the so-called "Epiphany frosts" (*kreščenskie morozy*), that is, after January 19 (New Style).

9.   Valentin Rasputin, *Povesti* (Moskva: Sov. Rossija, 1978), 81.

10.   In fact, the Christian and the folkloric elements in this story's structure, and, especially, in Nastena's consciousness, interpenetrate and complement each other throughout. Geoffrey Hosking suggests that Rasputin (and Belov) have "come to this vision of man as ruled by subconscious collective and ancestral spirits — ruled by them because he tries to deny them and has thereby lost his conscious, moderating, and creative contact with them." See Geoffrey Hosking, *Beyond Socialist Realism: Soviet Fiction Since Ivan Denisovich* (London: Granada, 1980), 80. In Nastena's case, the remnants of Christian ritual and her ingrained sense of moral responsibility provide a counterpoise to the hostile forces that threaten both her and Andrej from outside (arrest, punishment) and inside (fear, guilt).

11.   There are equally moving prayer scenes in Viktor Rozov's most recent drama *Gnezdo gluxarja (The Nest of the Wood Grouse)*, recently staged in Moscow, and in Nikita Mixalkov's 1980 film version of Gončarov's novel *Oblomov*.

12.   In Russian, "*u pokosivšejsja izgorodi*." The attribute *pokosivšijsja*, "slanted, leaning" is attached conspicuously to three wooden structures in the story: the Gus'kov house (*izba*), which has one leaning corner; the cross which Nastena grasps when slipping into the muddy grave; and the fence near which she is buried. This trait becomes a leitmotif for the Gus'kov family, and a marker, a symbol, of the apparently fragile, but potentially saving grace which Nastena's faith represents. We are reminded of the lowest rung of the Russian Orthodox cross, which slants, to accomodate according to legend, the one short leg of a slightly-crippled Christ. Both Andrej, incidentally, and his father Mixeič, limp slightly, having received leg injuries in their respective wars. The cross in question is sometimes referred to as St. Andrew's cross.

13.   Some are strictly ironical, such as: Vasilisa, nicknamed *Premudraja* (the Wise), the self-styled purveyor of folk wisdom who somehow manages to remain plump throughout the hungry war years; Konovalov (meaning farrier, horse-doctor, quack), the Karda village Soviet chief, and Burdakov, called "Bardakov" (from *bardak*, brothel, chaos) to his face by the Atamanovka villagers, the district policeman, who together conduct the initial investigation into Andrej's disappearance; and the family name Gus'kov itself (from *gusek*, the diminutive of *gus'*,

goose). Andrej's father Mixeič, in his last conversation with Nastena, having suggested that she warn him to flee before he is caught, conveys his vexation with Andrej by calling him a goose: "'I would curse you, girl, for not allowing me to see him, but you will have enough abuse on your head as it is. And this sin on you, you will never be able to get away from it.' And then the bitterness burst out, Mixeič added 'And he's a goose to boot — afraid to talk with his own father. Ah, the hell with you both.'" (197.) Here one is reminded of such Russian sayings as — *Xoroš gus'!* "A fine fellow indeed!" *S nas beda, kak s gusja voda!* "Like water off a duck's back." *Letit gus' na svjatuju Rus'* "A goose attacks our Holy Rus'." This is a reference to Napoleon and, possibly, to the Napoleonic theme of taking fate (one's own, and that of others) into your own hands. *Gus' lapčatyj* "a web-footed goose" (rogue, a sneak). *Gusej draznit'* "to tease the geese," to irritate, to annoy someone (often without purpose or reason), to provoke ill feelings, and the children's game called "geese" in which the mother goose drives her flock into the field, then calls them — "*Gusi domoj! — Začem? — Volk za goroju!*" They race home, and the wolf intercepts and catches them. All the meanings implicit in these sayings and games can be related to the Gus'kov family, to Andrej in particular, and to the tale's action.

14.　Serge Zenkovsky ed., *Medieval Russia's Epics, Chronicles, and Tales* (New York: Dutton, 1974), 47.

15.　Coincidentally, the land on the other side of the river where Andrej hides out is called "Andreevskoe," having been given this name after an early twentieth-century settler in the region named Andrej Sivyj (Andrew Gray). This Andrej, a true pioneer, had been the first (and the last) to cultivate soil lying that far from the village. He died in the 1920s, one of his sons had been killed in World War I, and the other son was dispossessed as a kulak during collectivization and sent with his family into exile. The fields of Andreevskoe were then abandoned as unworkable by the kolkhoz. This interesting sidelight in the tale is rife with implications that freedom, vision, personal initiative, and hard work are important for the well-being of the community and of the human spirit.

16.　"A peasant version of crime and punishment which happened in the twentieth century," asserts E. V. Starikova, "Žit' i pomnit': zametki o proze V. Rasputina," *Novyj mir*, 1977, No. 11, 243.

17.　Sergej Zalygin, "Povesti Valentina Rasputina," in *Literaturnye zaboty* (Moscow: GIXL, 1979), 175.

18.　Feliks Kuznecov, "Sud'ba Nasteny," in *Pereklička èpox: očerki, stat'i, portrety* (Moscow: Sovremennik, 1976), 340.

19.　O. A. Salynskij, "Dom i dorogi," *Voprosy literatury*, 1977, No. 2, 22.

20.　N. N. Shneidman, *Soviet Literature in the 1970s: Artistic Diversity and Ideological Conformity* (Toronto: Univ. of Toronto Press, 1979), 80.

21.　Ju. I. Seleznev, "Zemlja ili territorija," *Voprosy literatury,* 1977, No. 2, 59.

Xenia Gąsiorowska

Barbara Herring

Xenia Gąsiorowska was born in Kiev and received her secondary and college education in Poland. She had a career as novelist and poet in Poland, worked in the Polish underground in Warsaw throughout the German occupation, then in 1945 came to the United States as cultural attache and decided to remain here to begin an academic career. She earned the Ph.D. in Slavic Languages and Literatures in 1949 at the University of California, Berkeley. In the same year, she joined the Department of Slavic Languages at the University of Wisconsin, where her native knowledge of both Polish and Russian as well as her strong and balanced teaching and scholarly expertise in the language, literature, and culture of Poland and Russia have contributed to her success as faculty member.

Professor Gąsiorowska is an internationally known scholar in the fields of Polish and Russian literature and has published extensively in these areas. She is a foremost authority on the topic of women in Soviet literature. Her publications on this subject include *Women in Soviet Fiction: 1917–1964* (1968) and numerous articles in various publications in several countries. During the calendar year 1980, Professor Gąsiorowska was on research leave as a Senior Fellow of the National Endowment for the Humanities, working on a sequel volume which treats the years 1966 to the present. She is also a noted scholar on the Russian historical novel. Her most recent contribution to this field of research is her book *The Image of Peter the Great in Russian Fiction* (1979).

Upon retirement from teaching in Spring 1981, Professor Gąsiorowska received the status of Emeritus from the University of Wisconsin. She intends to devote herself to further research and publication.

University of Wisconsin at Madison

Publications

Books

1. Żytomirska, Xenia [Gąsiorowska, Xenia]. *Wiersze.* Warsaw: Dom Książki Polskiej, 1937.
2. ———. *Tłumaczone na wiersze.* Warsaw: F. Hoesick, 1938.

3. ____ *Jan i Małgorzata.* Warsaw: Wyd. Eug. Kuthana, 1945.
4. Gąsiorowska, Xenia. *Women in Soviet Fiction: 1917–1964.* Madison: University of Wisconsin Press, 1968.
5. Żytomirska, Xenia [Gąsiorowska, Xenia]. *Wiersze wybrane.* London: Oficyna Poetów i Malarzy, 1969.
6. Gąsiorowska, Xenia. *The Image of Peter the Great in Russian Fiction.* Madison: University of Wisconsin Press, 1979.

Articles

1. Żytomirska, Xenia [Gąsiorowska, Xenia]. "Oliver Twist Cruishanka." *Pion* 253 (32), 1938.
2. ____ "Kiedy Oliver Twist był nowością literacką." *Kurier Warszawski,* August 23, 1938.
3. ____ "O twórczości Johna Drinkwatera." *Kurier Warszawski,* March 3, 1939.
4. Gąsiorowska, Xenia. "Villains, Heroes and Superheroes in Soviet Literature Today." *Antioch Review,* 13 (March 1953), 14-22.
5. ____ "Recent Trends in Soviet Literature." *Modern Language Forum,* 39 (1954), 95-105.
6. ____ "The Soviet Postwar Historical Novel." *AATSEEL Journal,* 12 (1954), 70-79.
7. ____ "The Career Woman in the Soviet Novel." *Russian Review,* 15 (1956), 100-09.
8. ____ "The Postwar Polish Historical Novel." *Comparative Literature,* 9 (1957), 17-32.
9. ____ "Daša Čumalova and Her Successors." *Slavic and East European Journal,* 15 (1957), 260-71.
10. ____ "The Soviet Woman in Fiction." *Problems of Communism,* 8 (1959), No. 5, 27-35.
11. ____ "Aksin'ia Astakhova of the Quiet Don." *Studies in Russian and Polish Literature, in Honor of Wacław Lednicki,* ed. Z. Folejewski et al. The Hague: Mouton, 1962, pp. 217-28.
12. ____ "Bolesław the Brave by A. Golubiew, a Modern Polish Epic." *California Slavic Studies,* 4 (1967), 119-44.
13. ____ "Das Bild der Frau in der Literatur." *Sowjetsystem und Demokratische Gesellschaft,* 2 (1968), 646-58.
14. ____ "The Portrayal of Women in Literature." *Marxism, Communism, and Western Society,* 8 (1973), 351-57.
15. ____ "La femme liberée dans le roman soviétique des années vingt." *Revue de l'Est,* 4, 2 (1973), 141-151.
16. ____ "Die Neue Frau in der Sowjetliteratur." *Osteuropa,* 23 (1973), 903-16.

17. _____ "Solzhenitsyn's Women." Aleksandr Solzhenitsyn: Critical Essays and Documentary Materials, ed. J. Dunlop et al. Belmont: Nordland, 1974, pp. 117-28.

18. _____ "On Happiness in Recent Soviet Literature." Russian Literature Triquarterly, 3 (1974), 473-85.

19. _____ "Two Decades of Love and Marriage in Soviet Fiction." Russian Review, 34 (1975), 10-21.

20. _____ "Portrait of a Lady in Polish Positivist Fiction." Slavic and East European Journal, 20 (1976), 261-72.

21. _____ "Ungeschminkte Wirklichkeit. Zum Verhaltnis zwischen Mann und Frau im Jungeren sowjetischen Roman." Osteuropa, 28 (1978), 56-66.

22. _____ "Soviet Women Writers and Their Heroines." Folio, 11 (1978), 28-37.

23. _____ "Working Mothers in Recent Soviet Fiction." Slavic and East European Journal, 25 (1981), 56-63.

24. _____ Contributing Editor to Annual Bibliography of English Language and Literature (Cambridge, England), Soviet Linguistics and Literature, 1963–71.

Reviews

1. Gąsiorowska, Xenia. Rev. of Anthology of Eighteenth Century Russian Literature, by Clarence A. Manning. American Slavic and East European Review, 13 (1954), 275-77.

2. _____ Rev. of Through the Glass of Soviet Literature: Views of Russian Society, ed. by Ernest J. Simmons. AATSEEL Journal, 12 (1954), 55-57.

3. _____ Rev. of And Quiet Flows the Don, by Mikhail Sholokhov, trans. by Stephen Garry. Slavic and East European Journal, 18 (1964), 342-43.

4. _____ Rev. of A Bilingual Collection of Russian Short Stories, ed. and trans. by Maurice Friedberg and Robert A. Maguire. Slavic and East European Journal, 10 (1966), 479-80.

5. _____ Rev. of Reka vremen, by Boris Zajcev. Slavic and East European Journal, 13 (1969), 514-15.

6. _____ Rev. of Russian Futurism: History, by Vladimir Markov. Slavic and East European Journal, 14 (1970), 67-69.

7. _____ Rev. of The Oxford Chekhov: Volume 5. Stories 1889–1891, trans. and ed. by Ronald Hingley. Slavic and East European Journal, 16 (1972), 101-02.

8. _____ Rev. of Explorations in Freedom: Prose, Narrative and Poetry from Kultura, trans. by Rulka Langer, M. Czachowska, et al. Slavic and East European Journal, 14 (1972), 112.

9. _____ *Rev. of Przewodnik polonisty: Bibliografie, słowniki, biblioteki, muzea literackie*, by Jadwiga Czachowska and Roman Loth. *Slavic Review*, 24 (1976), 185-86.

10. _____ *Rev. of In Stalin's Time: Middle Class Values in Soviet Fiction*, by Vera S. Durham. *Slavic and East European Journal*, 22 (1978), 225-27.

11. _____ *Rev. of Soviet Russian Literature since Stalin*, by Deming Brown. *Russian Review*, 39 (1980), 270-71.

12. _____ Rev. of *Soviet Literature in the 1970's: Artistic Diversity and Ideological conformity*, by N. N. Shneidman. *Russian Review*, 39, 4 (1980), 522-23.

13. _____ *Reviews in World Literature Today* [formerly *Books Abroad*], since 1962.